Frances Ann Degnan

UNDER THE
Arctic Sun

The Life and Times of Frank and Ada Degnan

by
Frances Ann Degnan

Ada and Frank Degnan
1945 ~ Unalakleet

Cottonwood Bark
P. O. Box 33
Unalakleet, Alaska 99684-0033

ISBN 0-9669650-0-0
Library of Congress Catalog Card Number: 99-94636

Cover photo by June Degnan

Printed by A. T. Publishing & Printing, Inc., Anchorage, Alaska

Cottonwood Bark
P. O. Box 33
Unalakleet, Alaska 99684

*This book is dedicated
to the memory of my parents*
Frank Auvnue Degnan
and
Ada Quyan Johnsson.
*It is also dedicated to
the memory of our
Unalit / Kawerak ancestors
and all their descendents
living and deceased.
It is their collective story.*

Martha Annie Degnan (Apok), her son Frank Degnan,
and Lottie Burns at St. Michael

Francis Gerald Degnan

Table of Contents

Acknowledgements

Many thanks to all who helped me in this endeavor.

John Auliye, June Degnan, Alma Bradley Ivanoff, Mildred Otten Ivanoff, Linda Phillips Larson, and Sheldon Ryan for loaning photographs of our ancestors.

Laura Degnan Lawrence, Ida Degnan Harden and Dr. Dorothy Jean Ray for reading and critiquing the manuscript throughout the process.

Lowell and Betty Anagick, Beatrice Murray Daniels and Alma Bradley Ivanoff for helping identify photographs of ancestors.

John Auliye, Beatrice Murray Daniels, Alma Bradley Ivanoff, Hazel Mulluk Kotongan, Eunice Oyoumick Ryan and Elsie Kotongan Soxie for their historical perspective.

Frances Charles for spelling of Inuit names and words.

Dr. Virginia Breedlove Degnan for use of her electronic equipment and expertise. Jack Davis for solving my computer problems.

Agnes Ryan (Igailaq), Frank Ryan, Ada Johnsson,
Gertie Ryan, and Jessie Ryan

Eric Johnsson

Introduction

I am taking this time to share with you the stories of my parents and their parents. I believe that you would call them ancestors, and I believe that they are your ancestors too. One way to find out who your ancestors are is to ask your parents about them and as early as you can.

So that is the reason I am taking this time in my life to write some of the stories that were told to me by my parents. What I am writing about will have some words from our Unaluk (Yup'ik), and Kawerak (Inupiaq) languages as names for people, places and much-used phrases used to describe people, places or emotions. Because these stories are about our own world and how we view it, I will also use some of our Native words. Most importantly, the stories are from our own frame of reference.

My parents wanted me to make sure their children, and their children after them, would have an appreciation of the family's combined Unalit/Kawerak heritage.

The usual tradition of the Inuit (The Real People) is to relate the happenings through stories of actual life happenings, legends, parables, and songs. So since the songs and dances have gone and are shadows, the next best thing is the stories that incorporate the legends and parables.

The persons best able to tell the legends and parables are the grandmothers as they have the longest life experiences and understanding. The grandfathers have their stories and may have a different life view or come from another place. Whoever the storyteller is will clarify what he is going to relate and will give credits to whoever or whatever needs be credited. That is the way of our ancestors.

Somehow, from my own experience, it seems that the grandmothers had the best stories and legends and they would say, "I will tell you an Unipkaaq now." (Unipkaaq, meaning "story.") The atmosphere would be set for a grand experience. We did not need a radio, television or movie to entertain us. Who had radios, televisions or movies then in that time that seems so long ago?

These stories are from my parents about their lives and stories that they have passed on from their parents. At times I will weave in the stories as I understood them.

To introduce the family to you I have the following: My name is Frances Ann Degnan and I was born May 26, 1943, at 1:05 a.m., to my mother Ada Johnsson Degnan and father Frank Auvnue Degnan. I was born in the log cabin that my parents built in 1937 in Unalakleet, Alaska. They were so proud that Poppa had built it in only seven days.

I have three brothers and six sisters when you consider what the Inuit family recognizes as family. However I will list those siblings that were raised in our parents' home.

My oldest brother Charles Orville was born on June 23, 1941, and youngest brother, Maurice John, was born on October 3, 1947. My youngest sister, Shirley Kate, was born on February 28, 1945. They were born in that same cabin in Unalakleet that Poppa built in seven days.

My oldest sister, Marjorie Miller was born, on November 23, 1931, in Unalakleet. Eva was born on June 9, 1930. Gerald O'Brien was born on July 13, 1931. Ida May was born on May 29, 1935. Those three were born in Nome, Alaska. Ada June was born in Unalakleet at Aunt Gertie and Uncle John's log cabin on June 1, 1937. That was because Poppa had not finished building our own log cabin.

Marjorie Miller died August 22, 1932, of influenza at home. Maurice died, February 9, 1949, at the hospital in Nome of spinal meningitis. Shirley Kate died on March 7, 1945, of an intestinal obstruction shortly after birth at our home. Both Momma and Poppa said that if there had been a hospital near Shirley could have lived, as repairing the obstruction is a simple procedure today. Our oldest brother Gerald died, August 25, 1974, in Anchorage, Alaska.

Poppa died on Thanksgiving Day, November 27, 1980, at 2:20 p.m. at the Alaska Native Medical Center, Anchorage, Alaska. Momma and I were by his side when he left us. Momma died peacefully at home on January 4, 1996, at 7:50 a.m., and I was with her. Both Momma and Poppa are buried at the Unalakleet cemetery and their graves are side by side.

Poppa's mother Apok, also known as Martha Annie Degnan, died March 15, 1953, at the Mount Edgecumbe Hospital in Sitka, Alaska, and her remains are still at the mausoleum of the Native hospital. We will be bringing her home soon. Gerald O'Brien is buried in the city cemetery near the Sheraton Hotel in Anchorage, Alaska. Maggie Otootuk Degnan is buried at Belmont Point cemetery in Nome.

Momma's mother, Igailaq, also known as Agnes Anaktayuk Ryan, along with Henry and Marjorie Miller, Maurice John and Shirley Kate Degnan, is buried at Unalakleet. Igailaq died in her own home in Unalakleet on August 21, 1962.

Poppa's poppa, Francis Gerald Degnan, is buried at the Northern State Hospital Cemetery in Sedro Woolley, Washington where he died on December 26, 1942.

Momma's poppa, Eric Johnsson, died September 16, 1966, at Everett, Washington, at the Everett General Hospital. He is buried at Restlawn Memorial Park in Edmonds, Washington. Grandpa's wife, Margaret Harriet Johnson Johnsson, died May 10, 1980, in Edmonds, Washington and is buried there also. May they rest in peace.

1. Momma's Story of New Life

When Momma spoke about our family she was ever thankful to be living in Unalakleet. She said that she wanted all of her children to be born here. She ever marveled that all the children that were born here were healthy normal babies in her time. She was thankful that Thora Soosuk (Katchatag) had delivered Chuck, Shirley, Maurice and me; in fact, had delivered many of the children born here.

Thora was a skilled Unalit midwife. Her Inuit name was Naqhchuk. She was also a mother of many children. She was like Igailaq in that she trained her children well in the traditions and customs of our people.

Momma said that I was born at spring hunting time. My father Frank Auvnue Degnan was in Shaktoolik, a village forty miles north of Unalakleet. Momma told me that he had just taken another mother and newborn son to their home by boat.

As for Momma, she said that she and my oldest sister Eva had been busy all day planting potatoes in the garden. Momma had just gone down the steps of the root cellar in the log cabin when "the water broke and I really hollered for Eva to come. She came right away and I sent her to get Thora. Eva sure was fast. You were born early in the morning. That morning when your sisters and brothers saw you I told them that the swallows that they had been anxiously waiting for came and delivered you. They brought you in a diaper that they held in their little beaks. Your sisters Eva, Ida and June and your brothers Jerry and Chuck really believed that. It seemed that I sent Eva running for a midwife for each one of your births.

"So it was Apok, your dad's mother, that named you right away after her Irish husband Francis Gerald Degnan who had died in Sedro Woolley, Washington on December 26, 1942. Then that day your dad came back from Shaktoolik with baby clothes from Sophie Rylander that her son Allen had outgrown. That's the woman dad had brought to her home in Shaktoolik."

My mother, Ada Johnsson Degnan, had also been born at her mother's home in Unalakleet on February 10, 1910. She was the youngest daughter born to Agnes Anaktayuk Ryan and a Swedish mail carrier Eric Johnsson. Her Inuit name given to her at birth was Quyan, meaning Thankful, she told me that was her favorite name but she had many other names and some of them were Sapsugaq, Ahwahlik, and Kaalatuq.

Momma loved to tell me the story of her birth. She was born in her mother's little log cabin and the best friend of her mother named Lena Williams, whose Inuit names were Kakauraq and Aakanaagaq, attended the birth. When Momma was just born, Kakauraq cleaned her off and wrapped her in flannel and brought her over to her own son, Charlie Williams, who was sleeping in one of the beds and placed the newborn baby next to her son and said, "Keeh, now you two are married." Kakauraq then named her Kaalatuq after Kakauraq's brother. Kakauraq was Kawerakmiut like Igialaq. She had been the first wife of Nashalook, a Malemiut, and they had three children who were Marion, Joe, and Andrew. When Nashalook took a second wife, Kakauraq left him for Frank Williams. Kakauraq and Frank had two children who were Laura Williams, wife of Henry Ivanoff, and Charlie Williams. Momma always liked that story as told to her by Igialaq.

When Momma got older, Igialaq would tell her about her own life and about not knowing her own parents. Although Igialaq and Eric had not married, Momma was very close to both of them as they claimed her as their child. Eric Johnsson had come from Sweden to San Francisco, California and then made his way to St. Michael and Norton Sound on the Moran Fleet when he was only sixteen.

Momma always said that both her parents were orphans and therefore we were all so very lucky that we had our own parents for however long we had them. Much later in life grandpa wrote to Momma when I questioned him about his own childhood. He wrote that as a child he was raised by strangers in Stockholm, Sweden. He did not know his mother, and he said that his father had been in India. As a result he never knew his parents. That is why he left Sweden to come to America. After Momma died I learned that grandpa was born in Eskilstuna, Sweden on January 29, 1876, to Aaron and Clara Johnsson. That much we know today, thanks to our cousin Linda Larson, who sent me a copy of the information she had gathered, some of which was from Reverend Ludwig Ost who was a good friend of grandpa Johnsson. Momma loved her father dearly, so it was unfortunate she did not know this history.

Momma said, "Mother was born at a point north of Nome, Alaska, during the family camping time about 1876. The point was Igailuts so she was named Igailaq. Her mother was Killaun and her father was Anaqtuyuuq. They were both Kawerak Eskimos from the Imuruk Basin-Teller area. They were traditional Kawerakmiut in that he was a hunter-fisher-gatherer and she was his helpmate. They had a son named Aasuk and two daughters Aligiaq and Igailaq. I think that mother was born around 1876 because they did not have records them days."

Momma said that when her mother Igailaq was just an infant her father was lost on a hunting trip. He never returned nor were his remains found. Killaun loved him so much she died not too long after that of a broken heart. Her children were then orphaned, and since Igailaq was the youngest she was sent to relatives living at Port St. Michael. Aligiaq and Aasuk remained in the Teller area and there was no family contact or reunion for many years.

Momma said that whenever Inuit parents were not able to raise their own children for any reason there were always relatives that would step in and help rear the children. As a result no child ever became homeless or was without a family.

When Grandma Igailaq moved to St. Michael, she was placed with close relatives and their family name was Neumann. Momma told me that this couple that took her in had several other children and one of them was a girl who later married and was known as Lucy Newman Whitley. They also had a son named Willie Newman.

From my own checking around I found that the man that took Igailaq in was named Henry Neumann. He was the agent for the Alaska Commercial Company at St. Michael for many years. Momma always thought that he was an Englishman, but I recently found out that he had been a German. The Holy Cross Mission records show that Henry Neumann sent his children to the mission for their education. I learned more about this, thanks to Dr. Dorothy Jean Ray who had spent some time in Unalakleet visiting and interviewing Mayuugiaq (Marion Nashalook Gonangnan) while she was still living. Mayuugiaq's daughter, Martha Lucy Isaacs Nanouk, also spoke with Dr. Ray. Momma and Poppa spoke with Dr. Ray, too. That was in the mid 1960's.

Momma said that Igailaq was baptized in the local Russian Orthodox Church and given the name Exzenia and then the English name of Agnes Anaktayuk and also Agnes Egiluck, therefore, Grandma Agnes. We always knew her as Grandma. She was a short, soft-looking, warm-feeling woman. She always said that her tiny feet were too small for her frame.

Momma told us that Grandma had a tough growing-up life because she was orphaned and did not have a protector, although she had a home she was welcomed in. As an orphan she felt she was expected to earn her bed and board and that is just what she did. It must have been difficult, but she learned how to compensate for the aloneness and not to depend too much emotionally on others.

Grandma told Momma that she learned how to rein in her temper and that is a good thing. She said that one day when she was alone in the home a neighbor woman came to visit and found her alone. This woman badgered her about how poor a person she was. Grandma couldn't do anything right. Grandma said that was all she could take and "I Silaiqued," meaning she lost her temper. Dishes, pots and pans flew. However, no one was hurt; the woman left, and she never badgered Grandma again. Happily for Grandma, she never let her temper loose again, and she vowed that this shall never happen again. It never did, and Grandma felt better.

Formal education in the American style was not an option for Inuit of Grandma's generation. Day-to-day living was the challenge of the times. Women had to keep the hearth and home humming, keep the man of the house fed, his hunting equipment in good repair and all the other challenges put forth by Man and Nature. You have to know that travel was limited to the mode of the season, communications were rudimentary and public utilities were primitive. Grandma said that life was good and everyone knew everyone and their business.

Fort St. Michael was established in 1833 by the Russians for trade and commerce. In 1867 the Russians sold the areas they occupied to the United States of America. The Americans used St. Michael for military, commerce and transportation purposes. The Americans had that outpost in St. Michael from 1897 to 1917.

When the United States government opened the school for the Natives it was located near the Army outpost and was under the auspices of the Bureau of Education. In the reports written by the teachers assigned there they wrote about the conditions of the village from what they observed. In their observations it was the military and the traders that had the best of accommodations.

The local Natives lived in two villages near the post on St. Michael Island. Of course, each of the writers had their struggles just to keep the school operational on a minimal budget. It appeared that their understanding of their primary role was to protect the Natives from the 'evils' introduced by the Outsiders.

The teachers were charged with the education of the Natives, and also to provide medical help when called on. The military had their own post doctor, who was called on to assist when anything serious occurred. The head teacher was also charged with keeping account of the reindeer herds that were still under government supervision. The only way in and out of St. Michael for the teacher was by steamship. If they traveled to Unalakleet it would be by hopping on the mail carrier's dog sled or by private schooner, depending on the season.

Grandma had contact with Outsiders and some of that which was considered modern then. Apparently this sort of life did not impress Grandma as she pursued Kawerakmiut way of life with vigor. She knew that she was of Kawerak origins and she never thought to embrace the foreign ways for herself.

She was a remarkable woman in the sense that although she could not read or write the English language she had relationships and children with three different European men. The first man was a German whose name was Fred Bouker, and they had one son later baptized as Frank Ryan. The second man was Irish whose name was Fred Ryan. He did marry her and they had two girls, Jessie and Gertie.

Momma said that Ryan did not stay around too long. One day he upped and went down the Yukon River and found another woman. Igailaq accepted his departure and went on with her life. This was in 1909. She had children that depended on her. This was her family and her whole life. She was satisfied. She would meet the challenges one by one that she was to face raising Frank, Jessie and Gertie. She would make sure her children had a mother who would love and protect them.

About this time a Swede came along, and his name was Eric Johnsson. Since Ryan was gone, Igailaq accepted Eric into her home. In the winter of 1910 they had a child, a daughter named Ada Johnsson. That is Momma. Eric wanted to marry Grandma, but since she was not divorced from Fred Ryan, and there was no trace of him she said that she could not marry.

So that is how Grandma said she was finished with all men. She kept her word, Momma said, and she died peacefully in her own home on August 21, 1962 at the age of eighty-two or thereabouts. Uncle Frank Ryan put on her death certificate that she was born, January 22, 1880, and her parents were unknown. Momma said her mother told her about her parents and she had to be older than eighty-two, more like eighty-six at her death, but for sure she was older than eighty!

Village Elders: Nashalook, Etageak, Tomrun, and Chikliak

Dorcas Society, 1936
Top L-R: Mrs. Etageak, unidentified, Kiarok, unidentified,
Mrs. Nashalook, Mrs. Oyoumick
Front L-R: Mrs. Katchatag, Mrs. Tomrun, Mrs. Ryan, Mrs.
Muktuk, Mrs. Ayagiak, Mrs Neuksik singing

2. *Igailaq's Move to Unalakleet*

How Grandma got to Unalakleet is hazy, but we know she moved there after she married Fred Ryan. Her first child, Frank, was born October 15, 1896 at St. Michael, Alaska. He was given the Inuit name of Tagilgayak. Frank was baptized in the Russian Orthodox Church on December 19, 1897.

Momma said Grandma had a daughter May born in 1901 and died in 1902. She did not remember her Inuit name given at birth. Jessie was born on January 6, 1903, at a creek south of Unalakleet. Today that creek bears her name, Jessie Creek. She was given the Inuit name of Kuvsaq meaning Net. Jessie's father was Fred Ryan. Jessie was also baptized at the Russian Orthodox Church at St. Michael.

Two years later Grandma and Fred Ryan had another daughter, Gertie Ryan, who was born at Unalakleet on October 19, 1905. She was given the Inuit name of Tugragmiu.

Igailaq never talked about her husband to any of the children in our family. Since she did not speak of him, Momma did not tell about him except that he was the father of our aunts. I never thought to question anyone about him and I regretted that. On my part, life just moved so fast and we were all so busy. I think back now and realize we were just responding to Grandma. We never wanted to hurt her feelings by being inquisitive. Actually little children were to be quiet when the adults were speaking.

Trying to get events into perspective, Momma can be sure that she was born in Unalakleet. Momma remembered her mother telling her that she moved to Unalakleet from St. Michael but there was always a need to go to St. Michael. This is the place where marriages, baptisms and trading occurred. There was constant traffic between the two villages by foot, dog sled or boat.

Momma's father Eric Johnsson left Stockholm, Sweden and went to San Francisco as a cod fisherman. From there he got on as a crewman on one of twelve steamers, The Moran Fleet, that came to Alaska in 1892 and he was only sixteen years old. He got a job carrying mail on the route between Nome, Unalakleet and St. Michael. That is how he met Igailaq. Fred Ryan had abandoned Igailaq and when she was to have Eric's baby, Eric wanted to marry her. Ryan was nowhere to be found and Igailaq felt she could not marry. Momma was born at home on February 10, 1910, in Unalakleet. Momma said everyone knew she was Eric's daughter as she looked just like him.

Momma told me many times that the village was governed by a committee of elders who watched over the community. They found out that Igailaq was going to have a child and her husband was gone. They assigned Etageak to consult her. His assignment was to find out who the father of the child was. He made a visit to Igailaq. He asked her if she was pregnant. She did not answer. He then asked her to tell him the name of the father. She just responded with "Are you jealous?" He turned around and went out the door. Nothing was ever said again about that subject and the case was closed.

Igailaq was a protective and loving mother to all her children. She was firm and direct in her discipline. That discipline was tempered with love. She loved her children dearly. She was kind and loyal to her friends.

Momma said that her mother liked to have her women friends over for lunch or tea. They all would sit on the floor and enjoy the meal and companionship. It was a beautiful sight to see the women sharing food and conversation. They only spoke in their Native language. They would share news and happenings of the day or week. They would practice the gospel songs they were to sing at church the following Sunday. They did this regularly throughout her entire adult life until she died. These were pleasant and memorable times for all of the women.

Igailaq advised her children to be kind to the poor, orphans and helpless. She also told them as children not to go visiting at homes during the family meal time. She said that it was not respectful to do that unless you were specifically invited. She said that maybe they may only have enough to feed their own family. Momma said that they all respected their mother's advice. She also told her children that when they became parents that they were responsible for their care and upbringing, and that they should not let someone else take their children even for a short while. She did not know the word or meaning of "baby-sitting."

When Momma had her own children she followed her mother's advice. As a result we all went wherever our parents went. I think now that was the best thing that ever happened to us. We have so many memories of the things we shared with them.

Eric was a kind and responsible man and provided for the support and care of his child, Ada Johnsson. Two years after Momma was born, Eric then met and married a young woman, Margaret Johnson from Unalakleet, and they would have many children. They were married at Unalakleet in 1912. Margaret was the daughter of Anna Pukik, who was Unalit, and Maurice Johnson, who was a Swede. Maurice was born September 5, 1860, and died April 29, 1917, in Seattle, Washington. Margaret's Inuit name was Chikuyuk. Her Unalit grandparents were Yuyyaq, her grandmother, and Gasuanuaq, her grandfather. Eric and Margaret's children were: Aaron Alexander was born on September 12, 1913, at Unalakleet. He died on December 28, 1967, at Edmonds, Washington and was buried there. Anna Sophie was born on July 5, 1915, at Golovin. She married Harold Ford Phillips on May 8, 1937. She died on August 7, 1983, at Olympia, Washington and was buried at Edmonds. Ruth Katherine was born on January 26, 1923, at Council. Ruth married John T. Emel on August 5, 1943, at Fortuna Ledge. Peggy was born in Council and died as an infant in the 1920's. Maurice Calvin was born on September 19, 1927, at St. Michael. He died in 1947 in Seattle, Washington and was buried there. Peggy Clara was born in 1929, in Fortuna Ledge and died there as an infant. Clara August (Christmas) was born in 1932 at Fortuna Ledge and died there in 1938.

Momma said that even if her dad was married to another woman she still would go over to their house in the village to be with him. She said that she was so young she was not aware that she may not have been welcomed by Margaret. This relationship carried on Momma's entire life.

Eric then was hired as a United States Marshal for the Nome District. Eric and Margaret moved to Council, Alaska. While in Council, Eric was busy mining for gold with his friend Jepsen. He was forever talking about Jepsen but never about finding gold.

Momma kept in touch with them. Igailaq did not object and whenever Eric's work brought him to Unalakleet he would bring clothing, sweets and gold coins for Momma. Momma's favorite was a beautiful heavy wool red sweater. She said that since she was so rough at playtime her dad would bring her boy's work shoes and overalls for her play and work with her brother Frank.

Grandma Igailaq and her four children lived in a one-room cabin. The cabin was located near the south end of the village, close to the mouth of the Unalakleet River and along the coast of the Norton Sound. It was built of spruce logs and the floor was hewn cottonwood. She took pride in keeping the floor sparkling white. The cabin was heated with a wood cook stove. The roof was made of sapling rafters covered with sod. Momma always commented that in the wintertime a strand of grass always grew down. Momma called it her garden. For lighting the room Grandma had a kerosene-filled lamp. They had no radio then and the communication or news was by word of mouth. Even so, the news traveled fast.

Momma said that Grandma told her that she was living in her cabin before the Swedish Evangelical Covenant Mission and church buildings were constructed. Grandma told Momma that during her time all the houses were built of local spruce that grew in the Unalakleet River Valley. That was probably because the Russians had an outpost here at Unalakleet and the Unalukmiut learned how to live above ground from their example. Before that era they lived in underground winter homes. Their summer homes were portable tents made of skins, and the semi-permanent summer homes were made of driftwood. They moved into these homes to get away from the often wet and damp winter homes when the ground thawed. However, the winter homes, which were partially subterranean, were the warm ones for the winter season.

A census was conducted in 1880 by the federal government and it stated that there were only one hundred Natives living in Unalakleet at that time. In the book, *The Eskimo About Bering Strait*, E. W. Nelson writes that on February 12, 1880, he visited the village of Unalakleet and observed young teenage boys dancing their traditional dances in a kashim. Momma said that during Apok's life in Unalakleet it was commonplace to dance and have feasts. By the time Igailaq settled here the influence of the missionaries put a stop to all so-called "pagan rituals." As a consequence Momma and Poppa did not observe or participate in any dance and feast traditions of our ancestors at Unalakleet.

Igailaq was an industrious young mother. Her days were full of rearing her children as they were born to her. Her philosophy of life revolved around the traditions of her ancestors. She learned the skills of home management, time management and family budgeting from her time with her adoptive parents in St. Michael.

Momma said, "Mother never spoke much about her growing up or much about the men in her life. She sure knew how to take care of us. She always had plenty of food, fresh, salted, frozen or air-dried as well as preserved in seal or fish oil. She was such an amazing mother. She always knew what to do if anyone needed help, advice or just a place of refuge. She could always say "No I am sorry I cannot help you, but go and see…they know what to do,' if the situation called for it."

Unalakleet in Igailaq's time, was a quiet place. It was a good place to live as there were many animals, fish and plants. A person could be kept busy every day of the year in the harvest of foods. Like all good things, there were times that Mother Nature withheld her bounty. There was not much of a cash economy. One could live comfortably without cash but it meant that you would be a very busy person. Subsistence living was the rule of the day.

There were only a few paying jobs in the village. The persons earning wages were the teachers, missionaries, traders, mail carriers, reindeer herders, and those working in the freight-hauling business.

One of the first stores in Unalakleet was opened by Edward Bradley. Bradley, as he was locally known, was an Irishman from New York. He came to Unalakleet during the gold rush. After living in St. Michael and Golsovia, a village thirty miles from St. Michael, he moved his family to Unalakleet and made it his home. His store was next to the site where the old Alaska Commercial Company sheet metal covered warehouse had been located. Bradley's store was a wood framed two story building. His family lived on the second floor and his store was located on the ground floor. The building was torn down and the current Alaska Commercial Company manager's residence is located there today.

Bradley was a kind hearted man. He allowed many of his patrons to purchase on credit, so much so that he soon was out of business. He never went after them to pay their bills. Bradley bought Mischa Ivanoff's house. Here Bradley was to live out his life in Unalakleet with his family. Even if he was out of the store business his house was a busy place. He housed and fed many of the travelers and local people when they came to his house for help. All this he did out of the goodness of his heart.

Stephan Ivanoff was a half-Russian Yup'ik and he was the next local person to get into the store business. He established the next trading post in Unalakleet at the site where the current Alaska Commercial Company store sits. After some time in the business Stephan then sold the business to Stanhauser and Dwyer who operated the store.

Then in 1916 Charles Traeger purchased the trading post from Stanhauser and Dwyer. Charlie Traeger was to marry Eula Kootook some years later and raise a family in Unalakleet. Traeger's store was the only one in the village. Traeger was also the postmaster.

Stephan Ivanoff who had originally owned that store was now the commissioner after living many years in Shaktoolik. Before that the people had to travel to St. Michael for their marriage licenses and other business that required the licensing of the commissioner's office.

Momma would say that all the families were at the same level. It was the tradition for the community to make sure the widows and orphans were provided with the necessities of life such as food and shelter. Fresh water and wood for heating were plentiful. It just took hard work to bring it home for use. Everyone in the home had chores to do. The children learned at an early age to help out. Some of the children may have been mischievous, but there were very few problem children, what they label juvenile delinquents in the Western culture. Movies did not appear on the scene until the mid 1940's so the community provided for the entertainment. Many games were played by all the age groups after the day's work was done.

There was much time for visiting with family and friends. There was much travel along the coast throughout the year. Everyone knew their extended families and visited with them when they could. There were many small villages spread out around the Norton Sound area. People traveled a lot by foot. The people were physically fit because they did their travel by walking. If someone owned a boat they would take others if they were traveling the same direction. Time did not seem to be a problem. When you wanted to go somewhere you did not consult the calendar or clock. However, you would watch the weather closely. Almost everyone learned how to read the weather from observation of sky, sea, land and air.

3. Watching the Gold-Seekers

During Igailaq's days the most critical factors were the diseases and foreign illnesses brought in by the travelers that were on their way to Sitnasuak (Nome, Alaska) to seek their fortunes in gold. Igailaq liked to tell one certain story about the Outsiders and the craziness of their love of gold.

Igailaq said, "This old Inupiaq couple had a house in Ayasaruk, near Cape Nome and they would watch the 'Nalagmiu '(White man) keep go looking all around. One morning they wake up to noises, scraping noises under the house. The man go out and look and see a Nalagmiu scraping flakes of gold into a pan. The Inupiaq shrugged his shoulders and went back into his house and told his wife what was going on. They were amazed at what that White man was doing a foolish thing as he could not eat that gold." But, of course, any Inupiaq living then knew that this was gold fever and somehow or another this fever seemed to only plague Outsiders.

Another story was "This Inupiaq hunter was out in the hills near Sitnasuak (Nome) and he came across a prospector scratching a creek bed. Since neither were fluent in the other's language there was not much said. Finally the Inupiaq picked up a yellow rock, about the size of a walnut, and walked over to the prospector and gave it to him. The prospector looked at it, shook his head vigorously NO and gave it a giant heave. The Inupiaq hunter left with no more thought and the prospector hastily retrieved the gold nugget!"

There were many other stories about the gold seekers and other travelers making their way through Unalakleet. They said many went by boat but some walked. Some had makeshift boats and rafts thinking they would make it to Nome. The Inuit watched with interest and assisted anyone who needed help. According to the accounts kept by the missionaries, they too had an interest in the gold rush that was much different from the indigenous peoples interest. The mission was to benefit greatly from this event in many ways.

There are many stories and anecdotes about that Great Gold Rush to Nome. It seems that the libraries in Alaska and Washington are full of actual eyewitness accounts or stories remembered by friends and families. However, one would have to really search for anything written by the indigenous people about this era.

One would surmise that the cultural differences played a big part in the written collections. Also it appears that the indigenous people were so busy pursuing their own lifestyle they were not aware that their life was so different and interesting to those wishing to earn their way in life as writers. Since the actual people being written about could not read or write the other languages these articles were published in no one questioned the accuracy and authenticity of the articles.

Life goes on, and the saving grace for the indigenous people is that they retained their ancient method of oral history. In Igailaq's generation, the historian of the tribe held a special status in the group. The individual selected to be the historian had to have special calling and training for this position.

Igailaq was not one of those historians, nor did she claim to be one. However, there were two people related to her that were oral historians. The eldest being an Unalit named Apok who was to become Ada's own mother-in-law and a Kawerakmiut named William Oquilluk, Igailaq's own nephew, the son of Aligiaq, who lived in Marys Igloo. Later, William would publish a volume of Kawerak legends in a book entitled *People of the Kauwerak* published in 1973 by Alaska Methodist University, Anchorage, Alaska. Momma said that her aunt was an owner of large reindeer herds in that area and the name of her home became known as Marys Igloo during the Gold Rush era.

Aligiaq and Aasuk, sister and brother of Igailaq

Mary Aligiaq, sister of Igailaq

4. *Poppa's Start in Life*

Now we go back to Poppa's side of the family. Poppa's mother Apok was the only surviving daughter born to Auvnue and Nataguq, who were Unalukmiut, of the original indigenous tribe of Unalakleet, Alaska. Apok's father Auvnue was one of five Unalit brothers. These brothers had one sister. All of the brothers were from Unalakleet but lived along the Norton Sound coast.

The eldest brother was Im-ma-you-ak.

The next brother was Nathrook, who had a son named Oscar Natigook, who was the first husband of Lily Sacceus. Lily later married and was known as Lily Aukon.

The next brother was Auvnue who was married to Nataguq and they had one surviving daughter named Apok. Apok told Poppa that she had two half-brothers. Their names were Daniel Boone, (Tuungaiyaaq), whose mother was Qikiqtaq of Golovin and Reuben Paniptchuk, whose mother was Panigruaq, of Unalakleet. Auvnue and Nataguq lived in Unalakleet. According to Poppa, Auvnue died of the flu in 1900.

The next brother was Paneok. Paneok's wife was Siuvak and their children were: a daughter Atghaq, and sons Aaron Paneok, (Analgaq), and Ernest Paneok, (Kalluk). Atghaq, living in Koyuk, had sons named Sankey, John and Harold Charles and a daughter named Esther Charles.

The youngest of the brothers, U-goon-earik, was adopted by his mother's sister. He was born at Kwiniuk. His English name was Mike Murray. Mike married Helen Otton, (Inuit name Binegnoruk,) who was born at the mouth of the Koyuk River. She was the daughter of U-tan and Aqpayuk of Koyuk. Their children, living in Elim, were Esther Murray, Beatrice who became the wife of Harry Daniels, Mary Ann who became the wife of Sam Segock, Julia who became the wife of Andrew McCafferty, Mabel Murray, Joe Murray, Dan Murray and James Murray.

Chinglak was the sister. She spent all of her life in Unalakleet. She married Toghak and their children were Ellen and Alma. Ellen married Edward Bradley. Chinglak lived with the Bradleys after Toghak died.

Apok was born approximately June 15, 1870, during spring camping time at Wood Point, just north of St. Michael. Poppa said that his mother told him that when she was born the herring had just migrated into the St. Michael Bay area and were spawning on the rocks and seaweed.

Apok lived with her parents at Unalakleet up to the time of her father Auvnue's death about 1900. Their home and kashim were in the traditional fashion of the home of an Unalit. Apok told Poppa that he had two biological uncles from two other families. Her father, Auvnue, had a son with a Unalit woman, Panigruaq. The child's name was Nookuksaigahk. The other son was with Qikigtaq, and the child's name was Tuungaiyaaq. So Poppa grew up calling those men "Uncle." They knew what he meant.

As Apok was the daughter of an Unalit chief she was trained in the oral traditions of her tribe and since her father was also an active trader he was able to bring in oral historians from other tribes to teach Apok the history of the Inuit. Apok said that the Unalit tradition of training took about fifteen years to learn the role of the woman. Since she was the only surviving child in the family she had to study fifteen years more to learn the male role of the Unalit. She commented that the education she saw being practiced by the American way seemed simplistic.

Written records were never kept by the Unalit so they would tell of the events that took place at the time of birth, deaths, marriages so that they could be remembered. These stories were then related on down the line of generations. Also when a child was born they would be given the name of persons recently deceased and that were related to them biologically. This practice continues today.

Here is the Unalit story that my father Frank Auvnue Degnan told to me. To start with, Poppa was born in St. Michael, Alaska, on July 7, 1901, to Apok, also known as Martha Annie Apok Degnan, and Francis Gerald Degnan. Apok named her child Auvnue after her father, a name that means "cottonwood bark." His other Inuit names were Tipaq and a Siberian name of Noohk-too-yii, meaning "All Powerful," after a Yup'ik relative living in Siberia. Poppa was the only surviving child; an infant sister named Eva did not live long.

Poppa told us many times about the day he was born. His mother told him that he was born on a bed of grass in a barn, on the day the first ship of the season into St. Michael had arrived, and at the very moment the ship horn sounded. His mother told him he was no bigger than a ptarmigan, and she could put her wedding ring over his hand to rest on his wrist.

St. Michael was the largest port in Alaska when Apok lived there and it was there she met and married Grandpa Degnan. Grandpa was born on March 2, 1869 in Seabeck, Washington, near Port Orchard. There is no record of his birth at the Kitsap County Auditor's office in Port Orchard because their records for birth certificates did not start until November, 1891. His death certificate states that he was born on March 2, 1869. His given name was Francis Gerald Degnan. His father was Tom Degnan, who was born in Ireland, and his mother was Johanna Murphy, also born in Ireland.

According to Poppa, his father's grandmother O'Brien left Ireland during the Potato Famine by wooden clipper ship, approximately 1840. The ship sailed around Cape Horn, her final destination being a port in Washington state. The family settled there when Seattle was still a wigwam village, meaning, the Indians were in control of their own country.

Poppa told us that he knew his Irish relatives. We had family in Quilcene, Port Townsend, Port Angeles in Washington and in the San Francisco, California area. We also have Irish relatives along the East coast of the United States. After he left Nome, Alaska about 1934 grandpa

Degnan lived in Quilcene, Port Angeles and then finally, in Everett, Washington. When he became ill he entered the Northern State Hospital on November 18, 1940. He was at the hospital until his death from cerebral arteriosclerosis on December 26, 1942. Grandpa was buried at the Northern State Hospital cemetery in Sedro Woolley, Washington.

The family names were Degnan, Oatman, and O'Brien to name a few. Poppa said that Grandpa was the black sheep of the family, and when the gold was discovered in the Klondike in the late 1800's, he made up his mind to strike it rich. Grandpa moved along the Chilkoot Trail with all the other gold seekers, but he never staked a claim nor found gold. The only money he ever made was that that he made backpacking supplies for other gold-seekers. Grandpa Degnan said that he was in Skagway when Soapy Smith was there and knew him.

Grandpa Degnan then shook off the dust of the Klondike and moved by ship to Port St. Michael to find his fortune in the Far North. An industrious man, he was willing to work at any job available to support himself. He stayed for a time at St. Michael, where he met Apok.

As you recall, Apok left her home in Unalakleet to move to St. Michael about 1900 after her father Auvnue had died. Auvnue's wife, Nattaguq, had died in Unalakleet before her husband, but Apok never spoke of the cause of death either. Poppa learned that a flu epidemic occurred in 1900, which caused the death of most of the elders at Unalakleet. Apok said that her father's remains were placed at Five Mile Point just north of St. Michael.

According to Poppa, "My grandfather Auvnue was the last of the truly Unalit chiefs. After he died there were no more Unalit chiefs in the original tribal traditional way. This was the new era of the American intrusion into Unalakleet. In 1832 the Unalit's were besieged by the Russians who established a fort at the village as it was situated in a strategic location where there was plenty of trees, fresh water, fish, land and sea animals for food. The Russians introduced new diseases to the local people including the fatal disease of small-pox. This small-pox disease was in the blankets that they gave or traded to the Unalukmiut living in the fourth Unalit village site across the point of the mouth of the present Unalakleet River. There were only thirteen survivors of the epidemic and were the direct relatives of Apok. I have a relic that was handed down to me; it is a scrimshawed ivory drill bow with the picture story of the end of the village. (Later in life the bow was brought to Poppa by 'Taguyah,' Frank Insall from Shaktoolik.) All the people, except for the thirteen, died and their igloos are how they left them when they died.

"When Momma (Apok) left Unalakleet, it was located at the present village site. This is where the Russians had their log cabins and their so called fort. This is the fifth village of the Unalukmiut since time immemorial. Unalakleet means 'Furthest to the South.' This means to the Inupiaq that this is where you will run out of Inupiaq country and be in Yup'ik territory. After the Russians came then the Malemiut Eskimos came in from Kobuk River area and found this to be to their liking and sent for their relatives and took up residence in this Yup'ik village. The first Malemiuts to come were Talialuk, Maqtaq, Tuktuk, Paniptchuk, and Nashalook and they were all brothers. That is how Unalakleet moved from a Yup'ik village to a mixture of Unalit-Malemiut and other mixture of people and their culture."

When Apok lived in St. Michael it did not mean that she had forsaken Unalakleet; she was to return there to live again permanently in 1937 with her now-enlarged family. So Poppa, Frank Auvnue Degnan, was born in Tachik, a Yup'ik village, also called St. Michael. There were two main groups of people there, the indigenous Yup'iks and the Outsiders. Of course, the Outsiders then were Russians who ran the trading posts and church, and the Americans who ran the military outpost, port and commerce. The port was the largest in Alaska. It was a busy, bustling place and was the jumping off place for all the travelers that were headed for the gold fields in Nome.

Grandpa Degnan was an easy going man who would work for a wage to provide the household with the necessities. Apok followed her Yup'ik tradition of being the hunter, fisher and gatherer. She had received her guns from her father Auvnue and was known locally to be a sharpshooter. She fashioned snares from willows and seal-skin twines to harvest the small game in season. When the game was available she provided rabbit, ptarmigan, and small birds for the family to eat.

With the mixture of cultures, day to day life was a blend of the old and the new, fashioned to the needs of the day. Since cash could only be gotten from the American system; the local stores issued their own form of currency to the locals. Called 'bingles, they were just like cash and could be redeemed for fur, gold, fish or cash.

Poppa said that when he was born, the village of St. Michael was a very busy place. There were many steamboats that traveled the river carrying passengers, freight, mail and supplies. The steamboats were well equipped to serve the passengers and were like traveling restaurants. They used the local timber for fuel and had their regular stops to load up on wood. The riverboats had a regular schedule and went as far as Nenana. In fact, when he got older he worked on several boats.

Frank A. Degnan on steamboat

5. Two Orphans Meet in St. Michael

The people living in St. Michael in the early 1900's were a mixture of Inuit, European and American. Not too many of the outsiders married the Inuit but there were some marriages and some long-term relationships. The children born were often called half-breeds, and were often looked down on by both groups, with the exception of those who loved them. Poppa said that when he was little he had curly hair and his parents would try to tame his curls by using oil, but that did not last long.

Grandpa Degnan had Poppa baptized, on January 6, 1902, by Reverend A. M. Keyes, S.J.. His sponsor was Alexander Waska.

It was at this time in St. Michael that Igailaq and Apok were to become acquainted and become lifelong friends. In fact, Apok, known then as Annie Arpuk, married Frank G. Degnan on October 31, 1900, on the same day T. F. Ryan married Agnes Egiluck, that is Igailaq. What a coincidence! According to Poppa, we did not know then that we would be more than friends, we would become family. While Igailaq was raising her children, Frank, Jessie and Gertie with her husband Fred Ryan, Apok and grandpa went to Koyuk with Poppa.

It was about 1905 that the Degnan family moved to Ungalik on the Norton Bay shore. Later the family moved to Koyuk as Apok had relatives there and game was more abundant than in St. Michael. While in Ungalik they lived with Nagaruk and his wife Ooyan and their son Paul whose

Inuit name was Soolook. Poppa said that time in his life was especially enjoyable as he had fun playing with Soolook and later with Paul's sister Beda. Beda's Inuit name was Misiqaaqaq, meaning "little bird." He said that Nagarak and Ooyan treated him like one of their own children.

Apok was busy pursuing her Unalit lifestyle. Apok took her son everywhere she went. She told him that when they were in Koyuk, out hunting, he would climb upon a stump of wood and start talking like he was speaking to a large audience. She never scolded him but would say to him that if he only knew how little he was at birth he would not be talking so much.

Apok knew that she would have to teach her only child the ways of her Unalit ancestors, and that she did with enthusiasm. In this period of Inuit history the people were living off the land and there was very little employment as we know it today. In winter, the families might have lived in the village to be near the church and school, if they were available, but when spring arrived the families would move out to their traditional camps to harvest the animals and plants and to renew their spirits. Every member of the family had their work cut out for them and the children learned at an early age what was expected of them in order for life to be profitable. So, in essence, everyone kept the cycle of tradition alive.

Poppa was a good son to both of his parents for he knew that he was loved and cherished by both of them. Both of his parents had high expectations for him. His father wanted him to get a good American schooling and his mother expected him to be a self-respecting Unalit. Apok had relatives in Koyuk and Golovin and that was the reason for the extended visits to those villages because she wanted her family to know the extended family. Of course, these were good hunting and fishing grounds, too.

It was time for the family to move to Nome for work and school for Poppa. When I tried to verify that Poppa indeed attended the Nome Public School I was informed by the Nome School District that the attendance records from 1902 to 1908 were not in their files. They referred me to the Department of Education Archives in Juneau, Alaska and they in turn informed me that the records they have do not include 1902 to 1908 either. So we shall just have to take Poppa's word. I can speak from personal experience that you can take Poppa's word at face value as it was always the truth.

Grandpa Degnan tried his hand at staking gold claims and if he had a likely spot he would sell the claim to a person wanting to prospect. Since Poppa was getting to be of school age and curious, grandpa Degnan and Apok wanted him to go to a good school and enrolled him in the Nome Territorial School although it was closed to the Native children. The Natives were not allowed in this school as they were required by local decision to attend the Bureau of Indian Affairs school.

Since Nome was a result of the Great Gold Rush it was a typical American Frontier town not a Native village. There were several classes apparent in the town. First came the professional and merchants that called themselves the "Four Hundred,"; then the technicians, the miners; and, at the bottom, the Natives, with the "Half-Breeds" at the periphery. So Poppa's little family moved, in, outside, all around and sometimes in the middle of the life of the different groups. Poppa said that he did all right in school. Grandpa Degnan worked and prospected for gold in Nome and Apok continued her Unalit food-gathering tradition. It was then decided that the family would return to St. Michael for work and return to the land of the Unalit.

When Poppa, Apok and grandpa Degnan moved back to St. Michael in 1910 they knew that Igailaq and her children had taken up residence in Unalakleet. Since Igailaq was now living in Unalakleet and she and Apok were good friends, Apok and her family would take time out and visit her home village and stay with Igailaq.

Poppa loved to tell us the story about their visit to Igailaq in 1911. "Momma and I went to see Igailaq and when we were settled in the house I saw this beautiful baby girl playing with a fat roly poly puppy on the floor. I looked at that baby, she was as round and chubby as the puppy she was playing with. I knew at that very moment that one day she would be my wife. She was not even aware of me."

St. Michael was still a busy port when the Degnan family moved back there. Grandpa Degnan went to work for the A.Y.N. Company. He belonged to a local club called The Moose Lodge 1414. The membership elected him the head of the group, and he was called "Governor." Poppa was back in school in St. Michael.

Before Poppa died in 1980 he wanted to show me the place where he was born and where they lived as a family in the early 1900's. We went down by airplane, and as we circled the village of St. Michael he pointed out the place where their house had been. The house was gone, but you could see very clearly where the foundation had been set in. When we landed at the airport he pointed out to me where all the buildings had been. He said that at one time this place was the biggest port in Alaska. We walked all around the place. We walked the beach and found small remains of what had been a busy port. The steamships were all gone.

Poppa told me of the time that he was a boy living here. He said that it was a good place to live. He told me that he was always curious as a child and always had some adventure planned. One day he and his buddy, Ivan Sipary, decided that they would look for buried treasure. With all the people that had lived or passed through this place surely someone buried a treasure! He said, "So we scouted all around. Not too far from the boardwalk there was a spot that looked like it had something. So we got a pick and shovel and went to work. It wasn't long before we struck something. Sure was exciting. We found a fancy chest that was fastened to keep it shut. We sure had something there. We had to figure out who would open it. The other guy said I had to do it. I looked at that thing and popped it open. It looked like something wrapped in cloth. I pulled it out. Unwrapped the thing. It was a monkey. Sure didn't smell good either. We put it back in the treasure chest and buried it back. That was the end of the treasure hunts."

Poppa said that he decided that it was time for him to go to work and help his parents earn some money. So he got a job sweeping up the store. It wasn't a bad job. But he had thought that he would eventually be allowed to clerk and maybe make a few more dollars. He said, "I never got to clerk at that time because the clerk there was good and all they needed for the business they did. I got to work there until dad shipped me to Holy Cross. Dad wanted me to get a good education and Holy Cross Mission, run by the Catholic Church, at Holy Cross, Alaska was the best that was nearest."

Third from left: Aulagin, father of John Auliye
Far right: Mike Murray

6. *Poppa Goes to Holy Cross Mission*

Poppa entered Holy Cross Mission School on July 28, 1914. The school records have him entered as Frank Deignan. Their records show that he was baptized in St. Michael, Alaska. He had his First Communion in April 1915. He was confirmed on August 15, 1915. This was all at Holy Cross Mission. Their records show him leaving the mission, on July 18, 1916, and he never returned there to the school. Holy Cross Mission was established in 1886 by the Catholic Church and it was run by the Jesuits. This school was to educate and train the indigenous population of Western Alaska.

Poppa said that when he arrived at Holy Cross on the steamboat he was shown where the school was located. The first person he met was Father Sifton. Poppa said Father John Sifton welcomed him and asked him if he knew where he was. He said, "I looked around and there was a large cross and I said yes, I am in Heaven and that's how I got to Holy Cross."

"Sister Mary Bernadette and Sister Mary Thecla were the ones to figure out where I would stay. The first dorm I went in by myself was the girls' dorm. That's not where I was to stay. They took me to the little boys' dorm and then to the big boys' dorm. I was too big for the little boys and too little for the big boys so they decided to try me in the big boys' dorm. So that is where I stayed for the time I was there.

"I settled in and checked out the Mission. I could see that this was a village unto itself. The Catholic priests and the nuns were there to make sure we got an education, that not only included reading and writing the English language but an education in routine and work. We were all assigned our chores and tasks according to our age and skills. The girls were separated from the boys and the children from the teenagers. It seemed like a good place to be.

"There were kids from all over the Yukon and some of us from up North. It seems like we were a mix of all nations. Some of the other kids were Tim Twitchell, Ivan Sipary, Harry Brush, and his sister Hattie, and many others. I would have to look at the school list to tell you all their names. We all got along well together and we had fun. It was a good place and my dad always encouraged me to do my best. I always wanted to do my best for both my momma and dad.

"Time sure went by fast at Holy Cross. The boys were busy at the bakery, fish-house, laundry and garden. The girls were busy in the kitchen, dorm and schoolhouse. It really was a self-sustaining place where they really kept you busy. It was a good place for those who didn't have any place else to be. They sure made you learn your catechism and Bible.

"Like I said, It's just like coming to Heaven, I got to know a lot of good people there that were to be my friends throughout life. It was in the first week I was there, it was supper time, during the prayer, I threw my plate down the length of the table. Of course, that got everyone's attention. The Sisters asked me 'Francis, what is it?' I said, 'It's about time our prayers are answered. Where are the coffee, butter and enough sugar?' 'You'll see about that later.' I said, 'It can't be later, it's got to be now.' All my schoolmates were quiet and waited to see if I would be sent out, but the only thing that happened was that they brought me coffee, butter and sugar. I asked for milk and said that I would not eat it unless all the other schoolmates got it too. Also we could be eating more of the king salmon strips and bacon. In other words, we could be eating a little better of what we had. As it turned out we did

41

see a change in our menu and were able to eat more of the things that the older folks were enjoying. I don't know why I was not punished. I just guess that my timing was right."

Poppa said that the education was good for the times. At then some of his schoolmates were looking to the future and higher education. Poppa said, "I was fourteen then. My good friend Tim Twitchell said that he was going to go to college and come back to help our people, and I said, 'I am going to start now as we don't have the time as the time is now.' We all knew that the times were changing from that what our parents grew up in. There were many outsiders and they seem to be the ones running the show and making the rules. But we all knew that we would have to learn the ropes to keep our country and ways. Anyhow our ancestors always seem to have survived anyone or anything that came their way and they were not displaced from our land."

"During the time I was in Holy Cross I enjoyed my time there. Life was interesting and it was good to be going to school with kids all up and down the Yukon River. Many of us were sent there because our parents wanted us to be in a school where they knew we would be safe and well-taken care of by the Sisters and Brothers of the Catholic Church."

Frank Degnan (left front), Ivan Sipary (drummer), and boys in Holy Cross band

7. *On the Yukon River Boats*

It was at Holy Cross that Poppa said he learned the skills that would serve him well when he went to work on the steamboats that traveled from St. Michael up the Yukon as far as Nenana. Poppa got a summer job with the N.A.T &T. Company (North American Transportation and Trading Company) working for several summers on the steamboats plying the Yukon River. Some of those boats were named *Susie, Sarah* and *Hermann*. He said his first job was in the kitchen washing dishes, pots and pans and cleaning the restaurant. He liked to tell of the time that he was washing dishes.

Poppa said that the cook on the boat he was working on was a very moody fellow. There were times that the cook would fling a pot or frying pan out the window into the water along with expletives. He said, "You had to be careful around that man. If you crossed him or if he had a bad day he may just throw a French knife at you. I've seen him do it. I kept out of his way. One day when I was up to my elbows in suds and dishes he hollered at me to get right out and wait on tables. One of the waiters never came back to the boat from one of the stops. So I did just what he would do, I took the dishes out of the sink and threw them out of the window. He saw that but he never batted an eye or said anything.

"So I was promoted to waiter. That was a good job. Much easier than that of dishwasher. All I had to do was walk around to the tables, with a cloth hung over my arm and take the passengers' orders. Then I would go to the galley station and holler out my order and wait in line for the order to be filled by the cook. One time when I asked a man what he would like for lunch he said to me, 'Oh, a little bit of this and little bit of that, anything you'd like to bring.' So I brung him some hash. He said, 'I didn't order this.' I told him, 'Sure you did, you said a little bit of this and a little bit of that; that's hash.' Well, I had fun being a waiter. The next job I had in mind was that of Purser. That seemed like an easier job than waiter and certainly easier than dishwasher. But I didn't stay long enough on the boats to make that position."

Poppa said that he didn't mind the work and kept his eye on what other jobs he could do. The boats he worked on were the *Susie* and the *Sarah*. He said that they were modern for their times and treated their passengers well. In the dining room where he worked they used linen and tableware just like good restaurants on land.

After his summer work on the river steamboats Poppa was again working in the store business for Mrs. Franklin Moses. Since he was fluent in both English and Yup'ik, she stationed him at her trading post at Alakanak. He told us that he enjoyed working in that area.

Poppa always said that he had great respect for the people living in that area. He said that they were very smart people and were living in the traditions of their ancestors. They did not let on that they recognized the changes that were moving into their area and affecting their lives.

Poppa said, "Those people were very smart. If you thought they did not understand English, you were mistaken. They still practiced their old ways and I got to witness first hand the 'Anatkuqs' (medicine-men) and what they could do. Momma told me to be careful when I went there and to remember that powerful forces were still in existence. I knew what she really meant was that I was to respect the people and their beliefs. And I always did. They were my own people. I knew my momma was always right."

8. *Apok Moves to Nome Again*

About 1918 the Degnan family moved back to Nome, Alaska and took up residence there again. World War I had not ended, and although both of them were willing to join the armed services Poppa said that his dad was too old to serve and Poppa was too young. Nome was a lot smaller in 1918 than their earlier stays there. Poppa said that he was able to secure a job with the court systems as a court interpreter since he was fluent in English as well as in all the Inuit dialects.

This was the same time that Eric Johnsson was United States Marshal, hauling in the Eskimos from the surrounding villages to be processed for alleged infractions of law. Many of the prisoners spoke only Yup'ik or Inupiaq, and a rudimentary English that had its own flavor, a language the Americans could not fathom.

According to Poppa, many of the prisoners pled guilty to any charges because the system was foreign and the right side of the law did not understand the indigenous population. So as a result, many an innocent person was incarcerated. However, as long as Poppa provided the interpreting, the jail stays were minimized. He felt that with his assistance the poor people had a better chance at justice.

When Poppa was working as a court interpreter the Danish explorer Knud Rasmussen came to Nome and the surrounding area on his Fifth Thule Expedition. Since Rasmussen was not fluent in the Bering Straits languages, Poppa was retained to assist Rasmussen in his study of the local indigenous populations. Poppa said that the two companions of Knud Rasmussen were Miteq and Anarulunguaq. All three were Inuit from Greenland. Poppa said that although Knud said he could speak and understand all the Inuit languages and dialects, Poppa himself could speak and understand three more than Knud.

In Knud Rasmussen's book *Across Arctic America* he does not mention using Poppa as interpreter. Poppa told me that there was a picture of his mother Apok in Rasmussen's book and the picture was labeled "Woman of Point Barrow." But being the kind of man Poppa was, I take Poppa's word that he did work for Knud Rasmussen.

Also at this time in Poppa's life I found out from the court records in Nome some interesting details that I wished that Poppa had told me about. As a child I was very much interested in finding out all the family kinship and connections. I did not have much opportunity to ask questions and when I did many times I got answers that satisfied my curiosity. I knew as a child that everyone had a mother and father. Some people had brothers and sisters and some had none. Some people had one grandparent and some had many grandparents. Everyone seemed to have an abundance of aunts, uncles and cousins.

For me I wanted to find everyone that belonged on our family tree. I went so far as to search every letter that I found in the house. Some of those letters contained names that I never heard about. When I asked Momma to tell me about the mysteries she would tell me to wait. The time would come when I would understand. Of course, I was patient and eventually she would explain who the people were. They turned out to be her first deceased husband Henry Isaacs Miller and her daughter Marjorie Miller who died as an infant.

I found out that Poppa had a daughter named Kathleen who was born in Nome. She was born on July 4, 1925. She was the daughter of Margaret Becker who was supposed to marry Poppa but ran away with another man and married him. His name was Fred Yenney and he and Margaret had many children. Kathleen made sure she kept in contact with Poppa and when her mother died she made a trip to our home in Unalakleet in May of 1949 to meet her other family. Poppa had acknowledged his paternal obligations to her.

Poppa said that his dad was wanting to go back to his home and to introduce his son to the Degnan clan. Poppa said that he was eager to go but then reluctant to leave his mother Apok, who was still pursuing the Unalit tradition of fishing, hunting, and food gathering while Grandpa and Poppa worked at odd jobs to bring in cash.

It was time to get to know the other side of the family. A family conference was held and it was agreed that the trip would be made and Apok would keep the home fires burning. Poppa promised he would return. So the trip by steamship would take the two men to Seattle, and they would go and visit family, relatives, and friends in Quilcene, Washington.

Apok and Poppa in Nome

9. *Igailaq's Decision to Make Unalakleet Home*

We take leave of Apok, grandpa Degnan, and Poppa and go back to Igailaq's little family at the small Unalit village of Unalakleet. Igailaq had her first two children at St. Michael and she is married to T. F. Ryan,but everyone called him Ryan. He is the father of only two of Igailaq's children, the first being Jessie Ryan and the second being Gertie. Neither of these were born at St. Michael but Frank Ryan remembered his life in St. Michael.

When Igailaq and her son Frank moved to Unalakleet it was with her then-husband Ryan. One of the stories her son Frank had told to his children was that at Unalakleet, his teacher and mentor, a Mr. Van Ness, taught him a lot about time and money management. "He sent me to the store with one dollar to buy French bread for him. At that time one loaf cost ten cents. I could barely carry ten loaves of bread back to Van Ness.'"

There really are no stories told by Igailaq about Frank's biological father but his name was Fred Bouker and some say he was German and some say he was French-Canadian. In essence he was out of sight and out of Igailaq's mind.

We can be sure that Igailaq spent her childhood and young adulthood in St. Michael and moved to Unalakleet as a young mother in the early 1900's as that village was as good as any to raise her family. Momma said that their family always gardened even before the missionaries came, probably because of the Russian influence and presence

since the main vegetables grown with success were potatoes, turnips, lettuce, cabbage, carrots, and radishes. All
the children learned how to garden and when they had
their own homes they had gardens of their own.

Igailaq was a busy homemaker and spent all of her
time rearing her children. Since his mother was a single
parent, Frank took on the role of the family protector. As
schools were already on the scene all of her children were
enrolled in their time. The family lived in the spruce log
cabin house that was to be the family home for almost
fifty years. As Frank became old enough he built a large
dog barn to house his ever-faithful team of Eskimo dogs.
He built an elevated food storage cache and outhouses.
This was the winter permanent home for Igailaq's family.

During the spring season the family would go to their
usual squirrel and waterfowl hunting spots where they
used the dogs and sled for transport and canvas tent for
shelter. Much of the travel was on foot, and no thought
was given to the distances the family had to travel. They
did know where they were going and what they were going to do.

Momma had such pleasant memories of her family
and this is a reflection on the kind of mother Igailaq was
to all of her children. Igailaq had a very strong sense of
the kind of mother she wanted to be since she did not have
any recollections of her own mother or father or her sister
or brother. She never complained of her own childhood as
far back as Momma could remember.

Igailaq did not rely on outside influences as far as
her children were concerned. There was no such thing as
government welfare assistance then. She was such an
independent-thinking woman she would not consider applying for such assistance even if it were made available
to her. She provided a safe, warm and comfortable dwelling for them to live in; that house provided shelter for the
entire family for as long as they needed it. The original
house was torn down in the early 1950's when her son
Frank Ryan built her a new frame house through one of
the earliest Territory of Alaska housing programs. Then,
the materials for a modest house cost, at the most, five
hundred dollars.

Igailaq's house was the center of the family operation for most of the year. Come spring the activity and focus was for the little family to head to the southeast of the village in search of fresh food and to renew their spirits.

The following excerpt is a recollection told to me by Momma, Ada Johnsson Degnan: "As far back as I can remember, I have always spent the season of spring in Unalakleet. In my early years spring meant dog sled rides, tomcod fishing, squirrel hunting and the return of the birds. Oh what a joyous time for a child!

"I was the youngest child in the house so I had the advantage of having more teachers, and that I enjoyed. My mother was a single parent so she had much to do in the task of raising three girls and one boy.

"In the first days of spring our little log cabin was a busy place. While we children were in charge of the wood and water supply, our Mother was busy sewing or mending skin waterproof boots, parka covers and fur socks for the out of the village camping trips we were to make as a family.

"My brother Frank, as the eldest child, was the next in line as head of the household. As I recall he was a very busy person. He had a string of dogs that he took good care of; he even had built a dog barn next to our cabin for them. He always kept twelve dogs. He built a food storage cache right next to the dog barn. Here we stored the dog food. It sat high above the ground on stilts and had a ladder to get into it.

"I can remember that Frank had me help him with the dogs and getting driftwood for burning in our stove. As I got older he would tell me, 'I wish you had been a boy.' I know he appreciated what help I could give him.

"As the daylight became longer each day the temperature became warmer and we know that it would not be long that we would be heading south to the hills and mountains that surrounded our little village. Of course, as we got to six years of age we were required to go to school. In those days of my childhood we were able to intertwine our subsistence way of life with our required formal classroom learning.

"As the temperatures warmed and the camping preparations almost done we knew it was almost time to go to the hills in search of the parka squirrel, 'Siq-siq.' All during the winter months mother and my older sisters Jessie and Gertie had sewn boots, slippers, mittens and parkas for all of us and some for trade at Charles Stanhauser's trading post. The trading post had been previously owned by Stephan Ivanoff, a local Native."

As a result of the spring squirrel hunting trips each of the children and Igailaq was to enjoy and use utilitarian parkas and the beautiful traditional Eskimo woman dress parka with the Sunshine style ruff on the hood. Igailaq took pride in using all the material she collected or bartered for, and used every particle of material at her disposal. She taught this to each of her children, so when they became adults with families of their own they were well prepared to cope with any situation that confronted them. Even if they had their own families they had daily contact with their mother Igailaq and if they had to leave Unalakleet they always managed to return to live.

Igailaq was a spiritual woman. She was caught between two spiritualities, but she never lost sight of the reason she was put on Earth: to take good care of yourself, your family, your neighbors, your community and the Earth and all its bounties. Since she was raised in St. Michael she had been baptized in the Russian Orthodox Church, and then the Catholic Church came in when Alaska was sold to America. So, as an adult, married and with children, it was only natural that she would find it normal to have her children attend whatever foreign church was available.

The notion of God and Jesus Christ was not foreign as the Inuit acknowledged the existence of a higher being and Creator. He was known in this Unalit area as 'Silum-Inua.' The values and methods of the Outsiders may have been strange but they were still the available method to give acknowledgment to a higher spiritual being.

During the years all of the family became members of the local Covenant Church and through regular attendance, took part in the various choirs and other activities. This is what everyone else was doing in the community too. Igailaq sang translated songs with the other elder women. Jessie, Gertie and Ada all sang in the choir. They were very good singers. Jessie sang high soprano, Gertie sang soprano and Ada sang tenor and bass. Frank also helped in the church.

Momma said that as long as the family was in the village, and there was a church service being held, the family would attend. As it turned out, it was always an Outsider that organized any activity in the church and if it was to be a local Native they were still on the sideline.

It was however, Igailaq's neighbor, Wilson Gonangnan who volunteered his services for the Covenant Church, which were accepted and he traveled to organize the church efforts in Mountain Village. Mountain Village was in Catholic Church territory and Wilson had to live without a stipend or support from the Covenant Church. Wilson was a Kawerakmiut like Igailaq. His wife's name was Yulgaq, and she was Unalit.

However the women's group, known as Sewing Society by the elders, would send small sums of money raised locally by sales of their handicrafts to Wilson and his wife. Igailaq was a member and she called it "Sewing Secei," since she couldn't pronounce "Society." Later Wilson was to tell Igailaq that if it not been for the money sent by the ladies, and for help of the local Catholic priest in Mountain Village, he and his wife would not have been able to survive without begging. It was about that time that Wilson sold his house to Frank Ryan as it was next door to Igailaq and when Frank married he moved his family in there.

Igailaq was an excellent seamstress and she used all the Kawerak and Unalit traditions in her creations and had her own adaptations. For the girls she fashioned calico dresses and cloth parkas, and their favorite flannel undergarments. For her son, she made shirts, but was able to get trousers already made from the trading post. However, if necessary, she could have fashioned them too. The winter wear was all hand-crafted by her, and she successfully taught the skills to all of her daughters, who, later in life, were to be known for their good sewing and crafting skills.

Momma would tell us that she was not as good at sewing as Jessie and Gertie were. She said that it seems effortless for them to fashion any garment or footwear without any help from Igailaq. She said that since she was so embarrassed about her sewing, she would practice in secret so they wouldn't see her stitches. They made mittens, slippers, boots (plain and waterproof), parkas and backpacks, all of animal hides or fur. They were able to get the skins and furs with their own efforts by trapping, snaring or hunting. For more rare material they would trade clothing for a hunter's furs.

In all reality, this family's daily activities, was the same for many other families. Seasons dictated the activities. Traditions and customs of the ancestors were closely adhered to ensure continued plenty for harvest.

Dances and feasts were common before the arrival of the missionaries. With the arrival of the Outsiders these activities were to become a rarity. There was very little introduced to take their place. The last traditional Inuit feast to be held formally in Unalakleet was about 1911 according to the now-deceased elders.

Up Unalakleet River

10. Unalakleet's Kashims

Momma said that there used to be several kashims in Unalakleet. One was located near the site where Johnny and Emma Ivanoff built their house, and the other, at the site near George and Helen Lockwood's house. She said those kashims, or men's council underground houses, were in constant use until the missionaries came and introduced Christianity: The men worked there every day, and that is where the Unalit had their feasts, dances and storytelling. When Christianity was introduced the Inuit embraced it without question as the spirituality had linkage with the same values of the people. One of the Outsiders was responsible for the destruction of the last kashim about 1911 and was therefore given the name "Destroyer of Kashim" by the Unalit. After the church, mission and schools were established they became the focal point of the village social activity. This social activity was important along with the every day pursuit of food, water, heat and clothing.

Since the majority of the village pursued the same lifestyle there were only a few Inuits holding positions that brought in cash on a steady basis. Most of the positions were held by persons who came from outside the village. The local mission started the schools on behalf of the United States government and when the school system for the Alaskan indigenous people were instituted the Alaska Native Service took over the operation of the schools.

Many of the early Outsiders, who were teachers, were affiliated with a church organization. Later, teachers were recruited by the Alaska Native Service, subsequently known as the Bureau of Indian Affairs. A majority of these people did not mingle with the Inuit in the community, but stayed together in their own dwellings. From the outside view, an observer would think that there were two separate and distinct classes of people. However, the children of both groups played together and had fun.

Life was much easier materially in this harsh environment for the Outsiders. They were about the only people who had access to cash or subsidies. Their housing was subsidized by the federal government and whatever church congregations that sent them to Christianize and educate the people.

In 1884 the federal government offered various churches their choice of land in the aboriginal land of Alaska, thus began the populating of Alaska by Outsiders. The aborigines had no knowledge of what was happening. It was like the silent and subtle invasion of their territory. Whalers, navigators, and traders moved throughout their territory, but they were not permanent. The churches and schools that came would be permanent and would have a land base taken from the aboriginal people.

The Inuit still enjoyed the freedom of their territory. They moved along with the seasons. They followed their fish and game. They practiced their songs and dances and held their feasts and festivals at their designated times. The arrival of the strangers brought new ways, new ideas and new diseases. Many of the Inuit died before their time and the populations dwindled. But the spirit of the Inuit remained intact. They were not strangers to adversity. They would prevail. This was their homeland and they would not be displaced.

According to Apok, the Unalit had survived from time immemorial in their homeland. According to legend, Unalakleet was the first settlement on the continent. The first people came down from space to settle and the land was made good for their existence. They lived well, food and shelter were plentiful. Life was easy. They had many helpers with whom they communicated on a spiritual plane. That was just the way it was. Life was good. Time went on. Changes to come were seen ahead of time. The people were to prepare for these times.

Another Unalit legend was about the first man. These are Poppa's words in telling it: "This is the story of the first man. He came to life from a blade of beach grass, this first man. It was during the spring when the snow was melting on the side of a stream of water. By the stream was a new grown clump of grass. The man felt the warmth of the bright sun on him and it felt good to him. This man was the blade of grass.

"This man he bent over and looked into the water. He saw a reflection in the water and it frightened him. He put his hand to his face and the man in the water did the same. This was all very puzzling to him. He didn't know what was going on.

"Then he had a pain in his middle. He leaned over the water and put his face into the water. He drank the water and it was sweet. He drank some more because it was so good. It made him feel better. That's the story of the first man. This type of grass can be found wherever the Eskimos have lived. You can tell by this grass where the old campsites were located."

Centuries passed. The Unalit made it through the natural disasters that caused climate changes, famines and death of many. There were always to be survivors. Sometimes only a few people survived. As long as the Unalit know their roots and history there will be Unalits living on the earth that was given to them to enjoy along with all living creatures. To keep the land you must respect all that is in it. That is where your sustenance dwells. That is the wisdom of the elders. I believe that wisdom is much more important today as the world population grows and pollutants diminish the natural productivity of the land, sea and air.

Although the kashims were gone, the sense and enjoyment of song were carried on through singing in the church. The fun of togetherness and play moved out into the open with the adults joining in playing games of football, foot races and competitions either on the sand or snow depending on the season of the celebrations. During the summertime one would observe the adult men playing ball or "ma-na-man-na" every night after work of the day and supper until they got tired.

The Unalit had celebrations and festivals before the Russians and Americans came into their country. Today that tradition has vanished into thin air as the memories of the ancestors were shunned in the teachings of the Outsiders, and anything Inuit in tradition was looked up not to be treasured except perhaps in a faraway museum. Our people's way of life has had adaptations, but the basic values taught by our ancestors are still treasured by us. You can find descriptions in articles and stories written about the past by Outsiders. They give accounts of what they saw then. Those writings do not reveal the soul of the people or activities they witnessed. That is why the old stories from the elders are so important.

The following is Poppa's Unalit story about the settlement of the villages of Unalakleet. "There are no written records of the settlement of Unalakleet. However I will tell you the story as told by my grandfather Auvnue who was a famed Unalit chief known from the Aleutian Chain to Barrow and into Siberia. The history is by word of mouth told by my grandfather to his daughter Apok, my mother who then told it to me.

"The reasons for the Unalit settling on the shores of the Norton Sound and for the other Eskimo tribes in Alaska, on the coast of Siberia, the Arctic Coast and over into Greenland were for survival. They claimed that the sea foods were more vital for existence than land animals in that they were more nutritious and healthful. Also sea animals were more abundant in the areas they settled. There was an abundance of tomcods which were caught through the ice and at times were the only foods available during bad weather. They were able to harpoon the seal and oogruk on the ice during the winter. In the summer they harpooned and netted the whale, beluga, seal and oogruk (bearded seal).

"The Unalit hunter caught his game with bow and arrow. Ducks and geese were plentiful and tame. The caribou came into the village where they were able to corral them and shoot them with bow and arrows. In the timber they set snares for the caribou, rabbit and ptarmigan.

"Unalakleet, meaning 'the southerly community,' the first village had a population of over two thousand Unalit.

It was the first village and it had several kashims or council-houses dating back ten thousand years. (This first village was located north of the present community on the eastside of the current airport's north-south runway.) It was in existence before the Cape Denbigh village of Nukleet, At this time the sand spit, which present Unalakleet exists, was submerged. This sand spit came into existence after the glacial period and had been washed up from the Norton Sound. The first village was wiped out by some epidemic or tidewaters and this village was known as 'Inigluit' meaning 'big village.'

The second village was then built at the eastern edge of the present East-West runway. The second village was called 'Nil-lai-luit' meaning 'place of many houses.' However, the second village was not as large as the first village site.

"The third location was on the south side of the mouth of the Unalakleet River. The Unalit built a big mound with sand so they could observe their friends and foes. They built the igloos on this mound. They occupied this village when the Russians invaded their territory. This village site was called 'Inni-ghrok,' the place of old houses.

"The Russian American Trading Company established a trading post at the present location of Unalakleet. Here they built a fort, trading post, and a Greek Orthodox Church. They baptized the Unalit and gave them Biblical names. Some of the Russians married local women before 1867 wherein today you find such names as Kazeminekoff, Kameroff, Odinzoff and Ivanoff.

"About 1838 the Russians had also introduced to the Unalit across the village to the small pox virus. The entire population, except for thirteen survivors, died of the virus in their igloos. The survivors then moved across the river and into the current Unalakleet. These were all Unalit and were our ancestors.

"The main Russian forts were located at St. Michael about sixty miles southeast of Unalakleet. The Russian American Trading Company established trading posts to buy furs for the Czar of All Russia. The villagers called the Russians 'Gussapete' and they thought all white people were Cossacks, so during the Gold Stampede they met other people and called them 'Gussaks.'

"The Unalit village was found to be a desirable place to live and other Eskimos from further up North came here to live. These were Kawerakmiut from the Imuruk Basin and Malemiut from the Kobuk River area. So after the Russians came then the Malemiut and Kawerakmiut came and settled in Unalakleet as it was a bountiful place to live, plenty of fish and sea mammals and land animals. So it was the peaceful land of the Unalit became an international community. That was the oral history of Unalakleet as taught to me. Grandpa Auvnue died about 1900 at Unalakleet."

The following is Momma Ada Johnsson Degnan's story about how Apok left Unalakleet: "On these what we got from our mothers that Apok lived here with her father and he had an igloo right about the middle of this village. He was a trader and he had a kuzgree, like a council house, and so during all this time and up until this time they lived here and this is the part how when he died that they confiscated all his goods like furs and whatever he had and all the guns and such, he always had a gun for Apok, everything he had from his cache, and the people told them to leave this place.

"So rather than go into misery she up and took her gun and whatever she had and left. But when the village found out that she was gone, the people that were mad found out then and wanted to pursue her. This one woman was Mrs. Towarak, her name was Iikuluk. She had told my mother, she had a son-in-law, her daughter Bessie was married to a Native man...and his name was Ahlughnehk. And he told him, this mother-in-law told him, when he came in he was so excited. She asked him 'what is the matter' he said 'Well they have chosen me to go after Apok to bring her back.' Now Iikuluk said to him, 'Now I warn you do not listen to those mean people, if you want to save your life, you know Apok carries a gun. You will lose your life.' So he did not go, he listened to his mother-in-law. She was in earnest in what she was saying. That was the law of the Natives, every warning must be heeded. That's how Apok leave Unalakleet in 1900 when her father died and the missionaries came."

11. The Unalit Meet New Arrivals

The Unalukmiut, Kawerakmiut and Malemiut groups now were living at the present location when the white missionaries from America came into the village in 1887. The Unalit were the original settlers. The Kawerakmiut came next and the last Inuit to settle at Unalakleet were the Malemiut from the Kobuk River region.

The United States government under the guidance of Sheldon Jackson brought in the Laplanders with their reindeer herds in 1898 to teach the village people their methods of reindeer husbandry. The Laplanders were settled in the village, and then a reindeer station named Eaton Station, was established several miles up the Unalakleet River. It was a small community to house the people that maintained the reindeer herds in the valley. The Laplanders maintained their language and customs, but also learned the local languages. When the reindeer business declined, they moved into Unalakleet, and the children went to the local school. Momma knew most of the surviving Laplanders who settled in the village. Some of them were her classmates. She said that they were fluent in their own language, Inuit and English; had very strong family ties, and were very industrious people.

When reindeer herding was flourishing they had their reindeer fairs. These were very colorful affairs. The Lapps wore their traditional garments and even their reindeer that they used for transport were colorfully decorated. They were always singing their own traditional songs and chants. She also commented that they were very kind people. They were a small community within the community. Momma also said that she felt sorry that the government that brought them into this country, seemed to have abandoned them completely. They had to fend for themselves in a strange land, once their occupation of reindeer herding had vanished for good in Unalakleet.

Momma said that the Lapps always had dried reindeer meat and she was able to buy a few pieces at a time. She would save her coins and when she got fifty cents she would go and visit one of the families to ask for some of the dried reindeer sticks, and she said that they would be very generous. The meat had a lot of fat on it, and it was such a delicious snack!

The main Lapp families that settled in Unalakleet were the Bangos, the Boynes, the Klementsons, the Bahls and the Bahrs. They all had their homes at the south end of the village and at the mouth of the river.

In 1889, the Swedish Evangelical Covenant Mission established a school to educate the children in the village and region. They also had an orphanage connected with the school so many of the children were from the surrounding villages. During this time the mission trained all the young people that wanted to attend. At that time school attendance was not mandatory. The people were still living and practicing their yearly food gathering activities. The students that attended the mission became lay pastors and teachers in the communities throughout the region.

About 1903, the school function was turned over to the United States government under the offices of the Bureau of Education. During Momma's school years she said that some of her earlier teachers were those who were educated at the mission. Some of those early indigenous teachers were Aaron Paneok, Mischa Ivanoff, Kiatcha Ivanoff, Samuel Anaruk, Ebba Tomrun and Eva Rock, all from the village of Unalakleet.

Under the influence of the fur traders, missionaries and government teachers the villagers were gradually introduced to a new way of life. They had a desire to acquire this new and strange way of life as they saw it. They were to put a new twist to it.

The community had an informal method of governance. A council of elders set and enforced the rules so that the village could continue to live in harmony. These elders were well respected by the villagers. They were expected to take care of any grievances and annoyances throughout the year. Momma did not say that they were elected positions but the elders did their jobs well. It was just a normal part of life. To her estimation, during her early years, there were no major crimes at all.

In the village the people built log cabin homes replacing the sod igloos as they were accustomed to using. They spent more time in the village to be near the church and school. Their children were required to attend the school and the families remained in the village as they wanted their children to learn how to read and write English. The people gradually adopted the new ways and put their own stamp on the adaptations. The language was a mixture of Unalit, Kawerak and Malemiut and a new way of speaking English. Only a few people could speak Russian.

The village life revolved around the church and school throughout the year and especially during the long winter season when they were more or less confined to the village area. There was one trading post, one roadhouse and a small hospital besides the small cabins and fish racks in the village when Momma was a young girl. The hospital, run by the government, was called a dispensary. It was located near the school. In later years this building burned to the ground and was never replaced, although the community wanted to have a hospital built in Unalakleet to meet the medical needs of the people.

There was always a registered nurse stationed there, which was a big help. One of the nurse's projects was to teach good health practices and disease prevention. She would check the children in school to make sure that they kept themselves clean, brushed their teeth and learned how to clean their homes. They inspected the children every day and charted their progress. A child showing good progress was rewarded with what the children considered small treasures.

The nurses also made home visits to see what the cleanliness level of the home was that day, and made recommendations for improvement if they felt it was necessary. The families did not seem to be offended. They even gave prizes for different things. The nurse would also make a home visit whenever anyone in the home was sick.

There were times that epidemics of influenza, measles and diphtheria were in the region. The people did not want the sickness in the village so with the help of the teachers, nurse and missionaries they established quarantine zone around the village. Absolutely no person was allowed to violate those quarantines. Momma said that it was because of the people's cooperation those quarantines saved the life of the villagers. Even the mail carriers were not allowed to come near the village. Someone would be assigned to get the mail at a designated point during the quarantine period.

Lapp families: the Bahrs and the Bahls

12. Growing up in Unalakleet

Momma had many recollections of her childhood and growing up in Unalakleet. She said that since she was the youngest in the family she was lucky. She had many teachers, and learned a lot from all of them. She looked up to her oldest brother and her older sisters.

She said that Frank was always busy building and fixing things and always seemed to know what he was doing. He would find paying jobs when they were available. One of his earlier jobs was to backpack the United States mail to Kaltag following an established trail. At some places there was a cable-pulley crossing set up over the streams. Frank was physically fit and he performed his duties well. Years later he was to become the postmaster and welfare agent for the village.

However, Igailaq did not encourage him to become a seagoing hunter as her father had been. It was because he did not have a father in the home to teach him and that scared her. It was all right for him to hunt on land though. Each month of the year Frank was able to provide different animals and fish for the family to live on. The life the family lived was pure, simple and ingenious. It was same for all the other families living in the region. Momma said that the life we lead today may seem easier but is more complex and expensive with all the new ways coming in.

Since schools had become the routine in the village they were all required to attend some school but no requirements to finish. However, each of the children attended as far as the eighth grade. There were no high schools in the village but if a child wanted to go to high school there were places they could go to. The schools were a long way from home and none of Igailaq's children were interested in leaving the village and their mother.

All of Igailaq's children were bilingual. They could read, write and speak English, and could converse fluently both in Inupiaq and Yup'ik. Formal schooling ended at the eighth grade for all of them. Momma said that they all learned practical skills at school and at home.

In 1919, Igailaq's oldest daughter Jessie met Sam Otton of Golovin, when he was a resident at the orphanage at Unalakleet, which was run by the Covenant Church. Prior to that, Sam had been at the church orphanage at Golovin. Sam, whose Inuit name was U-gu, was the son of U-tan and his wife, Aqpayuk. Sam's father was Unalit and his mother was a Malemuit from Kotzebue. Sam was born in Elim, Alaska on January 9, 1892. They were well suited in temperament and Sam met Igailaq's approval. Jessie was old enough to leave home. She was sixteen years old. When they asked to be married Igailaq was pleased. They were married at Sam's village on March 7, 1919. They were to live there for several years.

The following is Momma's story to me about how life in Unalakleet was when she was a young girl. The words are close to her own words and when the reference to "I" is made, it will be Momma's story: When Momma was eleven years old an incident occurred that made her decide to look for work where she could earn some money. It was the time that Igailaq was out of the house and only Frank and Ada were home.

Frank decided to clean out the papers and proceeded to burn them in the stove. Ada realized that he had thrown into the fire an envelope that looked like the one Igailaq used for storing her paper money. She hastily retrieved it from the flames and found only coins remaining. She remembered that her mother had told her that she had only a ten dollar bill and some change left. Ada felt so bad that she wanted to cry, but she realized that it would not bring back the lost.

She told Frank that she was going to go to work to replace the lost money. She said "I went right away to

Anna Hagberg, the nurse at the dispensary, and told her what had happened. I said that I would work for her as long as she wanted me if only she would give me the ten dollars right now so that I could give it to my mother. She understood my situation and said that I was to come every day after school to clean the dispensary. I remember that Clarence Towarak was also working in the dispensary. That was my first paying job. I went home with the ten dollars and gave it to Mother. I told her what happened and she did not scold me. So after that I had a steady job and Miss Hagberg taught me lots. She even paid me more than those ten dollars."

Momma continued her story and said, "That time in Unalakleet there were not too many people living in the village. We did not have any electricity, radios, outboard motors and things like today that made a lot of noise. The village was so quiet you could hear all the natural sounds like people talking, children playing and birds singing. The ocean and river sounded so good. When the wind blew it made a lot of noise. These days now you can't hear good sounds as we used to.

"Everyone took time out to visit. The men would gather at the trading post to get news and tell stories. The women would take turns visiting each other and have their tea and practice singing for church. They were all active in the Sewing Circle and would make the different things that they would sell to raise money for the church and the needy.

"The children all had chores to do like getting wood, hauling water from the river and general helping around the house. Many times different children would go and help the elders, and they enjoyed doing that. The children always seemed to know who would reward them with a treat. I used to like to go down the beach with a gunny sack and fill it up with kindling for Mother.

"In the winter it was a little different as the children were required to go to school. One of my teachers in the early years was Samuel Anaruk. He was one of the few Inuit that were hired to teach in the schools. The other Inuit hired were Aaron Paneok, Kiatcha Ivanoff, Mischa Ivanoff, Eva Rock, Mabel Ivanoff, Emily Ivanoff Brown, Eva

Ivanoff Ryan, and Emma Kotongan Ivanoff.

"It seemed like most of the teachers were affiliated with the church or had relatives that were teaching in Alaska. I have no proof but that was what it looked like to all of us at that time.

"Sometimes when I look at what is going on in the later years of my life that practice is still continued. If education is to succeed it should be our own people teaching our own children. We have the most interest in the welfare of our children.

"One time when I was asked if I could be able to teach I told the principal that I was just as smart as the college punks and had more love in my heart that I could teach better than some of the teachers that are sent to teach our children. I guess that the point I was trying to make is that you must be interested in the children so that you could make sure they got the best education you could give them. I still feel that way today.

"Most of the ones I went to school with all finished the eighth grade. My classmates were my buddies and they were Martha Isaac (Nanouk), Sophie Anaruk (Lieb), Hannah Powers (Sambo), who we called 'Kidlets,' Esther Bradley (Webster), and Henry Nashalook to name a few of them in my school.

"In those days when we studied grammar we made sure that we got all the training we could. It seems today the students don't have that same training in grammar. Maybe it is just the times we are now living in.

"We learned our manners and what was considered 'social graces' and when I look around today it seems like this should be stressed in school once again. I see the children do not behave like we used to in that we had to respect all of our elders.

"When we were invited into a home we would stand quietly at the doorway until we were invited to sit down. We did not holler and scream when we were in the house or playing outside. The reason for that, as taught by our parents, in the traditional manner was that: If you holler and scream they will think you are in trouble. When they find that you are not in trouble the other times you do that no one will pay attention to you. Then when you are really in danger you can expect that no one will come to your rescue when you really need it.

"In school the ones older than us maybe went as far at the third or fourth grade and quit because they were needed at home. Those days we never thought about dropping out or drop-outs.

"We learned how to knit, crochet, cook, make nets, and many practical things. The boys learned how to make sleds and boats and carpentry. It seemed as we were very busy working at school the time really went by fast.

"We were lucky that some of the teachers knew their music and we learned how to play the piano. We used to almost fight over who would get to practice first.

"We also learned how to sing and all of us loved to sing. I think that is why the church choirs were so good in our time. Our mothers all sang in the church choir but they sang in our own language. My age group sang mostly in English but we sure could sing our own language too and love it. The men were very good singers too. During my whole lifetime I loved music. I can still hear those songs ringing in my ear when they were sung in church by the different groups. None of us really needed to use a music sheet as we could sing from memory.

"When I got big enough I was given a small dog sled by one of the men. On it was carved the word 'Fluffy.' That was the name of my puppy. I used to hitch up Fluffy to the sled and go for rides after school. I loved to take the sled out to go around a small island out in the ocean near the shore. Sometimes I would give my girlfriend Esther Bradley (Webster) a ride. We really had much fun. It was from helping my brother Frank with his dogs that I learned how to run my little sled.

"Since I was the youngest in the family I was able to tag along with my older sisters when they went somewhere. I went everywhere with our mother. I was always in and out of our neighbor's house with my playmates Chukkoothlook and Ballah. Their parents were Aaron and Edna Paneok. Their house was next to ours and Edna was the most patient mother I knew. She never scolded us when we went in and out of the house. I felt so welcomed there. Aaron was such a kind and gentle father to his children.

"Another house I loved to go to was that of the Toghaks. That is where my good friend Ellen lived. We were always in and out of the house. Ellen's Inuit name was Kitliq. Her father's Inuit name was Toghak and her mother's Inuit name was Chinglak. Chinglak was Apok's aunt. She was the sister of Apok's father Auvnue.

"When Ellen married Edward Bradley her mother lived with them. Bradley was an Irishman from New York who settled in Unalakleet. Their children were Alma, Ransom, Edward, and Allen. Years later Ellen's daughter Alma Bradley whose Inuit name is Mukkighuk, married my nephew Roland Ryan Ivanoff, whose Inuit name was Anaqtuyuuq."

Alma told that her grandmother Chinglak and Apok were close friends as well as close relatives. Chinglak told Alma that when she and Apok were young women living in Unalakleet, they waited until all the people had gone to sleep, then they hitched up the dog teams and go to haul wood for their mothers. Chinglak was well-known for her running ability and speed. When foot race competitions were held only the men participated. Chinglak entered these races. The men came from surrounding villages. The race started in front of the trading post and ran up to the reindeer station of Eaton Station and back to the starting point. Chinglak was the first runner to finish the race; she won every race she entered.

Momma said, "Our people loved their games and competitions. After supper the adults gathered to play games in the spring and summer. These were fun and happy times and provided good relaxation from the day's hard work. The children had their own games too. Many times the women and children watched the men play the competitive games. This all made a good feeling of community.

"When spring came along all the families would get ready to do their subsistence gathering activities. Some of them would go squirrel hunting up to the hills by foot and dog team. Some of the men would go out seal and oogruk hunting. Not everyone had a kayak or dog team but they could walk to where they would hunt. Some of the women would go after the tomcods. We would dry the seal and oogruk meat, make oil out of the blubber and then store it all in the seal poke. Sure made for some tasty eating. We liked our rendered blubber that we call 'duhn-ghnek' to eat with the dried seal or oogruk meat and dried tomcods.

"Springtime brought many ducks, geese and crane. Ammunition was not plentiful so the hunters had to be good shots to bring home the birds. The birds were so welcomed after all the fish and dried fish that pulled us through the winter. The hunters only took what they could use and quit hunting when it was nesting time. Nesting time was just wonderful. We used to go out to the nearby flats and look for all kind of eggs. I had so much fun looking for the snipe eggs. When we found them we would holler out, 'I Piq-que,' meaning 'I found an egg.' I liked to eat the first one raw if it did not have a bird in it. We only gathered enough sea gulls, duck and snipe eggs for a change of diet. We did not pick more than we needed so the birds could return. The lucky people that were brave enough to go a long distance to search for the cliff dwelling birds really had a treat when they found murre and puffin eggs. I think that eider ducks had the best eggs.

"During this same time the herring fish returned to Norton Sound. We had short nets to catch them when they came in the river. Some of the people would catch them up the beach. As the herring came near shore, they came in thick, you really didn't have to have a long net to catch enough of them. You would catch them on the incoming tide. That way they would be full of eggs. The herring fish is so good when it is cut, hung and half-dried and then boiled. We eat it with our good greens that are just coming out. We love to eat the herring eggs on seaweed and we call them 'kahg-ghra,' they are so delicious. When the herring spawn on the rocks, seaweed or sea grass, the eggs stay on for three days. Then they loosen their grip and wash away. Somehow it always makes me think of the resurrection story of Jesus.

"After the herring come the king salmon. That salmon is feeding on the herring. I like to think that every fish in our waters gets fat on the herring or their eggs. When the king salmon is here our family is settled in camp about two or three miles north of the village. This place is called Mek-kik-klek meaning 'a place of good water.' This spot was the place my family camped all the way until the 1950's.

"Mother had her summer camp at the same site each year. It was in walking distance from the village. Frank and whatever family members were home would go with her to set up the camp. She had her canvas tent that had a wooden floor and a wood stove. She used woven grass mats that she made for the mattress. On the grass mats she placed reindeer hides for warmth and cushioning. She made quilts from eider and goose-down for bed coverings. So the beds were warm, soft and comfortable. She kept the place cozy, clean and neat. Mother was a very particular woman in her living arrangements. She built a tee-pee style storage and smokehouse building of driftwood. She had Frank set up a windbreak all around the tent and work area. After this was all completed the family settled in for the fish and berry season.

"Mek-kik-klek was our summer home. When we needed supplies mother would send us in to get what was needed. On Sundays and special events we would all walk to the village. We never missed Sunday services at the church. Mother would send Gertie to invite our neighbor whose name was Evalu to have lunch with us. Since he was blind Gertie would escort him to and from the camp to his own nearby camp. Later Gertie would name her own son Richard Ivanoff after Evalu.

"Mother wanted to catch the king salmon fish that came right after the herring fish had spawned. She had a short salmon net that was set up on a cable pulley system so that she could operate it herself. Once the net was set in the ocean she would watch it carefully from her camp. As soon as she saw a splash and the net move she would carefully draw in the net to the shore. She would then wrap the net around the fish and bring it to shore. She would be satisfied to catch one king at a time.

"She would then go on to process the fish. She had her own method that used every particle of the fish. The family would enjoy the head and entrails cleaned and boiled for lunch or supper. The body would be filleted and hung to dry, shaded from the hot sun and rain. Some of the fillets would be salted and smoked in her tee-pee style smokehouse. When she had enough large fillets dried she would sew them together into a barrel shape. When the other salted and smoked pieces were done she would pack them down into the barrel she had fashioned. Once that barrel was full she would sew the top of the remaining dried fillets. Since the king salmon was a rich oily fish the barrel of fish would be preserved in its own oil. It was ready for cold weather use without fear of spoilage as long as it was stored in a cool, dry place. The fish was delicious. That method worked well for mother.

"Mother taught all of us that it was very important to take good care of your food as you harvested and prepared it for storage. It was especially critical when you were preparing fish, sea mammals and small game for long term use. When air drying the prepared pieces you had to make sure the sun and rain did not spoil the end product. She always stored the dried fish and meats in seal oil for long term storage. She made sure that the storage cache was kept clean and was always inspecting the place to make sure that all was in order.

"She advised me that if you did not take good care of your catch it would easily spoil if you were careless. The hot sun would cook the fish. The rain would ruin the fish. If you took proper care of the drying product and later in storage it molded that was okay. The spoiled product would never mold. She said that the mold would not hurt you and it was easy to wash or wipe off before you ate it.

"Summer seemed short. The days were pleasant because there was a break from the long hard winters. Fishing was good most of the time and all the families in the village were also at their favorite camping sites all along the coast. Later in the summer some of the families would go further up the rivers to catch fish and pick berries.

"Mother preferred her coastal fishing site. She operated her net until the end of summer. She caught king salmon, pink salmon, dog salmon and silver salmon. All the fish she caught was eaten fresh, salted, smoked or air dried. When the berries were ripe she would take all of us across the slough to the nearby hills to pick the berries. She built a raft of driftwood to cross the shallow water. When the tide was low we just waded across. We hiked for many miles with a pack on our back to carry the berries to camp. Our usual lunch was fish, tea and bread. She made a small fire to brew the tea. I would fill my bucket as fast as I could so that I could take time out to inspect and admire the flowers and plants growing in the area. That was the best part of berry picking.

"When we got back to the camp the berries would be stored in barrels placed in the ground to be kept cool. When fall time came and sometimes the berries were frozen; we would haul them into the village when camping time was done. Mother picked all the greens as they came into season. We ate the greens fresh. She also cooked them and stored them in wooden barrels and mixed some of them with berries. These would make good nutritious treats for the winter.

"In late summer Frank would go to the nearby lakes to hunt the fat ducks that spent the summer there. That duck soup was such a treat after a summer of eating a variety of fish. Frank was a good hunter. He was such a busy person and never seemed to run out of energy. Jessie and Gertie were so well trained by mother that they knew just what was needed to be done in the camp. The camp at Mik-kik-klek produced most of our winter supply of food.

"Frank's dogs would be brought to the camp when we moved there. Mother would feed them fresh fish that she cooked for them each day. She cooked the fish in a galvanized wash tub that she only used for cooking fish. It was kept scrubbed clean after each use. The fish cooked in the tub fed the family and dogs. The dogs would be fed the scraps from the family table too. The dogs would be used to help haul supplies in and from the camp. During the summer the dogs got nice and fat. I got fat too. However everyone else stayed trim for all the work they did in preparing food for winter use.

"In the fall and rainy season it was time to move back into the village. All the camping equipment was hauled in by the family. Mother was so efficient she had the packs well balanced so that the packing would be easy for her children, herself and the dogs to pack."

13. Igailaq's Family Grows Larger

Momma said that she was busy with her family and it was in the fall of 1922 that Gertie gave birth to her eldest son Roland. His Inuit name was Anaqtuyuuq after Igailaq's father. Momma said that the family did not know her sister was expecting to have a baby. Roland was born on September 22 at Igailaq's home. Igailaq didn't find out for a long time that the father was Sam Segock, Sr. of Elim, Alaska. Sam's Inuit name was Kiinaulook.

The baby was a good event for the family. Momma said that it was very nice to have a new baby in the home. Roland would call her Auntie and she liked that. She said that he was a mischievous child and made life very interesting for all of them.

One day she found an injured robin. She said, "I made a nice bird cage for that robin out of water willows. I took great pains in making the cage. Mother told me that I could keep the bird until it got well. I was happy that I had a pet. One day I went to check the bird. It was not there. I felt so bad. I asked mother what happened to it. She didn't know. Later that year Roland admitted that he let it out because I had scolded him for something. There was nothing I could do about it so I let the incident go. That Roland was such a mischievous child. I don't think that he even remembers that time."

Not too long after that, Gertie married Alvin Ivanoff and they lived in Shaktoolik. They were married on April 20, 1924, by Stephan Ivanoff the United States Commissioner at Shaktoolik.

Momma said that they were very lonesome for them.

Alvin was the son of Stephan and Amelia Ivanoff. He was born October 19, 1901, at the old village site up the Shaktoolik River. His Inuit name was Quqanaq.

All the Ivanoffs had moved to Shaktoolik where they operated a roadhouse. They even had Thora Soosuk (Katchatag) as a worker at the roadhouse. Alvin built his family a log cabin there. He was trapping for a living and their first child Alfred was born about 1925, but the baby did not live long.

Jessie had married Sam Otton and they were living in Golovin, Alaska. They had a daughter named Sophie, whose Inuit name was Took-fan. Sophie was born in Unalakleet on April 16, 1921, during a short family stay with Igailaq.

Igailaq was the kind of mother that wanted to make sure family connections were solid and in plain view of her ever-watchful eye. Momma said, "Sophie was our first baby. She was so little she looked like a doll to me. We all just loved her as she was our first baby."

Momma said that after she finished the eighth grade about 1925 her dad wanted to take her out to Chemawa Indian School in Oregon. She was not too sure if she wanted to leave home, and wanted to leave that decision up to Igailaq. Igailaq's answer was that it was too far away and she would be lost. Momma thought about that and then told her dad she would stay home. She always thought she wanted to become a registered nurse because of her cleaning work at the local dispensary. Momma said that in a way she was disappointed, but she loved her mother so much she could not leave her.

Her brother Frank married Susan Akan at St. Michael on January 29, 1925. Susan was from the nearby village of Egavik, just north of Unalakleet. He brought her home and they lived with Igailaq and Momma. Their first child was born on December 7, 1926, and they named him Wilfred Paul Ryan.

Then, on March 16, 1925, her dear friend Martha Lucy Isaac married Peter John Nanouk at Haycock, Alaska. Peter's Inuit name was Qapqan, and he was born on March 15, 1904. He was the son of Taituiq and Quinigiaq, who was adopted by a couple from Koyuk. Martha was the daughter of Marion Nashalook and Joseph Isaac and she was born on March 21, 1909, in Unalakleet. Her Inuit names were Apaachuaq and her Indian name of Ama. Martha and Peter lived in Koyuk several years before returning to Unalakleet to stay. Momma liked to tease Peter and Martha on their wedding anniversary that Martha had to wait until Peter was twenty-one before he could marry her. That was because they were married one day after his birthday anniversary.

Alvin, Gertie, Richard and Roland Ivanoff
Inset: Richard and Roland

14. Momma goes to the Johnssons

Momma said, "So after I was finished with school my dad sent for me to come and help Margaret with her children. Margaret's Inuit name was Chekuyyuk. Mother understood how I felt about my dad and urged me to go." So it was to be a lengthy stay at Fortuna Ledge for Momma. Eric and Margaret Johnsson now had several children and their names were Ann, Ruth, Aaron, Maurice, and Peggy. They were expecting another child to be born.

This was when Momma was sixteen years old. She was the oldest of Eric's biological children. His children were all under his roof and he was happy. Margaret was not too pleased to have Ada with them and she showed it in subtle ways. Ann and Ada were thrilled to be together again and renew their friendship.

Eric and Margaret lived in a big house. The Roy Hunter family lived nearby. Momma got acquainted with all the people in Fortuna Ledge. She also referred to the place as Marshall so I was under the impression that place had two names. Many of the Outsiders that settled there were expecting to make their fortune in gold. Grandpa had several gold claims in the area and worked on them during the summer. The other times he would be busy fishing for king salmon.

Margaret was a very busy woman and she appreciated that Momma was there to help out. She was an excellent seamstress and homemaker. Her kitchen was always busy. She fed all the people that traveled through their village. Grandpa was a kind and generous man and never refused help to anyone who would ask.

Momma said, "They had a piano in the house. I would play the piano and Ann and I would sing as long and loud as we could. We would sing both in English and Yup'ik. Ann was fluent in Yup'ik and was such a kind and gentle soul. All the people in the village loved her. I was fluent in English, Yup'ik and Inupiaq and did not have any problem switching languages." Momma and her sister Ann were so close, and they kept in contact with each other for their entire life. Ann's Inuit name was Yauh-huk.

The village was located on the Yukon and the people living there at that time were busy prospecting for gold in the area. Her dad still had great hopes of striking it rich and he would make his trips into the back country during the summer to find gold. Like all other villages the people loved to get together to socialize.

Momma said that they looked forward to the dances they would have. These were the modern dances not the traditional dances of the Inuit. She said that she and Ann never missed one dance that was held. She said that one of the old miners by the name of Pilcher would seek her out to dance. She danced with him but steered clear of him otherwise. She told her dad that she did not trust him. Her dad told her not to worry because old Pilcher enjoyed dancing with pretty girls. So she said she didn't worry about Pilcher anymore.

Momma said that she got a chance to sit on top of a horse to have her picture taken. "I never did ride a horse in my life and it took a lot of doing to get me on top of that horse. I sure was glad that he did not run off with me on his back because I would not know what to do with him. But when I look back on it that horse was just a worker not a riding horse. I had nothing to worry about."

After a year in the Johnsson home, her dad asked her if she would be willing to take care of some friends that were sick and needed help. That couple was Gus and Ella Bjornstad. Ella's Inuit name was Koomloo, meaning "thumb." Momma said she would do it. So she moved in with them and helped them on to the road of recovered health. When she was no longer needed she decided it was time to go back to Unalakleet and Igailaq.

Many years later Momma told me that she was glad that she lived with her father and Margaret that year. "I got to be with the father I loved so very much. I got to know my other brothers and sisters even if it was such a short time. I got to be with Ann whom I loved so much. Margaret got to know me a little bit and she acknowledged that I was really my father's daughter. That all meant so much to me throughout the rest of my life. I can thank my mother for allowing me to have this experience. I know that both of my parents loved me so very much. I have much to be thankful about and that is what life is all about."

Margaret and Ann Johnsson

15. Back to Unalakleet

When Momma came home to Unalakleet the whole village was suffering from illnesses. This was in 1929. She said that it was smallpox. Her sister-in-law Susan Ryan had just given birth to Mabel. The baby was covered with the rash and it was even on her eyes.

The whole family helped each other through the illness. Not all got sick. Momma said she went to the dispensary and the nurse vaccinated her on her leg. Her leg got so big and swollen she had a tough time walking. They all recovered without much incident.

Mabel was born on February 1, 1929, and her Inuit name was Kung-oiu-yuk. Her mother Susan's Inuit name was Paniuughuluuraq. Susan's maiden name was Akan. Her adoptive parents were the Akans from Egavik, a village fourteen miles north of Unalakleet.

Momma had told me that Susan had been adopted by the Akans when Susan's biological mother became ill. Susan's biological mother was Chikuk, a Kawerak woman who was married to Nasaunnoak, a Kawerak man living at Unalakleet. Another daughter Jessie was adopted by Katchatag, a Unalit man and his wife Dauquan, a Kawerak woman. Jessie's adopted bothers were Pesulthkok who was Joseph; Apaugruk, who was Stephan; and Daleeluk, who was Edwin. The eldest daughter was named Mamie who died of tuberculosis. Another daughter was Olga. There were two sons. John Akan married a Malemiut woman from Kotzebue and they had one son John Akan, Jr. When his wife died John married Jennie Paneok, the daughter of Thora Soosuk Katchatag. Jennie had been adopted by Ernest Paneok, (Kalluk), a Unalit and his wife Acheemuk. The other son was U-tan.

Frank and Susan lived with Igailaq until they were able to buy their own house from Wilson Gonangnan. It was right next door to Igailaq. Frank and Susan had several children and their combined heritage was Kawerak-German. Their first child was Wilfred Paul who was born on December 7, 1926. Their second child was Mabel. Their third child was Frank Stanley Ryan who was born on April 15, 1931. Stanley's Inuit names were Agibinik and Seatkoolook. Their fourth child was Fred Sheldon Ryan who was born on July 14, 1936. His Inuit name was Akan after his grandfather. Then Timothy Grenfell Ryan was born April 10, 1939. He later died of a broken back after he fell off a cache on July 25, 1944. Susan and Frank had another daughter named Dolly who died as an infant. Susan died of a lingering illness on March 26, 1941. Frank was left to care for the children. Igailaq helped him out with raising the children.

Karl Ivanoff, Susan and Wilfred Ryan, Olga Nashonak and child, Ernest Larsson, and Frank Ryan

16. Momma Sails to Washington

In 1929, Momma was working for Gladys Neelly, a nurse and teacher stationed at Unalakleet, doing house-keeping, cooking and baby-sitting. Gladys was planning a trip to the state of Washington and she asked Momma if she would be willing to travel with them and continue her duties. Momma said that she would have to think about it, so she asked Igailaq if it would be all right for her to go. Igailaq was agreeable. Momma made a plan to save enough money for the trip there and return home. Since she was good at beading she made beaded moosehide gloves and mittens to sell. She also knitted wool yarn gloves and cro-cheted baby caps and booties. She said that she saved what she thought was enough money to take care of emergen-cies. It was going to be an exciting time for her.

It was 1929 and it was time to leave Unalakleet. It was all right for Momma to leave. Igailaq knew she was in good company and that she would return home before long because her daughter promised her that she would. Promises were always made to be kept. According to an old Inuit tradition, if you made a promise it would be car-ried on your back for eternity if it were not fulfilled by the promise maker. Igailaq knew her youngest daughter would not want to be burdened for an eternity.

So Momma left Unalakleet with Gladys Neelly and her daughter on a small mailboat to Nome. There they booked passage on the last scheduled sailing of the *S.S. Victoria* from Nome to Tacoma, Washington. After that sailing, the ship was taken out of service. Momma had saved enough money for the boat fare and had enough money to return home. She worked for her room and board by caring for Gladys' daughter.

Momma said, "My dad was in Nome. He knew when we were leaving so he made sure he was there to see me off. He asked me if I was scared. I told him that I was not because I would be with the Neelly family. He asked me if I had enough money. I told him that I did. He reached in his pocket and gave me two hundred dollars. I took it because he was my dad. He asked me how long I would be gone. I told him that I would come back on the next ship. I knew my dad loved me. I was glad he came to see me.

"We left Nome and the trip was good. We went through the Aleutian Islands. We stopped in the ports along the way. I got to see the places where they had plants that took care of the whales and the big tanks they used to store the oil. When it got rough all the passengers got seasick. I didn't get sick at all. When it got time to eat, when I went to the dining room, the waiters put me up at the first class passengers' table. It was because they did not show up to eat. They were too sick.

"I was not scared on that trip. I was too interested in what was going on around me. I missed my mother and home, but I was comfortable with Gladys and her daughter. That trip was very good for me. I sure learned a lot of things and saw things I never even thought about before.

"When we arrived at our destination, it was at Olympia, Washington. I stayed with Gladys for a short time. I decided to enroll in a hair dressing school to learn another skill. The course would end just in time for me to board a ship back to Nome that year. This was in 1930. I enrolled in Madame Duncan's Beauty College. I found an apartment not far from the school. It was a small apartment owned by a nice couple who were Mr. and Mrs. Brown. I do not remember their first names. They had a young woman living with them. I found out she was their daughter. She was not married so she was still living at home. She was about my age.

"The Browns did not charge a high rent, so I was able to afford it and still pay for my school. They were very good to me. Each morning they would have a bouquet of cut fresh roses for me. They would bring me fresh milk, fresh fruit and vegetables in season because they knew I never had any of that before. For entertainment there was a movie house near by which I could walk to. Everything was in walking distance for me. If I needed to go anywhere else I learned how to take the cable car that operated nearby. The movie house always had free prizes if you held the lucky ticket. It seemed that I won something when I went there, like groceries, flowers and fruit. Some of the other girls in school liked to go to the movies with me because they might win too.

"It seemed that I was very busy at the hair dressing school. We had to learn physiology, hygiene as well as the methods of hair cutting and styling. We all got along well and it was a pleasant place to learn. Women would come in to get their hair done by the students for a small fee. When we worked on the customer we always had a supervisor checking on our work. The work was fun and they would send the tougher-to-do customers for me to work on. Maybe it was because I did not seem to get excited. I learned how to cut hair, and give perms with what they called Zota's wave. We did a lot of curling hair with curling irons. The basics were the same as today but the implements were different then. It seemed as everything worked out well for me. I got my diploma on August 26, 1930. I was so happy I finished what I had planned to do. It was time for me to go home. Gladys was glad that all worked out well too. I had written to my dad that I was coming back.

"I went to Nome by ship. When we arrived in Nome dad was there to meet me at the dock. After his welcome, his first question was, "Little One," he always called me 'Little One,' did you come home C.O.D.?" I told him I didn't. I even had two hundred dollars left. He said, 'If I were like you, Little One, I would be a millionaire now.' It sure was good to be back with him. We had a good visit and then I made my way back to mother and home.

"I never worked in a hair dressing shop but I did do hair cutting for men and hair cutting and waves for women in my home when we lived in Nome. No one complained and I was satisfied with my work. When we moved back home to Unalakleet I gave haircuts only, all the way until

I was eighty when I took a break. So I think that I used what I learned to a good purpose even if I did not make money at it."

Ada Johnsson and Ellen Neely

Ada Johnsson in black, third from right
Madame Duncan's Beauty School~Olympia, Washington

17. Back Again at Home

"It was 1930 and I was glad to be back in Unalakleet. Our family had grown much larger. My sisters and brother were married and raising their children, except for me. Frank and Susan were living at home with Wilfred and Mabel. Jessie and Sam Otton were living in Golovin with their children. Gertie had married Alvin Ivanoff and they were following the furbearing animals and at the time were living in Shaktoolik.

"This was the time that Henry Isaac Miller asked me to marry him. Henry's Inuit name was Kugluk. It was time to settle down. It was just fine with my mother. So we made plans to get married. We went down to St. Michael along with Franklin Soxie and Elsie Kotongan. Henry and I were married with Elsie and Franklin as our witnesses. We were then witnesses for Elsie and Franklin when they were married. Commissioner Herbert W. Johnston was the one that married us. We all returned home. We were married October 18, 1930.

Elsie Kotongan, was the daughter of Sarah and James Kotongan. Elsie's Inuit name was Ahghiagah after her mother's sister. Sarah's Inuit name was Goonoogglean. Sarah's parents were from Elim. Sarah's mother was a Unalit whose Inuit name was Chakanggnan. Sarah's father was a Unalit whose Inuit name was Ahmeghlaugook. Elsie's father was James Kotongan and his Inuit name was Kotongan. James' mother was a Unalit from Elim whose Inuit name was Ahpauchauk. James' father was an Unalit from Elim and his Inuit name was Igvian. Elsie and her husband Franklin Soxie made their home at

Unalakleet. Elsie's mother Goonooglean and Igailaq were the best of friends throughout their life.

"It seems that our marriage was so short. Our baby girl was born on November 23, 1931, and not long after that she became sick and died on August 22, 1932. Then Henry became sick. It was such a difficult time in my life. I lost my dear child, and my dear husband was not well. Since we were living in an old house we decided we would set up a new tent to see if good air would help him get well. His mother did not understand why we moved in a tent. It was summer time so it was not cold or uncomfortable. We all tried our best to get Henry well. His sister, Martha, was my very best friend. She was married to Peter Nanouk and she gave me a lot of support and help. She loved her brother very much too. I don't know why he had to die. He died on July 6, 1933. Henry was only twenty-one years old. I was so very sad. I did not know what to do. I turned to my mother and she gave me much comfort."

Henry Isaacs Miller was the son of Joseph Isaacs and Marion Nashalook. Marion was the daughter of Nashalook and Kakauraq, both of Unalakleet. Joseph Isaacs was the adopted son of the Isaac Kaleaks at Isaacs Point in the Norton Bay area. The Kaleaks had adopted the child from a half-breed Inuit-Caucasian woman and the child's biological father, Henry Neumann. Neumann and his Inuit wife has several children. From the accounts told by Martha and Momma, this was the same family that were the relatives that Igailaq went to live with in St. Michael when she was orphaned. The ones that Igailaq spoke about were Willie Neumann and Lucy Neumann (Whitley). Neumann's descendants lived in Unalakleet, McGrath, and down the Yukon.

About this time, all of Igailaq's adult children and their families would all return to Unalakleet. Gertie's husband Alvin Ivanoff had died in 1931. He got sick with pneumonia in Akulurak so they returned to Shaktoolik and there he died and left her widowed with three sons to raise. Alvin was buried at Shaktoolik, Alaska. Their first child Alfred had died as an infant. Richard who was born February 23, 1929, at Akulurak. Alfred was born on June 13, 1930, at Igailaq's home in Unalakleet. Gertie then married John Auliye who was living in Shaktoolik. John's Inuit names were Igugnek and Akivgouq. John and Gertie were married by the Commissioner from St. Michael on April 20, 1931, at Tom Power's Roadhouse at Unalakleet. John and Gertie built their permanent home in the fall of 1934.

Jessie and Sam Otton returned from Golovin with a larger family, which would grow even larger. Their eldest child Sophie was born on April 16, 1921, in Unalakleet and her Inuit names were Took-fan and Panigruaq. Myrtle Ada was born in Nome on February 23, 1925, and died in Unalakleet in September 1947, and her Inuit name was Akalook. Ralph Nathan was born in Nome and died in Golovin. Eva Elizabeth was born in Golovin on November 15, 1929, and died in Anchorage in 1997, and her Inuit name was U-tan. Ralph Henry was born in Golovin on November 2, 1934, and his Inuit name was Aqpayuq. Mildred Hannah was born in Golovin on February 26, 1932, and her Inuit names were Koongchuk and Anakpadak. Beatrice Jane was born on July 16, 1937, in Unalakleet and she was named Istalukka after a Lapp woman. Sam Jr. was born June 22, 1940, in Unalakleet and his Inuit name was Anisaaluk. Lois Ann was born July 28, 1943, at Tirakpak (Unalakleet) and her Inuit name was Noonghak and Lapp name of Ingarana. Sam and Jessie raised Sophie's children. Susie Patricia was born on March 17, 1938, in Unalakleet and her Inuit name was Panuughuluuraq. Susie's sister Ruth Marilyn was born on September 5, 1943, at Unalakleet and her Inuit name was Ahwiktak. Sam and Jessie built their log cabin next door to Gertie and John's cabin and there the family remained.

Igailaq was happy to have all her children under her wing once again. Each of the families had their own cabins and houses built, all except for Momma. However, it would not be long before Momma would marry Poppa. That would come later.

As Igailaq's children married they each established their summer fish camp sites away from Mek-kik-lek. The first place was about six miles up the Unalakleet River. This place is called Tirakpak, meaning "a big sand bar."

Here all of Igailaq's children, their spouses and children camped.

Later, Frank Ryan and Gertie Auliye moved their respective camps much farther up the Unalakleet River. Jessie Otten moved her camp up to an adjacent location. The remaining family at Tirakpak was that of Ada Degnan. In the summer of 1956 her husband Frank applied for a Native Allotment site of 160 acres of land under the Federal Indian Allotment Act of 1906. He did not get patent to that land until after his death in 1980.

Igailaq still maintained her summer camp on the coast. She told Momma that she did not like living up the river. She preferred being on the coast as there were more resources within walking distance. It was much more pleasant for her and the sea breezes kept the mosquitoes and biting bugs at bay. Also her best friend, Kakauraq (Lena Williams), and Apok shared the camp site with Igailaq. They got along well together and their camping time was pleasant. All of their children and grandchildren would check on them daily and help them when they needed help. It was so much fun to be with the three women. They were gentle and industrious women and they loved to work. They also loved to have visitors and the teapot and snacks were readily available at their tents.

Ada Johnsson, Henry Miller, Martha Nanouk

18. How our Ancestors Carried on Traditions

Momma related the following stories to us throughout the years: "In the long ago, but not the faraway, the ancestors of the Unalit lived along the shores of the Norton Sound but they had their own names for every point, hill, creek, stream, mountain, knoll, and place in their territory. The name of the place told what activity, event or advantages of that place were. All of these names were originally in Unalit.

"Later the Malemiuts gave another name to some of the places in their own dialect. And when the Russians and then Americans came into our country their own place names then showed up on their maps.

"But in our own tradition it was the name that showed that it was the traditional camping spot of a certain family for their seasonal outings. From the name you would know the aspects of the place and much respect was to be shown in the use of the land.

"The Unalit considered the land theirs to use and to use it well and share the bounty. The permanent settlements were in places that were accessible by waterways or by foot. Also these places had access to the day-to-day requirements of survival such as good water, fish, small game, heating supplies like driftwood or sea mammals which the oil was used not only for eating but for cooking the food, heat and light. You got to remember the ancestors lived underground.

"Your grandma Apok told me that the caribou used to come right near the village. The ducks and geese and birds nested all around the flats. All the game animals were not afraid of the people. It was because the people respected the animals and did not take more than the community could use.

"But many times there was scarcity of food resources and the Unalit knew this very well. With this in the back of their minds they knew that if they were careful they could cope. Sometimes, according to Apok, when the seas froze up solid during a very cold winter season and the hunters could not find open water the women could get their tomcod from the mouth of the river. And many times this was the only food that would pull them through the cold.

"Sometimes when the hunters traveled to get the oogruk (bearded seal) and seal they would wind up even forty-five miles out to sea and then they would meet hunters from the other villages around the Norton Sound. All this travel was made by foot and if the hunters had dogs they would use them to help with the transport of the oomiak or kayak and they also used a bobsled called a 'kumi-ghoun.' Not every hunter had all the transportation equipment and whoever was a skillful hunter and had an omiak, which is a large skinboat, was considered rich and was acknowledged as an 'Oomal-lik.'

"When the hunters were successful in harvesting seal, oogruk or whale the whole community would benefit from the bounty. The hunters at the site would enjoy the fresh liver and fat from the seal or oogruk and the tasty parts of the whale. They performed age old-ritual after the kill to ensure future success and they had a specified manner of field-dressing the kill.

"If the hunter was alone he would take the whole animal home uncut for his wife to cut and she would be the one to share the bounty with the community. But if there were several hunters at the hunting site the animal would be field dressed and the successful hunter would have the prerogative to do the shares.

"Upon return to the village the elderly and widows would enjoy their share. Much of the catch was air dried and surplus would be stored in specially prepared pokes made of sealskin or stomach of the whale. This was all dependent upon the availability of the resources.

"After a successful hunt, the community enjoyed the bounty and the tales would be told to the community through story and dance at the kashim. At the same time the surplus would be stored with the goal to provide for the anticipated forthcoming regional feasts. These feasts would be planned according to ancestral schedules and for specific purposes. In anticipation of these scheduled feasts the people readied themselves so that they could accommodate their designated guests in a fashion that would be long remembered.

"At the back of each person's mind they had pictures of how that feasting would transpire, so excitement slowly developed throughout the seasons. The women had much preparation to do. Every month had several foods to be harvested, prepared, consumed and some to be stored in the proper fashion and reserved for the feast. Every month of the year fish of different species was available for harvest. In the spring and summer months the different greens, roots and berries were harvested for short and long-term use. The women and children took care of the greens and berry harvest as well as getting the fish. The men took the task of harvesting the small and large game but it was mainly the women who had the task of preparation and storage.

"So each day of the Unalit year was full of activity. These activities did not all happen in the winter settlement but occurred over a vast territory. Each of the family units had their own camping and harvesting spots and all respected these well-identified spots. Much of the travel was by foot, and the natural trails were well known. Many of these places came to be the burial places for the Unalit that lived there and happened to die there."

19. Poppa's Trip Outside

Now we go back and visit the activities of Apok, grandpa and Poppa. I believe we left them considering a trip to be made by the men and they would leave Apok in Nome. The easiest way for the two men to travel was to take the ship at Nome and travel to Seattle. We imagine that they would travel steerage and it would take at least two weeks to get to their destination. The only place they ever talked about was Quilcene, Washington.

From what Poppa told me, they went out in 1924 and came back to Nome in 1926. Grandpa Degnan wanted his son to get more education and placed him with family friends in Quilcene who were Albert and Mabel Haradon. Poppa got acquainted with one of his paternal aunts whose name was Dasie Oatman. Poppa got to know the place his father wanted him to know and he finished the ninth grade in school. Then Poppa went to work for a short time in the logging camps and worked as a choke setter.

The stories that Poppa told us about this time sure sounded like he had a very busy adventurous time. After school he was able to get a job in a logging camp. He told many stories of the logging camps and one about this friend of his that said that he was going to quit the job and go home that day. However, he changed his mind and went back to the log cutting job the next day and he did not live to see the night fall. He was killed in an accident not uncommon for that occupation and times. So Poppa said he promised himself that when he decided that it was time to leave he would leave and not look back.

When Poppa left the logging camp, he went into a new job. But before he got the new job he decided to do as the rest of the loggers did and go on a vacation. Poppa said that he asked some of the chaps how do you take a vacation when you don't have much money. They told him, 'That's easy. All you do is to go down to the train yard and hook a freighter and get off where you want." So Poppa did just that. "I went down to the place where the trains were and looked them over. I seen a fancy looking one called The Shasta Limited. It looked like it would be a good one to hook. So before it took off I climbed onto the top just like the guys told me to and found a place to hang on. When the train took off, it really took off, I wound up holding on to dear life on the vents at the top. It sure did not take me long to get to California. Later I found out that it was only the freight trains that you could hook a ride on. But if you were caught it was not a good thing.

"When I got to California I looked up one of my dad's friends, a Mr. Dan Starrett, to see if I could find some work. He was able to steer me to a job I got on the Oakland Bay Bridge. They were building it then. So I can say that I helped build that bridge, but I worked as a laborer. At that same time there was a big commotion in San Francisco. I guess that the Humbolt Bank was robbed and the morning paper had a front page issue that showed a picture of 'The Machine-gunner' for the gang that held up the Humbolt Bank. Lo and behold it was a picture of me! Of course, I was nowhere near that Bank and would never think of such a thing. I showed that paper to Mr. Starrett and told him to please let my dad know that it was a case of mistaken identity. Nothing ever came of that incident. I guess that police and paper knew they made a mistake and since the paper said that the picture was of an 'unidentified man' they did not have to find me and tell me it was their mistake. Well, then I had made enough money to get back to dad in Quilcene, Washington in case he was worried about me. So I made it back but this time I rode the train, not hooked it. Dad sure was glad to see me. He told me that he believed me. "

So Poppa is back telling about his new job. "That job was to be in the moving pictures. I thought that that would be fun and easy since all you had to do was to do what they told you to do and make money at it. That sounded like a good deal. You can't lose. So I decided that I would try it. The director of the moving picture was a guy named W. S. Van Dyke and he was making a picture of the gold rush in Alaska Yukon for H. C. Weaver. We shot the film on location at Mount Rainier in the state of Washington. That was in 1926. That was just before the talkies came out. The name of that picture was *The Raw Country* when it was being made (but wound up to be renamed as *The Heart of the Yukon* when it was released in 1927 by H. C. Weaver Productions of Tacoma, Washington.)

"I was playing the part of an Eskimo dogteam driver and wore squirrel skin parkas and all the things they thought Eskimos wore. The people I worked with were okay. The main actors in the picture were Johnny Bowers and Russell Simpson. They did not have the snow at times and they had to use a lot of rock salt to imitate snow. It was not a bad job and I had fun at it and got to meet many new people. Van Dyke told me that he would like to take me to Hollywood, California and that I would have a good career in the movies. He told me that I was a natural born actor and could become a big star as the talkies were going to be the thing. I thought about it and I didn't think so, so I told him, 'Thanks for the offer, but I didn't feel like playing a Chinese person for the rest of my life. I am an Eskimo and I promised my mother that I would come home.'"

20. *Return to Nome*

Grandpa Degnan and Poppa came back to Apok in Nome. Poppa married Maggie Otootuk, originally from Elim, Alaska, on March 30, 1929, at Commissioner Thornton's office in Nome. She was born January 1, 1911, at Spruce Creek, Alaska near Solomon, Alaska.

Maggie's mother's name was Esau-ghak and her father's name was Otootuk, an Unalit from Elim who ran a roadhouse there. Maggie's Inuit name was Pihssauk.

Maggie had three sisters. One was Dora Buckley who had a son named John Buckley. The other sister was Ada Blackjack Johnson, Inuit name Nayoumouruk, who had a son named William Blackjack Johnson. The other sister was named Chuppeechaulook, who had three sons and a daughter who were adopted out. They were Edward Jackson, Eric Tetpon, Roger Nassuk and Ann Scofield.

Hazel Kotongan told me much later that her sister Thora Katchatag's father was Otootuk also. Maggie had one brother and his name was Albert Delutak. Poppa never told me anything about Albert except that he was living in Nome when his sister Maggie was alive.

Maggie and Poppa were married in Nome. Grandpa Degnan and Apok lived with them. Our sister Eva was born on June 9, 1930, in Nome. Apok immediately named her Natagug after her own mother. One year later our brother Gerald O'Brien was born on July 13, 1931, and Apok named him Dugh-lung-ghak after the Unalit Ta-Chiqmiut (St. Michael, Alaska) chief who had just passed away. Maggie Otootuk Degnan died on July 30, 1931, at Nome, and was buried at Belmont Point cemetery.

It was then that the task of raising the children fell on Apok, Poppa and grandpa. Poppa had been working on the various dredges in Nome as a winchman. He was very faithful in his duties and many times he walked to and from the work site.

Apok continued to harvest the bounty from the land and sea to feed the family in the Unalit tradition. Since Gerald was a male child he received her special attention, but that was not unusual as that was the manner of the traditional Unalit to rejoice when there was a male child in the family. Apok could relate to this as she herself was an only child and she was required to learn the roles of the female and male of the Unalit. So she was able to instruct the boy from the time of his birth.

Momma said that she never really thought of Frank Degnan but she knew who he was and that he was living and working in Nome and that his wife had died. She said that both of his parents living were with him, and that he had two small children. Poppa said that when he got word that Ada Miller had lost her husband he knew then that he was going to ask her to marry him. On his part he knew that his children needed a good mother to help him raise them.

At that time his own father, Frank Degnan, Sr., was talking about returning to his own hometown as he was lonesome for the old family. Since Apok never entertained the idea of leaving her homeland and her son, it would never do to take her to a foreign land that she had no desire for.

Apok was content to remain with her son and his family. Poppa said that he would never leave his mother and it would never do to have her live by herself; his home was her home, as her home was his home. That is the way of the Unalit. It is the tradition for one of the children to provide for the daily care of the parents when they became elders. No questions asked, that's just the way life is, and should be, for the Inuit. That's tradition.

21. *Momma Marries Poppa*

Poppa said that he wrote to Momma at Unalakleet and asked her to come to Nome to meet his family. Momma thought long and hard about the invitation and decided to see for herself. She went up by mail boat and stayed for a few days. She said that she saw the two young children with their grandmother and the father busy working. She and Poppa had long talks about their situations. She said that she would have to think about it. Poppa told her to go on home to Unalakleet and let him know before long what she wanted to do because he wanted to marry her.

Momma said that she came home and told Igailaq about the visit. Igailaq would support any decision she made. "It was not an easy decision to make for me. I had just lost my baby and my husband. Your dad had just lost his wife and he had those two little children to raise and his mother to take care of. I had always heard about stepmothers and how mean they were to their stepchildren and how they treated them different from their own. If I was to marry your dad, I did not want to become like those stepmothers. I prayed very much that time that God would show me the way.

"I knew that your dad would make a good husband and father, so I made up my mind that I would marry him. My mother and I went up to Nome and I told him of my decision. So we go to the commissioner's office, I believe it was Commissioner Thornton, and got married. That was on June 26, 1934. Our witnesses were Ella Bjornstad and Archie Wheeler. We never told anyone else that we were going to get married. I don't know how the kids found out so quick because right away a lot of kids came to our house and were very anxious and excited that we were married. So Dad went downtown right away and got a lot of candies and goodies to give to the kids. They sure were happy. We were happy, too. That's how we got married."

Momma said that Grandpa Degnan decided that it was time for him to move back to his old home town in Quilcene, Washington. Apok did not want to leave her only son. It was all right for Grandpa to go to his relatives. He kept in touch with his family through regularly writing letters throughout the years until his death on December 26, 1942. He had been a patient at Northern State Hospital in Sedro Woolley, Washington since his admittance on November 18, 1940.

Momma said that the little family got along well together from the beginning. Eva and Jerry had many little friends who always came over to play with them outside. Since Momma loved to cook and bake there always was some bread, cake, doughnuts, cookies or candy to share. Poppa had bought Momma a new coal cook stove and she was so proud of it. Igailaq stayed for the summer. Momma was glad to have her there with her.

When she was sure that all was well, Igailaq went back to Unalakleet in the early fall by boat. Frank Ryan was glad to have Igailaq back and wrote Momma that she "looked like a million dollars when she came home." He also wrote that there were four new houses being built at Unalakleet that summer. One of those houses was being built by John Auliye.

John was the new husband of Gertie Ryan Ivanoff. John was from the village of Shaktoolik. He told me that he was born June 15, 1900, at Moses Point. His mother's name was Ahlugnek and his father's name was Aulagin. John's Inuit names were Akivgouk and Igugnek. His father Aulagin was accidentally killed while he was beluga hunting in Norton Bay. After his father died the family was taken in by Sam Otton's parents, U-tan and Aqpayuk, in Koyuk. Here they stayed until George was able to get employment in Shaktoolik. George's Inuit name was Suttughin. John's family of Ahlugnek, George and Genevieve then moved to Shaktoolik. They remained there and made it their family home. John moved to Unalakleet when he married Gertie.

Grandma Apok had selected Jerry to be under her tutelage as he was the male child. She was instructing him in the Unalit tradition so that he could become a good hunter and provider. Since Eva was only a female Apok left her to Momma. Momma said that one day she came home and caught Apok as she was disciplining Eva very harshly.

Momma said, "I told Apok to stop right there, I will not raise a crippled child. You will never do that to any child again. And you know what! Apok never ever raised a hand to any of my children in our life again. It was then I knew for sure that I loved Eva and Jerry as they were my own. Apok and I never spoke of that incident either.

"Jerry was claimed by Apok as her own so he went wherever she went and I think that is how he came to be such a good hunter. And I tell you that Eva was my biggest help and especially when the rest of you kids came along. You will always have to be good to her, besides being the oldest she was the best help I ever had, and I always love her.

"The first year that we were in Nome as a family it was a busy time. Your dad was working on the gold dredge as a winchman. He had a steady job and we were doing fine. Apok was content to stay with us. Eva and Jerry had many little friends and they had fun. We lived in a house toward the east side of Nome. It was a small house that dad bought. He bought me a new coal cook stove and it heated the house too.

"That fall the King Island people were scheduled to put on an Eskimo dance that was authentic. The old folks said that whenever it was performed to an audience something drastic would happen. They were scheduled to perform this dance called the Wolf Dance at the Eagle Hall in Nome. We did know about this because it was a traditional dance that when they performed it was so realistic. It was a deep kind of story. You have to be knowledgeable and understand the customs to appreciate it. "Anyway, the dance was performed. Then a disastrous thing happened in Nome. A great fire was started. That day was

September 17, 1934. I think that it started at the Eagle Hall. The buildings were so close together that when one burned, the fire moved quickly to the next. They sure tried hard to put it out. You could see the business owners trying to get their stuff out. Everybody in town tried to help put out that fire.

"Since our house was a way off your dad didn't think it would reach us. Apok and I thought that since it was such a big fire the whole town would burn. So we started packing up to get out of the house. The heat was so great. We were scared. I got the kid's stuff packed and a box of food ready. Then Apok and I took down the stove to cart it out. I didn't want to lose my new stove. When we were doing that your dad came in. He set the stove back up and lit it. He told me to make lots of coffee and have food ready. The workers needed a break. So I spent the rest of the time providing coffee for the firefighters when they came in. After all when the fire was contained it did not reach our house. We felt bad for the others that lost everything.

"It was in the year of 1935 that your dad and some of the other men his age in Nome decided that it was time that one of them should seek a seat on the city council. They were successful in getting Duffy O'Connor to run and he was elected. We were so proud of him. This was the time that there was open discrimination against the Inuit at the public facilities. Most of these men were from families of mixed marriages. They did not like what was happening to the Natives and it was time things changed.

"At the same time someone should be seeking a seat in the territorial legislature. These men decided that your dad would be the one to submit a petition to have his name appear on the ballot.

"Your dad agreed to give it a try. So his friends took the petition to all the business houses in the town. They said they had no problem getting the signatures. Your dad asked if the head man at the Bureau of Indian Affairs signed. They told him that he would not sign the petition. So your dad took the petition and another man with him to the office. Your dad said, 'We walked in to his office. He greeted us and asked what we wanted. I didn't say anything, I put the petition before him. He picked it up, looked at it, didn't say anything, and he signed it. I thanked him and we left. When we got out of the door my friend said, "What did you do? He wouldn't sign it for us." I told him, "I guess he just needed to see me." So that is how we done it. I ran, but I didn't get elected. In all, I ran for twenty-six years before I got elected to the territorial legislature.'"

Poppa continued to work for the mining company as a winchman. Momma and Apok were busy with the children. It was springtime and their first child was born on May 29, 1935. She was born at home and Momma's midwife was Ida May Lehman, who was a registered nurse. Igailaq had come up to Nome to be with her youngest daughter for the time of the baby's expected birth. Igailaq and Apok also attended the birth.

As soon as the baby was born and the nurse had cut the cord the two grandmothers cleaned the baby's throat. First was with a ptarmigan wing feather, then with a seagull feather. They named the girl the Inuit name for Nome, "Sitnasuak", Seatkoolook, and Donnenah. Then the nurse gave her own name for the baby. So Momma named the baby Ida May. The grandmas said that because they cleaned her throat with those feathers that is why Ida May's laugh can be heard from one end of the village to the other.

Momma and Ida May in Nome

22. Moving by Skin Boat Toward Home

Igailaq stayed for a short while longer in Nome. It was time for her to return to Unalakleet. Momma said that if she left it will be so lonesome. She too wanted to return to Unalakleet. She and Poppa talked it over. They decided that it probably would be better to raise the children with both of the grandmothers at the same place. Poppa said that the price of gold had dropped and he had to figure out what would be the best way for him to support his family. He thought that he would try to stake gold claims farther down the coast closer to Unalakleet.

The plan was to move the entire family to a place near Moses Point just to the east of Elim. Poppa purchased a large skin oomiak from Owllana, chief of King Island Natives, on July 22, 1935. This was a twenty-four-foot-long and six-feet-wide skin boat, for which he paid fifty dollars. He outfitted it with a four-horse-power outboard motor. The family prepared for their journey by sea to a new place to live.

When they left Nome on July 24, 1935, there were seven persons besides all the household items Momma could squeeze safely in the walrus skin boat. Poppa was a fearless and skilled boatsman. The children were excited, the grandmas were eager to be on their way, and Momma was trying to be calm. She said that she was always afraid to be on the sea. It was okay as long as the sea was calm and no wind blowing. When the going was choppy she said that all she could do was to pray to God, "What else could

I do? When it got rough your dad would start singing. So when he started singing I knew that we would have to be ready to beach and I would have to be prepared for anything."

They stopped along the way several times to take a break from the boat and stretch. The going was good. They stopped in Golovin and visited there for a short while. They shopped for a few necessities at Joe Dexter's store. Jessie and Sam Otton were no longer living in Golovin, but had returned to live in Unalakleet. The family continued their travel. They stopped in Elim to see their friends Jennie and Roy Bradley. Poppa also wanted to get permission to build a cabin at Punuukutaq at Moses Point from the chief at Elim. Poppa was told it was all right for his family to live there.

They arrived at Moses Point. When they beached, Poppa immediately set up and lit Momma's cook stove. She said that while the boat was being unloaded she was busy making breakfast. The fire was roaring and sparks were flying out of the stack. She was right out in the open. The black brants were just coming in. She said, "The brants flew right over me and the smoking stove. I sure wished I knew how to shoot a gun. Your dad was too busy making camp that he let the birds go by. If it were today you folks would have had a lot of fun hunting. Anyway that was the only time I really saw brants so close to me. I will never forget that sight."

Poppa picked a site with the help of his friends, Roy and Jennie Saccheus Bradley. That place was called Punuukutaq by the local people living in the area. It was a little way from the mouth of the river at Moses Point. Momma said it was a good place and you could see all around. Roy helped Poppa build the log cabin. The grandmas had their own spot where they could relax from the bustle. This was the time of the eternally-optimistic gold prospector. Poppa and Roy thought they had just a good chance of locating good paying prospects. Momma was more interested in the survival of her family. She had the ones she loved living with her and she was happy.

She said that each day was filled with tasks to do for all of them. Apok would take Eva and Jerry out walking with her, looking over the countryside to see what its prospects were for game. When they went out, Apok always took her gun. Sometimes when they went for fish they would take their fishing gear.

Momma recalls this one certain day: "It was a beautiful day. Apok took the kids and her gun and set out to the lakes. She would be looking for ducks. They were gone longer than I thought they would. I was getting worried. I heard some shots but I didn't see them anywhere. Time went by. It seemed so long to me. They still didn't come. I got real worried. Maybe someone got shot. What am I going to do? Next thing I see them coming. There were three of them. I felt better.

"When they came home I asked them what happened. Apok told me that she saw a loon in the lake and she tried to shoot it. She didn't get it so they waited in case it came back. They didn't see any other ducks so they came home empty-handed. I told them they really scared me and don't go hunting any more. What I really was worried about was that Apok's eyesight was not very good anymore since she was old. I thought she just might hurt herself or the kids. After that she did not take her gun any more. She must have felt as I did. I respected her for that.

"There were times that I would go with your dad by boat to get supplies for the camp from Elim. The grandmas would watch over the kids. Eva told me that the grandmas sent her out for wood for the stove. She went out of the cabin and to the back. She saw some old wood neatly stacked so she started hauling them to the cabin. The shorter pieces she took in the house. She set them by the stove and went out. Next thing she heard was the door open and saw the wood fly out the door. The grandmas hollered for her to come right away. She flew in the house. They both immediately scolded her and told her to put the wood right back where it came from. The wood was from 'qunut' meaning ancestral graves. She learned her lesson well. They were not afraid but just being respectful."

When the family needed to go any distance they would travel by the skin boat powered by a Neptune four-horsepower outboard motor. Poppa had one of the few outboard motors in the area. It certainly made travel easier.

Momma told of one of the more memorable trips they made. She said, "We were going from Moses Point to Unalakleet by boat. It was a nice day. I was not afraid to travel. All I could think of was I was going home for a visit. Roy Bradley was coming with us. Everyone was bundled in the boat and was excited. Poppa crossed Norton Bay and was headed straight for Cape Denbigh. It wasn't too long a wind picked up. I could see the swells building. It started getting choppy. The grandmas and children were under the tarp and they were doing just fine. Roy and I were getting concerned. As the waves got bigger your dad said to me, 'If you are going to pray, you'd better start now.'

"I prayed and asked God to help Frank, guide him and give him strength. To take care of the children, the grandmas, Roy and all of us. I know your dad was concerned. I was scared and Roy said, 'You folks are lucky you are all together, but my family and wife are still at home.' I knew what he meant. We were in a tough situation. So I prayed and prayed. We kept watching the beach line. Poppa wanted us to look for a calmer spot that did not have boulders so that we could land.

"The water looked pretty tough. As we approached Cape Denbigh on the north side we all saw a shining spot. Poppa headed straight for it. He told Roy and me to be ready to jump out and hold on and don't let the boat go. He was going to beach. We all had to do our part. Poppa headed straight for the shining water. He hit the beach, we jumped out and held on the boat for dear life. A big wave crashed over the boat and almost pulled us all out. Poppa was out of the boat in a blink of the eye. Next thing I know is the boat is up on the beach. Everyone piled out of the boat. We were safe and sound. I thanked God for his providence and care again.

"The place we landed at was an old hunting camp site and it was called Utkusinnaq. Since this was to be a short outing we did not have any food with us. All I had was a can of milk and some cereal for the baby Ida May. We were all hungry. Roy looked around and found an old seal poke in the tumbled down cache there. The poke looked and smelled like it had been there for a long time.

Roy was the only one brave enough to sample it. It is a good thing we had water. When the sea calmed down Poppa said it was time to head on out. We traveled and stopped at Shaktoolik. There we were welcomed and fed by the families of Saul Sockpealuk and Simon Bekoalook. We stayed long enough to visit and we went on our way.

"Since the weather was still not entirely settled we stopped on the beach about five miles north of the village of Unalakleet. We pulled up the boat and turned it on its side. We then hiked into the village. It was good to be on solid ground. Poppa brought the boat to the village when the weather calmed down. We got our supplies from the trading post. We stayed at Igailaq's house. Frank, Susan and their children were there. We did not stay long as we had work to do at Moses Point. We were on our way. The weather was good and we made it back to Punuukutaq without incident."

The family was settled at their new home. Momma said those were busy times. They had a lot of company and her coffeepot was always ready. She said that the fish and game were plentiful and they had a variety of foods to eat as long as they harvested them in season. The grand-mas were busy, too, and kept the children entertained with little chores, and in the blustery weather, entertained them all with stories. Poppa had in his mind to search for gold up the rivers in the area. He was not the only one that was doing this. Jerome Trigg, his wife Nellie and their children stopped by and stayed for a short while. They too were looking for way to make a living off the land and its resources.

Roy and Jennie Bradley came often to check on the family. During the summer many of the people wintering in Elim would spend their summers at camp at Moses Point. Here they would put up their winter supplies of fish, greens and berries.

Momma said that she enjoyed their company. Roy and Jennie would bring them reindeer meat. "We sure enjoyed the fresh reindeer. What a good change from fish. But then we always liked our fish. The grandmas and the kids would go fishing for grayling in the fall after freeze up and we stored them in the cache. One time in the winter the grandmas wanted to eat frozen grayling. I sent Eva to get the fish. She came back running, all excited. She brought in what looked like grayling but they were just skins. Here the shrews had gotten into the box and ate all the meat of the fish and just left the skin, like shells. That was so funny it made us all laugh so hard."

The family was so busy the time flew by so fast at Punuukutaq. Momma was expecting another child. She did not want to have the baby out there and she asked Poppa if she could go to Unalakleet. She wanted to be where there was a nurse. That was all right with Poppa. Igailaq sent word to her two sons-in-law, Sam Otton and John Auliye to pick them up.

Eva, Jerry, and Ida at Moses Point with Polar

23. *Momma Gets Her Wish: Home*

Momma said, "On April 15, 1937, Sam and John came from Unalakleet, each with their own dog team, to pick Mother and me up to take us home. I had Ida May with me and was in Sam Otton's sled. John took Mother. We left the family to come later with the boat after spring break up. When Sam was traveling past one of the rocky points his dogs ran right into the rocks. The sled hit hard and we were tossed out of the sled. I really hit hard on a big boulder right on my abdomen. I was so scared. I was certain my baby was killed. Ida May and Sam were okay. We made it to Unalakleet. We arrived safely and found out that John and Mother were already there.

"The nurse checked me and there was nothing wrong with the baby. I sure was glad. We stayed with Momma. When it was my time to give birth I moved over to Gertie and John's cabin.

"On June 1, 1937, I gave birth to a healthy baby girl. I was so happy she was okay. The nurse was so proud of a new baby scale that weighed almost up to ten pounds. She was going to break it in for the first time. The nurse held up the scale. The midwife put in the baby. The scale went 'click.' It broke. My baby broke the scale at ten pounds plus. That baby was Ada June Degnan. She sure was a tough one. That's why I always say that June is tough. We named her Ada June and her Inuit names are Eetooghillgha and Tumgun.

"My sister Gertie wanted me to give her my new baby. Gertie only had boys and she wanted a girl. Her youngest son Vernon was born February 10, 1933, (Inuit name is

Anakpadak), and she thought it would be nice to have a girl. I told her I could not give any of my children away. Years later I was glad that Gertie and John were able to adopt a little girl. Her name was Linda Marie James and she was born on April 6, 1948, to Rena James, originally of Koyuk. Linda's Inuit name was Situqtun. Rena James had been the daughter of Henry Ivanoff so she was already part of the family. Vernon married Patricia Kotongan in April, 1955, at Unalakleet. Their children were Marlene, Debra, Verna, Diane, Genevieve, Cheryl, Vernon, Jr., Glenn, and Curtis. Vernon died on April 6, 1969, at home.

"So Poppa brought the rest of the family with the skin boat when the sea was ready to travel. Soon as he got here he set up a tent for us near Igailaq, right where the Covenant Church has its buildings today. This is the place where all of Igailaq's daughters and their families pitched their tents as they were building their cabins."

Momma said, "That time all the kids got whooping cough. It was terrible. I didn't get much sleep. Your dad was busy trying to get us a house to live in. I was scared for our new baby. I put her in a separate bed with a netting over it. I put cloths wetted with a disinfectant solution of water and Lysol around the netting hoping it would keep her from catching whooping cough. You know what? She never got sick. That June sure was tough.

"We decided that we would build a cabin here at home. Poppa did not want us to live in an old house. He got permission from the council and the church. The only place available was at the edge of the village that was covered with willows and 'qunut,' which are 'graveyards.' They were satisfied. Poppa set to work to clear the place for the log cabin. He consulted the elders and got their advice as how to take care of the graves."

He gathered his logs and Uncle John helped him. Momma said that it took Poppa only seven days to erect the cabin. She and the kids gathered moss to chink between the logs. Poppa put in the windows. It was fall time and freeze-up. Momma said that she moved everyone in even before Poppa put up the doors. "We only had a canvas to cover the door openings, but it was new, clean and home."

That fall Eva was enrolled in the first grade at the local school. Her first teacher was Mabel Ivanoff. Jerry would go to school the next year but he was already getting his Unalit education by living with Grandma Apok. Those two were always going on day trips out of the village for fishing, hunting and berry picking.

Beginning in the spring of 1938 Momma's own garden area was large. Poppa worked very hard to initially break the sod so that it would be easier for Momma to work the soil. Since the site they were given to build on was covered with willows Poppa worked very hard to clear the land. The site was an old grave site, so he and his uncle Aaron Paneok reburied all the remains they found in the village cemetery. Momma said that she told Aaron that she wanted to cry for the moving of the ancestors. She said that Aaron told her, "You don't need to cry for them now, we already cried enough for them."

Poppa also dug a well below the cabin so that it would be easier for the family to get wash water and water for the gardens. He said that the fresh water table was twelve feet down at the spot he chose. The water was cold and not at all salty. We never used it for drinking. Momma was very particular about our drinking water. We had to haul water from the river and collect rain water in the summer. In the winter Poppa hauled ice from the river or a nearby spring-fed lake. Our drinking water had to be boiled before we drank it. That was Momma's rule.

Every year thereafter Momma and all the children in the family dug and planted the gardens quickly. The expected reward was to be annual trips to the Cape Denbigh area to live off the land. The alternate camping place was near St. Michael called Canal. The excitement and anticipation were always great, so the gardens were planted with great speed. The camping trips were such wonderful events and produced great memories as the gardens produced good food.

The villagers had contact with several teachers and missionaries who had an active interest in the welfare of the villagers and one of them was Ernest B. Larsson, known as E. B. Larsson by the village. He taught the people how to improve their gardens and to raise vegetables for home use; and any surplus was sold mainly to Nome. He built a greenhouse near the mission house, where he grew different vegetables for transplanting by the village gardeners. He went so far as to tend the different gardens when the owners were at subsistence camps.

Every home in the village had a garden. The soil was very good for raising vegetables. At the end of the summer right near harvest time the community would have a garden fair. Each person that had a garden would enter their best vegetables. Momma said that it was a lot of fun to see how good and big the vegetables got. First, second and third place ribbons were awarded to the ones judged best in those categories. Momma kept all the ribbons that she won, and she was so proud of them.

Larsson was such a compassionate and industrious man. Momma thought very highly of him. She said, "He actively showed his love and concern for the people all the year long. If more people were like him this would be a different world. He did a lot for our village." E. B. Larsson left the village in the mid 1940's to return to his home in Sweden. On his way back to his own homeland he completed one last act benefiting the local Inuit by stopping by the church home office in Chicago and making sure that the church turned the village area they claimed as a reservation back to the Native Village of Unalakleet. This was on the specific request of Nick Riley who was on the Village Council at that time. If it had not been for the concern of Nick, I don't know what would have happened to that land title. If it had not been done then, it never would have happened."

All of Igailaq's children were now living in Unalakleet. They all had their own homes and she had many grandchildren. This was a busy time for all of them. She visited with each of them each day and they would all check on her during each day. All of her grandchildren loved and respected her. She was an independent woman and made no demands on anyone. She had her daily routines and many chores to do. I think that all of her grandchildren had their own special reasons why they liked to stop by her house. Somehow she always managed to have a different treat for each one of them.

Momma said that even if she was an adult she thought she could not sew as well as her sisters or mother. She said that she had to make all of our clothes since the trading post didn't have what she wanted for us. She had to make her own innovations to keep her husband and children warm for the cold weather.

When we went on our spring camping trips she would have us collect the eggs and nests. We would bring back the nest with its down and she would keep us busy cleaning the down. When she had collected enough down from the nests and the waterfowl that Poppa caught for food she would make down quilts for all the beds in the cabin. When the quilts were done her next innovation was to make pullover down parkas. The main parka was for Poppa.

When Poppa needed warm trousers she had an idea to make a pair of sealskin pants for him. She wanted them to be water-proof and wind-proof. She collected the sealskins and tanned them. When that was done she took a larger pair of Poppa's pants and took them apart to make her pattern. She said that she did not want Igailaq to see her at this work. Whenever Igailaq came visiting she would hide her work under the bed. When she finished her project Poppa tested out the pants. They fit well as overpants. She used buttons for fasteners and she put in front and back pockets. She said she made the pants just like the original trousers. Poppa went out seal hunting wearing those pants. When he came back from the trip Igailaq was at the house. Momma said, "Poppa came in the door and Igailaq noticed the pants right away. She told him to come and show them to her. He said that he would take them off first. Later he brought them out to Igailaq. She looked them over real good. Then she asked where did he get them from. I asked her if they were good. She said that they were real good. Who made them? I told her that I did. She said she never see me sew on them. So I told her that every time she came I would hide them. She then told me that I really sew good. That made me feel really good. After that I was not ashamed of my sewing. Yet I still did not sew as good as my sisters. I could accept that we just did different kind of sewing."

Momma said, "When we settled at Unalakleet I did not anticipate any more moves. I was back where I belonged. Your dad was back where he belonged. Apok was back to her hometown. In my estimation, Unalakleet was the best place in the world to be for anyone of any age. It was a place of freedom. We would be able to continue our own way of life. As a mother there were a lot of things that I was responsible for and had to do. My children were normal children and I was thankful for that. Your dad was concerned that we had a clean new house to live in because there had been a lot of people dying from tuberculosis. I was concerned too because we had both lost our spouses to what I thought was 'TB.' Since we did not have ready access to hospitals and such we at least had a nurse stationed here. That I was thankful for and it gave me some peace of mind.

"Mother's theory of disease prevention was that you had to eat our native foods, keep your home clean and have peace in the home. She taught this to all of her children. I tried my best to follow her instructions. It was not hard to do because your dad felt the same way. I felt fortunate that all of you kids were healthy. I always thank God that we women who delivered our babies at home had normal births. When I look at what is available today with all the clinics, hospitals and such, I think that God took care of all us women who gave birth to normal babies in those days."

24. *Local Government, Our Style*

Momma continued: "When we moved back home the village was functioning in its own form of government very well. The place was nice and peaceful. The rules were not written down but each family had an understanding that the community was governed informally by a committee of respected elders.

"It was in 1937 to 1939 that there was talk that we could form a government that would be ours and be recognized by the United States federal government. This information was brought out by the school teachers as part of their job with the federal government.

"It would be up to the people to decide what they wanted. I remember we had well respected people like Myles Gonangnan, Aaron Paneok, Henry Nashalook, Nick Riley, and Walker Asicksik considering this issue.

"Your dad and I talked about it. We thought that they would do real good and we would support their efforts. We were very proud of those people. They had all of the village interests and concerns covered. Your dad told me that he would help out when they asked him to and he thought that they would manage well as they were doing."

After a few years Poppa built an addition to the log cabin so that Apok would have her own room. She was slowly losing her eyesight and needed assistance to do some things. However she was a fiercely independent woman and would not ask for help. She had taken charge of our oldest brother Jerry's upbringing and he was her helper. Poppa and Momma let her carry on with her ways as she was still living under the same roof. Apok and Jerry would go off on their hunting and fishing excursions depending on what the season offered for harvest.

Every summer season from 1937 to 1943 Poppa would go to Camp Creek and the Tubuktulik River to look for gold prospects. He would fly up to Nome to get ready for the season. Then he would travel either to Golovin or Elim to get supplies for the camp. His usual partner in these ventures was his friend Jim Baldwin of Nome. Even Uncle Sam Otton helped Poppa in 1937. Sam also worked at the other mining camps in the area. One story is that when he was working in Bonanza he had a hankering to check on his family. Since there were no boats, airplanes to catch he just hiked his way home to Unalakleet from Bonanza, many miles away.

The prospectors were ever hopeful of finding gold and find a good enough prospect for an investor to back with equipment. Poppa said that they were not the only ones looking for the pay streak. They lived in tents all summer and put in a lot of digging. They lived off the land and the streams during this time.

Poppa was able to put in a small landing field for an airplane and the field was called Degnan Field. In his files he had pictures of his times there and all the claims he filed or had a proxy file for him.

Later he was to tell his children that because of the war and the fallen gold prices it was difficult to continue in that venture. So that was the end of his search for gold at Camp Creek. He said that the price of gold would have to rise to make it profitable.

Momma said, "I remember well that we were asked to vote on several different forms of government and the one that got the most votes was for organization under the Indian Reorganization Act of 1934.

"When we had our first elections for the Council in 1940. We elected Myles Gonangnan, Aaron Paneok and Henry Nashalook. The school teacher at that time was Mr. E. B. Fisher, who helped them fill out the necessary paperwork to comply with the government regulations.

"This was in 1937 what Nick Riley told me about. He said that he was only seventeen years old then. He was the only one that could understand the English language so he would interpret for the elders.

"So the Natives in the village had an election on December 30, 1939, to ratify the constitution and by-laws and charter for the Native village of Unalakleet, Alaska. That is how we became an IRA council.

"This was the time that the village was talking about getting their own store too. There was supposed to be moneys available from the federal government that the village council could apply for. The reason for wanting their own store was that a lot of times the trading post would run out of supplies. If we had our own store there would be competition. The only way that the village could get a loan would be they would have to pay for part of the business. The people got together and said that they would build the store with local materials that they would gather. The men would build the store building and that would be the village investment.

"This was a serious undertaking for the village. We believed that we could do it. Even the women and children took part in the construction of the store. We went out and collected a lot of moss for the chinking of the logs. They built the storage building or warehouse out of local timbers. This is where the moss was used. We were promised that the children would be able to get candy and goodies once the store was built and stocked. I know that we hauled a lot of moss. I can't remember if the children got any candy. That doesn't matter, but the store got built in 1938.

"Myles Gonangnan was the first store manager. The store was supposed to be under the management of the village council. The original store was right next door to the Nashalook's home. Across the street was the old Alaska Commercial Company trading post warehouse and Bradley's old store.

"The new Native Store building was a two storied place, the store and part of the warehouse were on the first floor. The second floor was used by whoever was the manager for their home. It was part of the manager's pay to live there rent free. The other store managers through the years were Fred Katchatag, Jack Koutchak, Charlie

Towarak, Andrew Nashalook, Millie (Otton) Ivanoff and Chuck Soxie. We went through three different store buildings from the 1940's to 1974 when the village council made an arrangement with the Unalakleet Village Corporation to take over the operation of the Native Store.

"After the Native Store was built and in operation the school teacher kept the communications open between the Alaska Native Service and the village council. Sometimes that communication was not clear. The village council had applied and received a loan from the federal government to stock the store with supplies. There was not much cash in the village. Very few people were getting any pensions from the territorial government and it was not very much. The people made money by trapping for furs and selling dried fish. The council tried very hard to make the store successful but that was difficult to do in the early days.

"The store was stocked with the basic necessities and they tried to price the items competitively with the trader Traeger's store. It was decided that the council would offer to buy Traeger out. To finance the purchase they attempted to secure a loan from the federal government. They were not able to be in a position to buy Traeger's store. The idea was good but it did not work out. So the village had two stores in the 1940's.

"These stores had their stock replenished during the summer season. When the barges and ships came in the groceries and hardware everyone turned out to off load the cargo. Also just the event of the ship arriving on the scene brought many people out to view it on the sea. When the time approached children loved to run down to the beach to be the first one to spot the ship. When the ship was seen you could hear the yell, 'Oo-mahk-pou-rak' said several times. This meant the ship was seen. In the early days you could smell the vegetables and fruit when they were coming in to port. It was such a wonderful smell. There was always a sense of excitement and expectation by all when the freight was unloaded. Everything was unloaded by hand. The workers used hand carts and wheelbarrows to unload the heavier items.

"When most of the men were away from the village working in the fish canneries at Ekuk and Koggiung it was the women and the teens that did the longshoring for the stores. This was about the middle part of the years in the 1940's. The children would be anxious to see what the new items in the store would be. Much interest was in the fresh fruits like apples and oranges and the ever-popular candy bars.

"Even with the stores being stocked in the summer the shelves would need restocking in the early spring. The most-used items were canned milk, coffee, tea, flour, sugar, onions and eggs. It used to be a custom when the cook in the family ran out of an item a child would be sent next door to borrow. Items usually borrowed were milk and homemade bread. Today you don't see that happening.

"Both stores were gathering places to visit when the weather was bad. You could find the men gathered around the stove during the winter. They would be talking about the events of the week and day. However, you did not see the women gathering and gossiping in the stores. They would rather have their gatherings in their respective homes.

"The post office was located in Traeger's store. I believe that Charlie Traeger was the first postmaster we had. Later my brother Frank was the next postmaster. The post office was in a small section of the store in the back behind the dry goods section. The mail was sorted and put in what looked like cubbyhole shelves."

Momma said that Unalakleet got more mail service during the week and month compared to the surrounding villages. The mail was carried by dog sled in the early days in the winter and spring. Her own father, Eric Johnsson, was one of those mail carriers using a dog team. Her older brother, Frank Ryan, backpacked the U. S. Mail to Kaltag when he was a young man. Sam Otton and Justius Pitmitalik were also mail carriers between Unalakleet and St. Michael. During the summer it went by mail boat to Nome or St. Michael. Then in the later years, like in the 1930's, by mail plane.

Momma said, "After the Native Store was built and in operation we felt good that we had our own store and it was being run by our own people. There still were not many jobs to be had in the village. That did not stop the shopping for needed supplies by all of us. We women were busy making hand-crafted items for sale or trade in the two stores. We also put up a lot of dried fish that we used for our home use and as cash. All the families were busy with their subsistence way of life. There were a few more boats with outboard motors so that we could go farther away from the village on our food gathering and camping outings."

Our store built in 1938

25. Spring Camp

Momma loved to tell us about the camping trips that we made as a family during our childhood. She said, "Our whole family looked forward for the time that we would go out to the Cape Denbigh flats and into Norton Bay. This one spring we went on a trip back to Punuukutaq. I was expecting another baby at this time and knew that I was going to give birth sometimes late in June. This time was in the year of 1941. Still I was eager to go camping. There was a lot of food that we had to gather. Your dad took us out in his long wooden riverboat that he had managed to buy. He was very proud of that boat and the nine-horse-power Johnson outboard motor.

"That trip was good and it seemed that the weather cooperated for once. It was not windy or stormy this trip up to Moses Point. We got to gather our duck eggs, pick our greens and had a good time. The kids had a lot of fun and we had plenty to eat. It was so good to be out. I told your dad that it was time to go home as the baby was getting close to being born. He agreed with me and we started for home about June 20, 1941.

"When we got close to Cape Denbigh the wind kicked up. Now it seemed that what I feared most was coming true. We were going to ride a fierce storm. Your dad had all of us covered under a canvas tarp. He was singing his usual tunes. I got out from under the tarp and he said that I should start bailing water as it washed into the boat. You kids were doing good. I tried to stay calm for the sake of the unborn baby. I tried to be brave. I say, to this day, that you have the best seaman in the world as your dad. We made it through the giant swells and waves through Cape Denbigh and into the Shaktoolik River. There we were greeted by our friends and they took good care of us. Your dad and I decided that we would leave as soon as it calmed down a bit.

"We arrived home at Unalakleet on June 22, 1941, in time for the birthday party for my nephew Sam Otton Jr. who had just turned one year old. His Inuit name is Anisaaluk. I hurried up and made it to the party. I had made him a pair of denim coveralls. When I gave him his gift he came over to me and placed them on my tummy. Jessie immediately said that he was predicting that the new baby was a boy. That sure sounded good to me because so far we had only one son in the family. It was good to be home.

"The next morning I had to send Eva running again for Thora Soosuk. It was time for another birth. This birth was acting much different from the other births, maybe it was a boy after all. My baby was born. Thora was very excited. She told me that it is a boy baby.

"My sister Gertie came running in the house. She was all excited. She took one look at the baby and shouted, 'Qaiguq tikittuq,' and 'Charlie.' That is how Chuck was born and how he got his name. He was named by Gertie after Charlie who lived in Golsovia, a settlement south of Unalakleet.

"What Gertie said was Qaiguq came. Qaiguq had passed away not too long before Chuck was born. I always thought that it was a fitting name for Chuck because his namesake Charlie always came to me to mend his parka and mukluks. I used to wonder why he chose me to repair his clothing even if I was not a good seamstress like my sisters. He always thanked me for helping him out and I didn't mind it at all."

26. Airplanes

Momma said that the first plane over and into the village was quite an event. This was in the early 1930's and in the summer and everyone had their own version of what they saw in the sky. The noises of the first planes were awesome. The village was so quiet that the airplane approaches and departures seemed to be thunderous.

She told me one special story about one of the elders. This family was across the river at their summer fish camp. Sukki and her husband Tuktuk were in their tent when they heard this big noise. It was like humming. They went out and looked up in the sky. They saw this big thing in the sky approaching them like a giant bird. Sukki happened to be wearing her best red cloth parka that day. The giant bird saw her in her red parka and he stopped in flight right above her. He stopped his flight and stood still in the air right over her. She supposed that he was admiring her beautiful red parka. Momma loved that story because it was a true story told by Sukki.

Another first airplane arrival story Momma told about was that Utuayuk, the wife of Sarren, had been unable to walk for many years. She was known to have a hard time to walk so her husband Sarren devised a reindeer sled to take her to church and other community activities. Everyone knew of her condition. When that first airplane flew into the village to land everyone knew a miracle had taken place. Utuayuk heard this great noise and raced out of the house to see what was going on. From that time on she was able to walk on her own power and everyone in the village was amazed.

When airplanes became commonplace at Unalakleet they were generally small planes. Some of them were on floats and pontoons. The small-wheeled airplanes would land on the tundra at the edge of the village. When the missionary plane landed it would taxi down the middle of the village and park near the church site. Like the early arrivals of the ships, the airplanes were great events. Almost the whole town would turn out to see who would come out of the airplane. In the latter part of the 1940's an occasional airplane would land that carried a load of tourists. These tourists would spend a few hours in the village taking pictures of anything they could find. Apparently this was not a likely destination for tours as that type of flights did not come often.

*Chinglak with Bud Hagberg
and Alma Bradley, granddaughter*

Frank, Sheldon, Stanley, Mabel, and Wilfred Ryan

27. World War II

When World War II started the news was slow in bush Alaska. Poppa had installed a wind charger generator to power batteries for a few lights in the house and for his Atwater-Kent radio. This was a short-wave radio and he would listen to worldwide stations and get the latest news. Momma said that he was at home alone in the evening when he heard a short-wave BBC broadcast that Pearl Harbor was being bombed. This was on December 7, 1941. He found out that Pearl Harbor was in the Hawaiian islands and it was on American territory. The Japanese had bombed the place. He told Momma that we were in serious trouble and that we had much to be concerned about. That scared the daylights out of Momma. She said that learning this brought the horror of world war to the quiet, peaceful little village.

There were quite a few of our local men who were drafted and served in the Armed Forces during the course of the war. Momma's nephews Roland Ivanoff and Wilfred Ryan served in the Army. The families had fear for their safety. Fear for the safety of the village and for Alaska was on the minds of many.

The Alaska Territorial Guard was formed at this time and all the adult men of the village joined and formed a local unit. Poppa said that he was happy to serve in the ATG and at the end of the tour he had the post of lieutenant. He said that Henry Nashalook was the captain of the Unalakleet ATG unit and held them together. He liked to refer to the ATG as the 'Alaska Tough Guys.' He said that they were issued military rifles and they had their training sessions. Colonel 'Muktuk' Marston was at the head of the Guard and he traveled throughout the North setting up local guard units. It was at that time the territory was on the alert for a Japanese invasion. After Pearl Harbor they heard about the Japanese invasion in the Aleutian Islands. To them it seemed like the war was getting closer. They would have their local drills and practiced what they would do if the war came to their doorstep.

Thankfully the North Country remained quiet, local villages were put on blackout alerts. During these blackouts, all the windows were covered so lights would not show through. They were to report any unusual activities. People thought that they saw Japanese fighter planes, but these sightings were not confirmed. They also stated that they spotted Russian bomber airplanes over the village. The people were happy when the war came to an end. Some of the older people were suspicious about Japanese for a long time after the war.

Also at this time, Grandpa Johnsson wrote to Momma with the news that Ruth had married John T. (Jack) Emel at his home on August 6, 1942, and that they were planning to live in Marshall. Grandpa Johnsson wrote often to Momma and she kept all of the letters that her father and father-in-law, Francis G. Degnan, ever wrote to her and Poppa.

Also, this was the year that Apok received Old Age Assistance from the Territory of Alaska. Frank Ryan was the welfare agent. Grandpa Degnan wrote to verify Apok's age. He said that he was told by Frank Kameroff that Apok was about the same age as Frank and that Frank had gone to school with Apok in Unalakleet when they were young. Also, that Molly Dexter of Golovin had a sister who was the same age as Apok. At this time Grandpa Degnan estimated that Apok was older than sixty-six years of age.

28. Sinrock Mary and Eunice Arrive to Stay

At this time Sinrock Mary had moved from her reindeer grounds in Klikaterek to St. Michael. Sinrock's Inuit name was 'Sanuyaaq.' Sinrock Mary had her granddaughter Eunice Oyoumick living with her. Eunice's Inuit name was Natiqaq, after the wife of Golsovia Charlie. Eunice's mother was Mary Waldron. She was the biological daughter of Istaluka. Sinrock Mary adopted Mary. When Mary Waldron grew up she met and married Gunner Oyoumick. When Eunice was a young child her adopted grandmother took her in with the consent of Mary and Gunner. Eunice had sisters named Katherine, Annie, Eva, and Julia. Her brothers were Fred, David, Harold, and Alec.

In earlier times Sinrock Mary and her husband Charlie Antisarlook had managed and owned large herds of reindeer in the Sinuk area. In 1909 Sinrock Mary moved her herds from Unalakleet to Klikaterek. Klikaterek was to be their home for many years. After Charlie died Sinrock Mary married Aanguyuk who was known as Andrew Andrewyuk. They continued to live at Kliketarek. This is where Eunice grew up with her grandmother. After the passing of her husbands and the reindeer industry, Sinrock saw no reason to continue to live in Klikaterek. It had been a good home to her. However it was time to move to where there were more people. They lived in St. Michael where Sinrock Mary had a nice big house. Eunice said that her grandmother was getting older and wanted to move to Unalakleet. So they picked up and moved there.

Eunice found a place to stay with Myles and Marion Gonangnan. Formerly Marion had been married to George Antisarlook who was the son of Charlie Antislarlook and Sinrock Mary. Sinrock Mary was taken in by Oliver and Nannie Anawrok. Sinrock Mary's first husband had been Charlie Antisarlook who was the brother of Oliver Angalook Anawrok. At the same time, Sinrock Mary and Eunice looked for a house to live in. They located Nashalook's old house with the help of E. B. Larsson, the missionary.

Eunice said that her grandmother was getting old and not feeling too good. This was about 1942. Igailaq offered to take care of the grandmother so they moved in with Igailaq. Igailaq was a lady of great compassion. Momma told me that she had a special affinity for the poor, ill and homeless. Since Igailaq was living alone it seemed to her the only right thing was to offer help and shelter to her friend.

Sinrock Mary lived with Igailaq until she died on November 22, 1948, at Igailaq's home. Igailaq told Momma that when Sinrock knew her time was coming she called Igailaq to her side and said, "I want to bless you for being so good to me. I will bless you with long life."

Igailaq replied, "I do not want the blessing. It is not good to get too old where you cannot take care of yourself. So I refused her blessing."

Momma told me she said to Igailaq, "Mom, how come you refused that good blessing, it would be a very good thing to have."

Momma said Igailaq replied, "I don't want to become so old I become helpless."

Many years later Igailaq was to get her own wish. She was in good physical health so that she could care for herself at her own speed. She had her children around her with all their children. She had her same sharp mind and wit. Igailaq lived a full life and she died peacefully in her sleep in her own bed in her own home on August 21, 1962.

Igailaq was very concerned about her only son and his children now that his wife Susan had died. Igailaq helped out the best she could but she knew the children needed a good mother. Also her son needed a good wife and helpmate. Igailaq took it upon herself to speak with her son. She told him that it was time for him to find a good wife. If he opened his eyes he would see that there was a young woman living next door to him that would make a good wife. Those children needed a mother to love and care for them. He listened to her and did not reply. However he let his mother know that he understood what she was saying.

It was not long after this talk that Frank asked his mother if she approved of his asking Eunice Oyoumick to marry him. Igailaq was very happy. This is just what she wanted to happen. Eunice had all the skills of what she considered to be a good wife and mother. So it happened. Frank and Eunice were married by Reverend Emory Lindgren at the old Mission House at Unalakleet. Eunice had a young child that Frank adopted as his own son. Henry was born on October 9, 1944, and his Inuit name was Kinik. So Frank, Eunice and all the children became one family. Igailaq was content. Frank and Eunice had two more children. Timothy Grenfell Ryan was born on September 24, 1946, at home. His Inuit name was Ahkalook. Glen J. Ryan was born on June 24, 1948 at home also. Glen died when he was a toddler. He was killed by the neighbors' dogs. That was a sad time for the family.

Igailaq, Apok, Edna Diatweaque Paneok
Sinrock Mary

129

29. Village Government in Action

During the war period the federal government, through the Civil Aeronautics Administration (CAA), selected Unalakleet as a site for their station and airport. On July 17, 1942, the village council members, Vice President Stephan Katchatag, Henry Nashalook, Joshua Tuktook, and John Auliye met with the principal teacher Mr. E. B. Fisher. The purpose of the meeting was to give permission to the Civil Aeronautics Administration (CAA) to enter the reservation. At this meeting the council voted in favor of allowing them to enter on the reservation.

Poppa was hired by the CAA to help site and survey the runway. He said that it was not a hard job to do as he has a lot of experience from his years of staking gold claims in the Camp Creek and Tubuktulik River areas. After the runway was set in, the construction of the CAA station began. This brought in some good employment to the village. Many of the men were able to work as carpenters, laborers, and later, at the station. Poppa worked as a carpenter and helped build most of the CAA buildings.

The summer season was the only time there was a chance for employment for the people in the villages. The Territory of Alaska did not spend much of their budget in the remote areas. Much of the projects that did come into the area were financed by the federal government.

During the winter season there was the hunting and trapping. Beavers were available in the area so many of the men went trapping for them. Poppa did trap beaver and some seasons he sold enough to purchase necessities for the home. Some of the years there was bounty put on

wolves and then sometimes for seals. So, many of the hunters were able to get a few dollars for these animals. However, that did not last long either. This did not bother the
hunters as they were also concerned about the viability of
the resource. They liked to see that the animal population
remained healthy, and they knew that the bounty situation was only temporary.

Much of the local winter travel was still by dog and
sled. So summertime meant that you caught the salmon
so that you would have enough dried fish for dog feed.
Some of the men set out fish traps during the winter to
catch the local trout. This was a welcome food after many
days of the dry fish for both man and animal. Of course,
the ever plentiful tomcod could be easily caught at the
mouth of the rivers that emptied into the Norton Sound.

Momma told me the story of my birth many times.
She said that it was early in the morning, on May 26, 1943,
that another baby girl was born and she was named after
grandpa Degnan and Sophie Ann Klemetson. That baby
was me. I was given the Inuit names of Kitliq, after Ellen
Bradley, Alvan, after Mrs. Anagick, Killegnek, after Mrs. Dave
Gray of Nome, Nunnouk, after Mrs. Etageak, and Amauguaq,
after Emily Brown's maternal aunt, Mrs. Neuksik.

Now there were six children and one grandmother
living with the parents. She said with so many mouths to
feed she had to do a lot of planning. She said that it was
all subsistence living. She canned many cans of stews,
soups and vegetables from the garden produce and reindeer and wild duck meat. She used tin cans processed in a
large pressure cooker that she had Poppa buy on one of
his trips to Nome. She said that she and the older children made sauerkraut from the cabbages they grew. She
salted barrels of salmon bellies. She even salted walrus
meat, ducks and geese for later use in soups and stews.
All of the vegetables harvested in the fall were stored for
winter use in the root cellar in the cabin. Momma always
commented that we lived a pure subsistence way of life
and that the land was always good to all the people. We
just had to take advantage of the resources and make sure
that we properly harvested and prepared the harvest so
that it would not spoil.

30. Native Stores

On April 22, 1944, a special meeting of the Native
Village Council was held. At the meeting there was as re-
port and discussion on the status of a loan for the Native
Store.

President Frank Degnan stated in the minutes: "Why
do we always fail to get help from the schoolteacher concerning our Native Store? That is one reason why I made
the trip to Juneau. To find out. Left Unalakleet the first of
April en route to Juneau. First stop was at Fairbanks.
There was no room to be got. Walked the streets for hours.
April 2nd I went to Anchorage. Hotels were all filled up.
Was up to see Mr. Broadwell. He asked me where I was
going? I told him I was going to Juneau to try and (get) a
loan for the Unalakleet Native Store. He said it was a
good idea. He told me George A. Dale of U.S. Office of Indian Affairs and Ralph W. Mize construction engineer were
in Anchorage from Juneau and would be a good idea to
see them for advice. Which I did. They advised me to see
L. C. Peters Credit Agent at Juneau. Left Anchorage on
April 4th. Arrived at Juneau same day. While in Juneau
called up Gov. Gruening. was invited to dinner. met Mrs.
Gruening. also Mrs. Day from Skagway. After dinner had
talks with Governor about loan for Unalakleet Native
Store. Gov. Gruening said it was a good idea and wished
me luck. Back to L.C. Peters, field agent of Credit Office.
asked for loan of $30,000.00. Peters said it was too much.
Offered $10,000.00 I said not enough for a big village. He
agreed with $15,000.00. While in Office Mr. Virgil Farrel
said, 'Received a wire from Mr. Fisher. School teacher of

Unalakleet wanting a transfer. Had papers made out in Juneau. Ready for Mr. Fisher to sign for grant of loan. Arrived home April 18th. Had council work on loan papers. The council sign their names. Except Mr. Fisher schoolteacher. Saw Mr. Fisher at the ball game with the schoolchildren at the landing field at 2:30 p.m. Shook hands with him. Told him I had papers for a loan for him to sign. The first thing he said, "I will not sign the loan." I said, "WHY?" He replied that he got a wire from Don. C Foster., Gen. Supt. Alaska Ind. Service, asking him if he would approve the loan. Mr. Fisher said he wired back. He would not sign as yet. I said "Alright, we can send a wire, too." Fisher said, "Wait a minute. Let's talk. How much was the loan?" I said $15,000.00. Fisher says NOT ENOUGH. I said, "Meeting Saturday 7 P.M." The final outcome of the meeting was that the school teacher E.B. Fisher would notify his superiors in the Office of Indian Affairs that the council requests that they be the one authorized to sign the loan papers with bonding of the individuals signing."

On May 24, 1944, there was a special meeting of the village to discuss the status of the Native Store. It had been closed by the local school teacher for the duration of the war. The people wanted the store opened but they were not able to secure credit to purchase supplies. It was time something was done. The men at the meeting formally organized the Alaska Native Brotherhood of Unalakleet. Poppa had been down at Juneau and saw the Alaska Native Brotherhood and Sisterhood organize to fight for their rights as Native people. The Southeastern group was willing to help their northern brothers and sisters to improve their living conditions and protect their rights. It was up to the people in the village to decide what they wanted.

It was decided at this May 24th evening meeting that they would organize their chapter of ANB. The organizing members were: Frank Degnan, Frank Roberts, Franklin Soxie, Henry Nashalook, John Auliye, Axel Oyoumick, Harold Charles, Nick Riley, Karlson Norman, John Oyoumick, Walker Asicksik, Harold Ivanoff, Wassilie Evan, Richard Benjamin, Pete Kotongan, Abraham Takruk, Joshua Tuktook and Stanton Katchatag. The elected officers were: President Frank Degnan, Vice President Walker Asicksik, Secretary Henry Nashalook and Treasurer Axel Oyoumick.

Their first goal was to get the Native Store opened and stocked or get the native store as a cooperative. This is where the first steps of many steps that were to be taken to start the Native Store cooperative idea that was to become a reality in 1947 as the ANICA or Alaska Native Industries Cooperative Association. Poppa was also the president of the Native village of Unalakleet Council and he was elected as Director for ANICA from Unalakleet. He did not run for president of the Native Council of Unalakleet in 1949 and Frederick Katchatag was elected President. So when Poppa was no longer on the village council the ANICA manager L.C. Peters advised the Village Council to select his replacement, and election was held and Fred Katchatag was elected director.

Top L-R: John Auliye, Moody Douglas, Jacob Soxie,
Stephan Katchatag, Nick Riley
Bottom L-R: Aaron Paneok, Arthur Soxie,
Wassilie Eakon, Axel Oyoumick

31. Discrimination Laws

The Grand Camp of the Alaska Native Brotherhood through its Grand President Roy Peratrovich advised the Unalakleet ANB, on March 8, 1945, that the Alaska Territorial Legislature passed a law pertaining to Equal Rights. The ANB had sponsored this bill at the previous session of the legislature, but it was defeated then. This session the same Bill was introduced by Edgar Anderson from Nome, Alaska. The legislators from the Northwest that voted and fought for the law were Bess Cross of Deering, Edgar Anderson, mayor of Nome, Wallace Porter from Haycock, O. D. Cochran and Howard Lyng from Nome.

Anyone knowing the history of discrimination in Alaska would understand the tremendous importance of the law. Momma said that discrimination was bad when they were living in Nome. The Eskimos were not allowed in many places and if they were, they had to be in their own section. This was an important part of our Alaska history.

According to a letter sent to the voters of the Second Division (where Unalakleet is located) dated May 1, 1945, from William L. Paul Jr., secretary of the Grand Camp of the Alaska Native Brotherhood the following was written: 'This law is a good example of the steady pressure that should be applied by every fair-minded person in the Territory for-'Equal privileges of public inns, restaurants, eating houses, barber shops, hotels, soda fountains, taverns, roadhouses, beauty parlors, theaters, transportation companies, etc.' This is what the Equal Rights law related to was discrimination."

Poppa said that the places where discrimination was seen and felt were in the larger towns and cities in Alaska. Discrimination was of a different sort in the small villages. He felt that the discrimination was that the opportunities for employment through the governments fostered was for Outsiders and not for the indigenous peoples. From the outside looking in it appeared that there was no problem. The Outsiders' operating myth was "The indigenous just do not want to work; besides they do not have the necessary qualifications for the jobs that exist in their village. They do not have the initiative to create jobs. They are ignorant."

Poppa said that if the governments truly had the indigenous welfare at heart they would do their jobs right to make sure the schools they taught in had effective programs. They would hire the local people to run all the agencies in the villages. This was not happening because the governments that sent these people and programs had their headquarters too far away. Also in the special reports to the Congress that were done by the Department of the Interior even went so far as to comment that the indigenous people had the mentality of a seven-year old child. Since we had a form of government that was recognized by the federal government, it was time our voices were heard.

From their earliest arrival, the Outsiders, depended on the goodwill of the indigenous peoples. In the Norton Sound any stranger was given shelter and assistance for as long as they needed it. This was not true in other parts of the country. The local people were not prone to run strangers out. The cultural values of the indigenous population were strong. Human life was respected. The world of nature was respected. Spiritual values were strong. The people were in charge of their world.

Both Momma and Poppa commented that our way of life was ever changing. We live through the changes and learn new ways to live with the land, sea and their resources. The health of the people was very important. To have good health the families needed good housing, good sanitation and nutritious foods to eat. At this time there were many illnesses and people were dying. Poppa said that it was because of malnutrition. Momma agreed with him.

Village of Unalakleet in the winter

Our home in winter during the 1940's

32. Camping Out

In 1945, Momma told me that she was going to have another child. This time that baby was going to be born in the winter. At this same time Elizabeth Paniptchuk, whose Inuit name was Aanauraq, was also expecting a child. Momma said that both of those babies were born on the same day. Elizabeth had a boy whom she named Walter; his Inuit name was Chinlialuk.

Momma gave birth to a little girl on February 28, 1945. Momma said that she was such a beautiful baby, and named her Shirley Kate. But there was something wrong.

Momma said, "I did not give her her Inuit name. Thora was my midwife again. The birth was normal but Shirley could not hold her food in, and I was just worried. She did not live very long. She died on March 7, 1945. It was then we found out that it was just a closed membrane in her intestine that was the cause of her death. Today that would be such a simple thing to correct.

"This made your dad and me really think that our people need a hospital where these things could be taken care of. Now whenever I see Chinlialuk I think that is how old your sister Shirley would be today."

That same spring the family readied to go to the annual camping spot at Cape Denbigh. This trip they invited Mabel Ryan to go along. This would be the last spring camping trip for Eva. Momma and Poppa had decided that they would send her off to high school at Sheldon Jackson school in Sitka, Alaska.

The entire family set off in the wooden river boat. It was a good trip. For the entire family it was always a great time to go egg hunting and they called it "Piq- qu-naq."

Momma said that the camping time was busy. This was the first time, that she had found white goose eggs. When Sockpealuk, one of the elders from Shaktoolik, was visiting at the camp, he told her that he had never heard of anyone finding white goose eggs before on these flats. He looked at the eggs and confirmed that they were white goose eggs.

Momma said that I was just a little girl and I was suffering some kind of sores in my mouth. She said that she didn't know what to do, but she thought of an old remedy her mother had told her about.

Momma said, "I went down to the seashore and picked up as many tiny clamshells as I could carry. I brought these to the tent. I scrubbed them good and put them in a pan and roasted them in the oven. When they were toasted I put them into a cloth sugar sack and pounded them into dust. Then I took that dust and put it on the sores in your mouth. I didn't know if that would work. But you know what? It worked. In a few days you were back to normal and eating regularly. That time too we ran out of bread in our grub box. Maybe it was because the bread tasted so good that we ran out earlier than usual or that I did not plan too good for this trip. Anyhow we were out of bread. Chuck was just a little boy, about four years old, and he was wanting bread. I did not want to cut our camping trip short just for some bread.

"Right at this time your dad had found a fresh maklasauq, (young bearded seal), that had washed up at the mouth of the Ching-iat Slough below our tent. He was butchering it for the blubber. I went down to help him. When Frank threw some of the blubber scraps into the slough I noticed that there were fish jumping. It gave me an idea. I got out my im-goo-you-tak, (sewing kit), and got a piece of twine and a safety pin. I put them together on a pole and made fishing tackle. I baited the safety pin with the fresh blubber and tossed it in the water. Immediately I got a strike and pulled in a large Dolly Varden. I hooked a few more and cleaned them right away. I brought them back to the tent and fried them up right now. Chuck got the first piece and everyone enjoyed the fish. It sure tasted good. Chuck never said, 'I want bread,' anymore on that trip.

"On that trip, like all the other camping trips, we had so much fun finding duck eggs. There were so many little sloughs and lakes we would spend most of the day in and out of the boat. We had to be careful of watching the tides so that we would not get high and dry and not make it back to camp. We all wore rubber boots and carried our backpacks and buckets. I always had all of you bring back any eider duck nests along with the eggs you found. I had a purpose for the nests. With the down I was planning to make winter quilts and maybe parkas.

"This one day your dad was a long way off and I noticed that the tide was dropping fast. I sent Mabel and Eva, since they were the oldest of the kids, to run after your dad to tell him we had to get back to camp. Eva and Mabel were running as fast as they could and hollering, 'Dad, dad,' at the top of their lungs. That sure made me smile. It took them a while to catch up with him. They all made it back before the tide went too far out. We made it okay back to the beach camp.

"The next day we went back to that same place to search for nests. The tide was much lower that day and when we were making our way through the mud to the bank we all got stuck. Ida had to help June out of the mud. When she got loose she left her rubber boot in the mud and would not go back for it. I had to go down and pull it out to save it. I got it out and made it back to the bank. I had a very tough time of it. I kept getting stuck. I got to the top of the bank and fell down exhausted. An eider duck flew out from under me. I had landed on her nest. It was full of eggs and I didn't break them. It was all worth the effort. After that day I started to call June by the nickname of 'Boots' because of that day.

"After our stay at Ching-iat your dad wanted to see old man Simon Sagoonick at Ungalik. So we all broke camp and loaded the boat and moved out. It was a beautiful day and the trip to Ungalik didn't take us too long. When we landed at Ungalik we were greeted by Simon Sagoonick and his dog, which he called Dossel. I made coffee and lunch right away. I remember well that you and Chuck went right in the water because you had seen schools of smelt and were catching them with your hands. Next thing I know is that you fell in the water and were screaming your head off. You thought you were drowning. But that water was so shallow I didn't worry. We got you out and put you near the fire in dad's clothes to get warm. I hung out your clothes to dry. Anyway that dog Dossel kept you company when you waited for your clothes to dry out. That reminds me of the saying that your dad always said when we talked about smelt and it was: I went into a restaurant and I ordered me some smelt. The waiter brought me some smelt and I never smelt any smelt like that smelt, smelt. You kids always laughed when he told that story.

"We had a good lunch, coffee and visit with Sagoonick. He was living by himself. Your dad asked him if he needed anything. Sagoonick said that he was doing okay and that he was glad we stopped by. After visiting for awhile your dad said that it was time we go home. So there we were. We had a good trip and now it was time to get back to the village. We had a good trip home. We were lucky that time that it was glassy calm all the way home to Unalakleet from Ungalik. But like all the other trips we just had to stop in Shaktoolik. We would never just pass by. We had to stop to visit our friends and see how they were doing. I always treasure those visits with all the old folks like Nizzek, Bekoalooks, Takaks, Sockpealuks and of course my dear friend Lizzie Beeson. Lizzie was so tiny I always called her 'Uutukuuraq' which means 'little one.' When we were children we had such fun playing together. Throughout my life it seemed like Lizzie never changed and was so very nice."

33. Leaving Home for High School

Momma said, "Eva had just finished the eighth grade at Unalakleet. We had a teacher by the name of Bessie Lambkin Smith who was very interested in helping the children get more education. That year Ida Kootuk Traeger and Eva were encouraged by Bessie to go to Sheldon Jackson School in Sitka, Alaska. Your dad and I talked about the need for our children to have more education then we ourselves had. We knew that it would take cash to send Eva away to school and that she would have to stay away until she finished school.

"We talked with Eva and Bessie and it was decided that Eva would go. It was her decision and we were supportive of what she wanted to do. Since the decision was made now we had to prepare for her trip. I wondered where we were going to get the tuition and the air fare. Eva and I set out to make her school clothes and to prepare emotionally for her expected departure. Somehow we were able to make and save enough cash for her air fare. Bessie told us not to worry about the tuition as that would be her project and contribution, but that Eva was to finish high school. That Eva agreed to.

"It was exciting to all of us that our oldest child was going on a new adventure. We were all so confident that she would succeed and do so well. Thank God we all had high expectations! When Eva left home, Poppa always said that she left the reindeer hide on our cabin floor to go to Sheldon Jackson to gain her sheepskin. Anyway we would all miss Eva. I especially would miss her and her cheerful, willing and helpful ways. She was a big part of my life and I would miss her very much."

Eva left Unalakleet on August 12, 1945. Eva and Ida Kootuk Traeger left Unalakleet on an Alaska Airlines two-engine large airplane. Poppa had made arrangements for them to stay with Mr. and Mrs. Sam Troutman who were living in Anchorage. Before that they had been school teachers on St. Lawrence Island. Eva said later that she was impressed that their two children had learned to speak St. Lawrence Island Yup'ik.

Eva and Ida arrived in Anchorage on V. J. (Victory over Japan) Day. She did not know what that was all about but they witnessed the part of the mass hysteria of celebration at the end of World War II. She recalled that it was such a shock to see adults behaving in unbelievable ways.

The Troutmans had planned an evening outing at the movies for their guests. They were on their way to the theater but the activity on the street was so rowdy their hosts cancelled the outing and they spent a quiet evening at home.

Eva remembers that they flew to Juneau on a big airplane. Poppa had made arrangements to have them stay with Mr. and Mrs. Walter Soboleff. Eva was impressed that Genevieve (Mrs. Soboleff) was the first of the Tlingets to become a registered nurse.

Momma said, "Eva and Ida then made their way to Sitka and their final destination being Sheldon Jackson School. They were to remain there for the purpose of getting higher education, another great challenge and adventure for our eldest child.

"Now that Eva was gone, your dad and I talked about the need to have our own high school here. It would not do to send all our children away to a far and distant land to get an education. We knew that times were changing and the children needed all the education and training they could get to succeed in their futures.

"It was also at this time in our lives that Apok had lost most of her vision and eyesight. She said that the house was too noisy and crowded for her. Poppa knew that there was a cabin next door to us that was vacant. He contacted the owner who was living in Nome and asked him if he was willing to sell the cabin. That man was Justius Pitmatalik. Justius was willing and he sold Poppa the cabin, on May 4, 1944, through the law office of C. C. Tanner of Nome, Alaska. That was where Justius was now living."

Apok's new abode was a small one-roomed spruce log cabin with a small attached shed. Apok was glad to move. When she moved she took Jerry with her. They were next door so it was just like a bedroom. They were to continue to eat and live with the rest of the family.

Momma said, "Now that Apok had lost most of her eyesight it brought another change into our lives as a family. There were very few hospitals in Alaska. No matter where we sent her it would take much planning and money. Outside of her loss of eyesight she was in good physical condition. She wanted to stay home. Poppa knew that he would have to do something for his dear mother.

"In Poppa's search for help he was also advocating for the rest of the indigenous peoples in Alaska. He spoke many times to the Alaska Native Service Superintendent Don C. Foster in Juneau about the need for hospital care availability and educational opportunities for the people and the extreme lack of those institutions that were accessible to a majority of the people living in rural Alaska."

Eva, Momma, Frances, and Frank Ryan
1945 ~ Eva goes to Sheldon Jackson School

34. Eskimo Mothers Club

Also in 1945, Emily Ivanoff Brown was a school-teacher for the Bureau of Indian Affairs at Unalakleet. Momma said, "The women of the village were very interested in how their children were doing in school. They wanted the best for their children and make sure that the school would do right by them.

"Emily came up with the idea of forming a Mothers Club and all the other women in the village agreed that it was a good idea. So it was that year the women formalized the idea and organized the Eskimo Mothers Club. Their goal was to improve the health and education of all the children. They would support the IRA Council's efforts to get a high school and hospital established in Unalakleet.

"At then the only places the children could go to school was at the boarding school at White Mountain, Alaska and to the Chemowa Indian School in Oregon. Also some of the older ones had attended the boarding school at Eklutna, Alaska. The goal of the community was to establish a high school at home so that the children would not have to travel away from home to get a high school education. Another important goal was to have a hospital established in Unalakleet so that the people could be treated at home. The way it was they were lucky only if they remained healthy. There were no nearby hospitals, besides no one could afford the transportation costs to any medical facility in the world.

"The charter members of the club were: Emily Ivanoff Brown, Martha Isaac Nanouk, Marion Nashalook

Gonangnan, Virginia Soxie Nashalook, Eula Kootuk Traeger, Elizabeth Pazgataagaq Sarren, Thora Soosuk Katchatag, Isabelle Tomrun Towarak, Ifgenia Eakon Roberts, Marie Soxie Anagick, Ethel Sarren Toshavik, Virginia Toshavik Agibinik, Selma Etageak Lockwood, Mary Eakon Paneok, Jessie Katchatag Paneok, Lillian Nashalook Ivanoff, Helen Nashalook Lockwood, Florence Savetilik Sarren, Hazel Mulluk Katongan, Ada Mike Kootuk, Frieda Anawrok Riley, Ellen Paneok Soxie, Elizabeth Paniptchuk, Esther Anawrok Agibinik, Marie Eakon, Frances Bannuk Ayagiak, Anna Mixsooke, Clara Paniptchuk Oyoumick, Guerie Paniptchuk Towarak, Ebba Paniptchuk Katchatag, Edna Atchak Koutchak, Irene Koutchak Katchatag, Nannie Okillaq Anawrok, Jennie Paneok Katchatag, Carrie Soxie, Elsie Kotongan Soxie, Betty Nanouk Anagick, Bessie Towarak (Larsen), and Ada Johnsson Degnan (Momma.)"

Momma said, "We were concerned about the welfare of the children. We approached the principal of the elementary school and got permission to hold our meetings in the school basement. The club would invite and welcome the teachers at the beginning of each school year through a party and meeting. We got the approval to use the school after hours on a regular basis for our monthly meetings. We met each month of the school year."

During these meetings they concluded that the children needed to be healthy to learn. To be healthy they had to have nutritious meals. The best place to have those meals would be right in the school. They decided they would sponsor a hot lunch program in the school. They designed the program and got the approval from the principal E. B. Fisher.

The Bureau Indian Affairs Alaska Native Service did not have a lunch program in the school, so the building was not set up to house the program. That was no problem for the mothers. All they needed was a place to cook, feed the children and clean up the place after the meals. They did not think that was hard. Of course, they did not have any money, so whoever was going to be the cook would have to be a volunteer and would need helpers.

The mothers did not think that the lack of food would be a problem because they would supply the food too. They had visions of serving all local foods to the children. They figured that they had vegetables that they grew in their gardens. The river and the sea would provide the fish. The land would provide the wild game along with reindeer which would be the source of meat. Of course, this meant that they and their families would have to fish, gather, hunt, and plant their gardens to produce the foods they needed for the program. The will was there, they would do it. What a wonderful group of mothers we had.

Momma said, "So when we first got organized and okayed to do our part in the school, the first order of our business was to see what kind of education our children were receiving. We agreed and selected mothers that were willing to go to the school and sit in the classrooms to observe what was going on. That was no problem as the principal had okayed it. So our mothers went in the classrooms.

"The principal told us that one of the teachers was upset that our presence was there. That teacher came to the officers of the club and told us that he knew that he did not spend enough time in the classroom. We told him that we just wanted to know what was going on. Next thing we knew is that this teacher packed up his things and took the next plane out of the village. There was no explanation so we figured he didn't like us taking an interest in the education of our children.

"So when it came time to set up the hot lunch program I was selected as the volunteer cook and my helper was Ebba Katchatag. There were to be many volunteer cooks and to my recollection they were: Susan Shafter, Alma Bradley, Mabel Ryan, and Gertie Auliye. We were to open the lunch program in the basement of the elementary school.

"Shafter Toshavik was the janitor. There was a small room next to the boiler room where we would cook. It was between the bathrooms and large empty space that we had tables put in. The stove we cooked on was a large coal cook stove. We also used the stoves in the teachers and nurse's quarters on the third floor of the school building to cook the children's lunches. We would use large tubs to wash and sterilize the cooking and eating utensils. At first we brought our own pots and pans from home to cook in. We had the children bring in their own dishes and silverware for them to use.

"What were we going to cook for them to eat? Since we had a plan we were ready. Them days we did not have freezers or refrigeration so the foods had to be dried, canned, salted or fresh. Just like at home. That was no problem. We had all the grades from primary to eighth grade to feed.

"We had to have lots of water to cook with, to clean up with and for the children to wash up with. This was not running water out of a tap. In the winter many chunks of ice would have to be hauled in from the river by the men. The cooks would have to melt the ice on the stove or let it melt in barrels in the basement. Not an easy task as we would require gallons of water each cooking day. All of this would have to be heated on the single stove in the kitchen. We would do it all.

"Shafter the janitor, the volunteer cooks, the children in the higher grades and the principal all helped to make it work. The families provided the food. We never had any complaints because everyone played a part in this whole production.

"When we started this nutrition program, the plan of the club was to collect a small fee from the families for each of their children eating at school. This would be paid to the cooks if we collected anything. The club selected a committee to collect the fees. The club would do the collection, the accounting and then the payment to the cooks. Whatever they could collect.

"Everyone understood that this was a village where there were very few jobs. Most of the population was living a subsistence style of life. But there was hope that the program would be successful. Maybe that way the Alaska Native Service would incorporate the program as part of the educational system.

"Finally, in 1947, the Alaska Native Service became interested in what we were doing and started sending old military surplus foods to feed the children. The dry foods were okay and that included milk, eggs, flour and cheese.

We had a hard time with the canned goods. When we opened the cans we had to inspect the can and the contents. Many times I threw out what was in the cans because the lining was black and that meant it was spoiled. Also if there were bubbles or bad smell. We did not have trouble with the beans and noodles.

"I had to make up the menu from what we had available. So I made breads, biscuits and doughnuts from the flour. I made bean soup, split pea soup and vegetable soup from the dry stuff. We had a lot of cheese so I made lots of cheese and macaroni. We still had reindeer and fish supplied by the families. We mixed up the powdered milk and that was our drink. We also made hot cocoa for a treat. Of course, we made rice and raisin puddings, chocolate and vanilla puddings. I guess we just had to have a lot of imagination to figure out what we would cook.

"The children were just wonderful. They were always happy and willing to help us set up the tables for the meals. They did a good job of clearing the tables too after eating. I did not have any trouble in the kitchen and dining room. I can truly say that cooking for the children was my joy.

"So when Chuck started school it was then I took Frances to work with me. That was because I did not have a babysitter at home. She was not content to stay in the kitchen but would rather be with her brother in the classroom. After the first year of that the teacher just put her in school. That is how she went to school so early.

"It was on March 21, 1946, that my nephew Roland Ryan Ivanoff married Alma Bradley at her father's home. Alma's Inuit name was Mukkiguk.   Gertie and I were so happy about this grand event. We baked the cakes and Alma baked, too. Flora (Dalaq) Auliye made the doughnuts. Old man Charlie Traeger got Alma a pretty rose-colored dress from his friend Polet in Nome as a gift to her. Traeger gave the wedding rings from his store as a gift. Reverend Emory Lindgren brought a portable organ for the music and he performed the marriage ceremony. The doors were open for the wedding and many people came. I was the bridesmaid and brother Frank (Ryan) was the best man. It was a wonderful event." Roland and Alma's children were: Ellen Ann, born on January 24, 1948, Inuit name

Kitliq; Maurice, born on August 2, 1949, Inuit name Tetpon; Myrtle, born on August 19, 1951, Inuit name Ahkalook; Darlene, born on November 11, 1953, Inuit name Aayu; Mary Jane, born on December 15, 1955, Inuit name Nowlinnak; Woodrow Merlin, born on November 28, 1957, Inuit name Ookitniq; Ruth, born on July 7, 1960, Inuit name Maqtaq; and April, born on April 6, 1965 and her Inuit name was Tuqaq.

Some members of Eskimo Mothers' Club
Front L-R: Ada Degnan, Martha Nanouk,
Marion Gonangnan, Virginia Nashalook, Eula Traeger
2nd Row: Elizabeth Sarren, Marie Eakon, Mary Paneok,
Emily Brown, Isabelle Towarak, Ada Kootuk & child
3rd Row: Florence Sarren, Thora Katchatag, Selma
Lockwood, Virginia Agibinik, Ethel & Ruth Toshavik
Back Row: Frieda Riley, Ifgenia Roberts, Jessie Paneok,
Lillian Ivanoff

35. Villagers Organize a Buying Cooperative

In 1947 Poppa was in Juneau on a trip representing the Native Village of Unalakleet as president of the village council. Poppa said that nobody, even the village council, had enough money for air fare to Juneau. The people decided that since this was very important they would send him down by donating a few dollars from those who could give some money. This trip he was to advocate for many services that the council felt was important. These included medical care, local high schools, job opportunities and development of local natural resources, both renewable and non-renewable, to benefit the indigenous peoples. It was important that the people enjoyed the benefits of newer methods of sanitation, health care, and that the students be educated at home. All in all, the entire community was able to buy his airline ticket. The village council kept track of who all donated.

As an outcome of these efforts to assist local indigenous populations, the Alaska Native Service was able to secure the deactivated Naval Base at Japonski Island near Sitka, Alaska and planned to turn it into a vocational training school for indigenous students from the entire state. This school was to become Mount Edgecumbe High School.

It was also time to consolidate the native stores in the rural areas into one unit to take advantage of combined purchasing power that would bring an added benefit to the families in the villages. There were current existing public laws and loan programs available through the federal government. Poppa said, "It was time to act to get an organization formed. There were several villages and leaders willing to form what they called a cooperative. The cooperative concept was not foreign to the indigenous peoples but the management of cash and resource in the Western sense was the concept that was foreign."

Poppa was elected to a leadership position in Unalakleet, and with the consensus of the council he set forth to try out methods that seemed to work for other peoples and communities. Poppa said, "The council was willing to try out the new method so that their village store could be better and provide better goods at lower costs to their customers. The council decided that they would send me to a meeting of other village council leaders to form an organization that would help us all keep our stores stocked with goods that we all needed at competitive prices."

A meeting was scheduled and held during the summer of 1947 in White Mountain, Alaska. The participants were Roy Ashenfelter and Abraham Lincoln representing White Mountain, Simon Bekoalok representing Shaktoolik, Xavier Pete representing Stebbins, David Saccheus representing Elim and Frank Degnan representing Unalakleet. The group organized and founded the Alaska Native Industries Cooperative Association.

The goals and mission of the cooperative were to provide a vehicle to be in the business of supplying native stores in rural Alaska villages for the benefit of all the member stores. This cooperative was to be known by the name of ANICA (Alaska Native Industries Cooperative Association). Poppa was elected as the president of the executive board. At that time, the Alaska Native Service in Juneau administered the program and each of the member Native Stores ran their own business, but had their financing through loans that were funneled through the Alaska Native Service, to later be known as the Bureau of Indian Affairs.

Poppa said, "We were a group of men who were born and raised here. We were elected by the people in our communities to find ways to keep up with the modern ways. We all had experiences in our different lines of work but we had one common goal. That goal was to give the people in our communities a chance to find work. If there was work in our communities it would mean that the entire community would benefit. The students, when they got their education and training, would be in the position to find jobs in their own communities.

"You know, we Eskimos, we love our families. We all know one another. The way our parents taught us, we all got to know who our relatives are. We are all related one way or another all the way from the Aleutian Islands into Siberia, up to Barrow, across Canada and into Greenland.

"So when we organized that summer we knew that we had our work cut out for us. We tried to hire a local Native from Juneau, I believe that he was Tlinget. His name was Roy Peratrovich. He was well educated and would do the right job for us."

Poppa served as the president of the governing board at the beginning. The organizers wanted to bring the benefits of lower prices, greater selection of goods and more employment to the local people. Since the local economies revolved around a subsistence existence they thought that the village store business was the most logical place to start in their efforts to improve the economy that would affect all the people.

Abraham Lincoln was elected as the next president of the cooperative executive board. The board felt that it would be best for him to track the operation of the new system since the headquarters were in Juneau. Juneau was so far removed from the Norton Sound villages that had organized this new venture. Time would tell if they were to succeed.

That summer there were a lot of people traveling to work in the fish canneries in Bristol Bay. In order to get to their destination, workers from the surrounding villages had to travel through Unalakleet to get to Bristol Bay. These workers needed a place to stay and eat while they were waiting for transport. Momma said that she was called on by the school teacher to feed the workers at the school kitchen.

Momma said that she got her sister Gertie, niece Mabel Ryan, and daughter Ida May to help her. Momma was paid for her work, but she had to get her own help for which she paid herself. She said that she was glad to do it because it helped the other families in the region. To make the work easier she and Gertie baked all the bread at their own homes. She said that they were lucky that they had fresh fish, reindeer and fresh vegetables from their own gardens. With these foodstuff they were able to make delicious homestyle meals for the travelers.

This same year Momma was expecting another baby. She said that this was not going to be a spring baby like all the rest of us. I was four years old now and I knew that she was going to bring us another brother or sister. I can still see the scene in the log cabin. Since Eva was at Sitka it fell upon Ida May to run for Thora Soosuk. Momma was busy right up to the moment that Thora came in the cabin door. She made sure that she had plenty of hot water and clean rags. That was no problem as Momma had everything ready.

Thora shipped all of us to bed and told us not to bother, but to stay in bed. As usual, Poppa was not in the picture as it was clearly understood that this was a job for the women only. It was later in the evening and they assumed that we were all asleep. Being curious, I got out of bed quietly and quietly opened the door to take a peek.

I could see Momma on the bed and Thora pushing and pulling at her. I remember feeling maybe she was hurting Momma. I knew that something was very wrong. I ran to the bed just as my brother Maurice was born. I knew that Momma had died because she had just let out a scream then fell quiet. There was the baby and then a lot of blood.

I will never forget that fear. Then a miracle happened. Momma called me over to the bed. I was so happy that she was still alive. The rest of the family was then let in the room by Thora. Life was so good. Momma named the new baby the Inuit name of Kaukutaq, after Monroe Gonangnan, the son of Grant and Excelia Gonangnan. That day was October 3, 1947.

Momma told us later that Maurice was such a good and beautiful baby. She knew that he was going to be here only for a short while. She said that he was very smart and aware for his age. We had a painting of Jesus in our kitchen and she said that Maurice was always pointing and saying, "up a Highs," or "hi Jesus," like welcoming a friend, and that he could see him.

Eva was down at Sitka, and she was very faithful in writing home. Poppa made sure that he went to Sitka, at least once a year, to see how his eldest daughter was progressing with her high school education. While he was in Sitka he took the opportunity to visit with the local indigenous leaders there to find out how they were faring on their aboriginal rights issues. Eva got used to his trips to Sitka, and continued to work her way through school.

Eva learned many years later that Mrs. Bessie Lambkin Smith, the schoolteacher, had provided the tuition for her and Cecilia Soxie (Borbridge) at Sheldon Jackson School in Sitka. Cecilia was the daughter of Victoria Mulluk and Arthur Soxie of Unalakleet. Cecilia was born on October 15, 1926, and her Inuit name was Chugiayaq. Cecilia married Ted Borbridge on February 1, 1952, in Sitka and they made their home there. Ted was originally from Juneau. They had five children, who were James Theodore, Harold Gene, Alan John, Donald Arthur and Kay Denise (Simmons). Mrs. Smith also provided the tuition for several other students throughout her lifetime. Momma said that Bessie Smith died in a hotel fire while she was in Bethel, Alaska. She never got to see any of the students graduate that she helped.

Poppa continued to put his name on the Territorial election ballots for the House of Representatives. He had a strong belief that it was time that the native indigenous peoples should fill the Legislature and help shape the destiny of our land. Since we were living a subsistence lifestyle like all the others in the land, it was difficult to reach all the communities to campaign for office in person.

With a shoestring budget Poppa was able to get a few picture postcards printed and mailed out to his hoped-for constituency. There were no local radio stations so he had less media to work with. He said that the time would come where we would have instant communications and people would have the chance to know just what was going on anywhere in the world at their fingertips.

In the spring of 1948 Momma told me that her nephews Richard Ivanoff and Wilfred Ryan were out of the Army. Then, on April 2, 1948, Commissioner Stephan Ivanoff performed the marriage ceremony for Richard and his new bride Marjorie Excelia Agibinik. Stephan was also the grandfather of Richard. Margie was the daughter of Virginia Toshavik and Walter Agibinik. Momma liked to tell the story of Stephan when he was instructing the couple to go through their marriage vows at the actual ceremony. Stephan said: Do you take this man for Richard or poorer...? That was one of the memorable sayings of the ceremony that tickled everyone that was present. Richard's Inuit name was Evalu. Majorie's Inuit name was Nugattaq and she was born at Quigaheq (Beeson Creek) on August 11, 1930. Marjorie's mother Virginia Toshavik was the daughter of Ethel Sarren and Maurice Johnson and was the half-sister of Margaret Johnson. Virginia was Malemiut and Swedish. Her husband Walter Agibinik was a Kawerakmiut. Richard and Marjorie's children were: Agnes Amelia was born on June 16, 1948. Janice Jane was born on January 2, 1950. Gerald Walter was born on July 27, 1951. Katherine Eleanor was born on September 28, 1952. Floyd Davis was born on February 19, 1955. Richard J. was born on June 4, 1957. Walter Lonny was born on May 27, 1960. Ronald Davis was born on August 20, 1962. Burton Lee was born on February 2, 1964 and Gertrude Jay was born on January 25, 1965. Richard and Marjorie raised their family at Unalakleet.

Momma and Poppa had always been proud of the accomplishments of their nephews. They said that Richard was a natural born mechanic and engineer. He could figure what made any engine function and was ingenious in fixing and getting to run any piece of equipment and machinery.

Momma said, "That year, in 1948, my sister Gertie started to take in patients from the surrounding villages and providing food and lodging for them when they went to go to the government hospital in Kotzebue. That expanded to housing traveling students and prisoners on their way to jail in Nome. Gertie did this all the way until 1972 when it became too much for her. She and John used their own resources to provide food and bed. Gertie also provided diapers and used clothing for those needing them. She treated all the people like her own family and they will not forget her kindness. I don't know how she managed to do all of that. She sure had a big heart. She did not get paid for all the travellers but the Public Health Service would send her a small pay when she sent her billing. If she did not send a billing she did not get paid."

Momma said, "It was at this time that your sister Eva had been begging to come home. Your dad and I talked about sending for her as she insisted so much. We didn't have much money, but that was not unusual. I told your dad that we could do it. So your dad went and got a ticket for her to come home. Eva left Sitka on January 21, 1949, and arrived home on the 24th. With Eva being home it made it much easier on me because I could go to cook at the school without worrying about my babies."

Poppa was on his way to Juneau to advocate for village improvements. On February 7 Momma sent a distress telegram to Poppa in Seward trying to reach him as he was on his way to Juneau. Momma told us many years later that if it had not been for Eva coming home when she did Momma would not have survived the events that were just around the corner. Baby Maurice was not feeling well. Momma had the nurse check the baby and they were watching his progress.

On February 7, an Army plane was sent in to pick up Momma and Maurice to go to Nome. Momma said that the weather was terrible. The wind was blowing so strong and the snow was drifting. She said, "I had no choice but to leave it to God to take care of us all. Thank Heaven that Eva was home to take care of you kids. I don't know how, to this day, the Army pilot made it through the storm. But we landed at Nome.

"I took my sick baby right up to the Maynard Columbus Hospital and waited. I waited and prayed. I was glad that Lottie and Johnny Bahnke welcomed me again in their home. Lottie was my dear friend. I spent all the time at the hospital. My baby was not getting better. The doctors told me he had spinal meningitis. I didn't know that sickness but it sounded bad. All I could do is pray. I didn't know what to do to help my baby. It was late in the afternoon when Maurice died.

"There was nothing more I could do. I wanted to cry real loud. I went out of the hospital and as I was crying a whole pack of loose dogs made a circle around me. I thought that it was very strange for them to do that. They didn't hurt me. They just looked at me. After walking for a while I made my way back to Lottie and Johnny's house. Lottie was a big comfort to me.

"That night I know that folks from home, who were now living in Nome, were going to have a prayer meeting at Esther and Tom Brown's house. I wanted to see people from home, especially Abigail Eben. So I went over there. They all welcomed me and I told them what happened and they prayed for me. They made me feel a lot better.

"They said that they were expecting someone from Unalakleet to come in. Then there was a knock at the door. The door flung open and this big man come in stamping the snow off his boots. As he was taking his coat off he said, 'I've just come from Hell; I've just come from Unalakleet. You know that they have that devil Frank Degnan running that town.' I stood right up. I said, 'Denny Ost, I'm sure glad that I was here. Otherwise these poor folks here would have believed you. I am Mrs. Frank Degnan. I came here because I just lost my baby and I wanted to be with my folks from home. You can't say anything about Frank because you don't live with him; I do. Frank is a good man and he only does what he thinks is right because the people want him to do it. That's why they elect him.' That's all I said and I sat down. The meeting was good and I am glad that I was there that day.

"I went back to Lottie's home and spent the night. They were so good to me. The next day I went home with my baby in a coffin. It was my thirty-ninth birthday and that's one day I will never forget. Your dad came home from Juneau so it was a sad time for all of us. When you are a parent it is so hard to lose a child. But you know, life has to go on. So Eva was a big help again. As a result of her coming she lost out on some of her schooling but your dad and I decided that she had to finish her high school education.

"That fall we sent Eva back to Sheldon Jackson School in Sitka, Alaska. Ida May had just finished the eighth grade and she applied to Sheldon Jackson and was accepted. In the meantime we found out that she could go to Mount Edgecumbe. We decided that both of them would leave for high school. Eva would go to Sheldon Jackson and Ida would try Mount Edgecumbe.

"But before Eva headed back to Sitka she went down with a group of people from here to work in the fish canneries at Koggiung, Alaska. In fact she went with her dad. There were Wilfred Ryan, Richard Ivanoff, John Ivanoff and Eva Ivanoff that went from home too. Your brother Jerry went down that way too but he wound up working at the cannery at Ekuk, Alaska.

"So when it was time for Ida May to leave for high school we all knew that it would be a long time before she would come home. In those days we did not have ready cash for air fares. Ida said that she wanted to go with her other classmates.

"When the day came to travel the children that left the village were Ida May Degnan, Henrietta Nanouk, Roger Riley and Jerry Degnan. Since Jerry had made enough money at the cannery he decided that he would try the vocational classes that were offered at Mount Edgecumbe. Those kids wound up traveling to Nome, to Fairbanks, to Anchorage, to Juneau and then to Mount Edgecumbe.

"They left here at the end of August on Alaska Airlines to Nome. There the kids stayed with John and Lottie Bahnke in Nome. They traveled to Fairbanks and stayed at the Salvation Army quarters. Ida always said that it was the first time they saw flush toilets and running water. She told me that the lady there had to get after her for flushing the toilet over and over. She told me that it was fun to see the water moving so fast. Those kids traveled to Juneau and then by Grumman Goose airplane to Sitka. That is how they got to Mount Edgecumbe from Unalakleet.

"We all knew it would be a very long time that they would be there since none of us families had money to bring them home. If they wanted to come home they would just have to earn their way home. Our one consolation was that all of our older children would all be close together. Your dad and I knew that it was probably true for most of the families that sent their children away from home just to get a high school education."

It was at this time that Wilfred Ryan married Eva Ivanoff. Eva was the daughter of May Tetpon and Paul Ivanoff. May was the daughter of Fina Kenick of Shaktoolik, a Kawerakmiut and Tetpon, a Unalit. May's Inuit name was Ahwiktak. She was born at Shaktoolik on October 30, 1901, and she died on October 7, 1996, in Nome. Paul was the son of Chalavaluk and Malgway (Stephan and Amelia Ivanoff). Stephan was Yup'ik and Russian and Amelia was Malemiut. Paul's Inuit name was Yungak. Paul was born in Unalakleet on September 22, 1894, and he died in June of 1957. Wilfred and Eva were married on August 15, 1949, by her grandfather Commissioner Ivanoff at Unalakleet. Momma had another story to tell of the wedding. She said: "It was a very nice wedding. We were all there, the relatives, and Chalavaluk was very proud to do the honors. We were all wondering what he was going to say to these two couples. Anyway, it was going good. Then when he said, 'Say after me, say, I do. Will you Wilfred Paul take Eva Paul....' We all had to laugh because it reminded us of Richard and Marjorie's wedding the year before. It was so good to see young people get married."

Wilfred and Eva moved to Kaltag as Eva had been hired as a teacher there by the Bureau of Indian Affairs. After a year and a half, they returned to teach in Unalakleet. Their children were: Susan, born on July 6, 1950, at Nome. Her Inuit name was Paniuughuluuraq. Linda, born on September 16, 1951, at Nome. Her Inuit name was Kakauraq. Wilfred, born on April 10, 1953, at Nome. His Inuit name was Apok. Glenda, born on August 28, 1954, in Unalakleet. Her Inuit name was Malgway. Adrian (Chat), born on April 3, 1955, at Anchorage. His Inuit name was Chalavaluk. Pauline, born on July 7, 1957, at Anchorage. Her Inuit name is Yungak. Dennis, born on December 17, 1959, on an airplane en route to Anchorage. Loretta, born on August 2, 1961, at Anchorage and Stephanie, born on November 22, 1963, at Anchorage.

Eva continued to teach at the school in Unalakleet until she retired in 1980. Wilfred was hired to work for Alaska Airlines in Unalakleet doing various jobs. He decided to learn how to fly an airplane and succeeded in his efforts. In 1955 he founded the Unalakleet Air Taxi and operated a successful local air charter service. Unalakleet Air Taxi was granted the mail service contract from Unalakleet to the Yukon River in 1960. Wilfred died on March 7, 1977, while he was a patient at the Anchorage Alaska Native Medical Center. His family continued the air taxi business and expanded it into a state-wide transportation company known as Ryan Air. Today the company operates as ATS (Arctic Transportation Services) in the air cargo hauling business.

Momma said that Grandma Apok had lost most of her eyesight. Poppa located an eye doctor in Anchorage who thought that he could help her recover her sight.

Momma said, "Your dad loved his mother so very much. When he told Apok that maybe she could see again, Apok told him that she was willing to try. So, again we scraped up enough money to see what could be done. Your dad took his mother to Dr. Milo Fritz in Anchorage. We will always be thankful for Dr. Fritz. He was the one that gave back her eyesight to her. Your dad said that it was cataracts that made her blind. When she came back home to us she was wearing real thick glasses and she looked so good. The first thing she did was laugh when she saw you kids. She knew what you sounded like but this was the first time she saw you. That was another big miracle in our life.

"It was also in the fall of 1949 that the Mothers Club was approached by a lady who was traveling Alaska to get the organization of Girl Scouts started. She was Mrs. Marjory Kafer and she was the field advisor for the National Girl Scouts organization. How she found us was through the recommendation of Mrs. Elizabeth Peratrovich of the Alaska Native Sisterhood in Juneau, Alaska. The local chapter of the Alaska Native Sisterhood, Unalakleet ANS Camp 23 had been the one that Mrs. Peratrovich had intended to sponsor the Girl Scouts.

"The Club discussed the issue and thought that it was a worthy thing to get involved in so Lillian Nashalook

Ivanoff and I (Ada Degnan) volunteered to be troop leaders and the other members would serve as assistant leaders and troop committee members. Along with the Girl Scout program the Brownie Scout program was established. Mrs. Selma Lockwood volunteered to take the younger girls. She did such a wonderful job with the young ones. They loved her gentle spirit. She taught them the old traditional ways. They even learned how to do grass mats and baskets. Frances was in her troop along with the girls of her age. Selma held all of the meetings at her home and that was so good for the children."

Mrs. Ada Degnan and her assistant Mrs. Ebba Katchatag were assigned to lead Troop 3. The troop committee was chaired by Mrs. Martha Lucy Nanouk and the members were: Mrs. Marion Gonangnan, Miss Louise Klassen and Mrs. Sara Eben.

In the following years the volunteer assistants were: Martha Lucy Nanouk and Elizabeth Sarren. Troop committee members that served were also Mrs. Mary Stepp Croell, L. C. Ferguson, and Lillian V. Russell.

The first girls that were in Troop 3 were: Janet Agibinik, Helga Anagick, Jessie Anagick, Margaret Anawrok, Ada June Degnan, Amy Eben, Theresa Etageak, Hilda James, Myrtle James, Amy Katchatag, May Kotongan, Elsie McCaffarty, Swanhill Milligrok, Ruth Carol Nanouk, Kay Nashalook, Beatrice Otton, Susie Otton, Elfie Paneok, Irene Paneok, Maurine Riley, Bertha Sarren, and Nancy Wilde.

As the years passed the other Girl Scouts were: Rose Anagick, Alice Auliye, Helen Ayagiak, Frances Degnan, Lorraine Eben, Mabel Eben, Mary Eakon, Lena Gonangnan, Hilda Katchatag, Irma Lindstrom, Rachel Nanouk, Lois Ann Otton, Ruth Otton, Julia Oyoumick, Ebba Paniptchuk, Gladys Riley, Anna Riley, Blanche Sarren, Adeline Soxie, Sarah Soxie, Mildred Soxie, Grace Tom, and Ruth Toshavik.

The troops had sponsoring committees from the community to give help and advice. The Girl Scouts were involved in projects of their own choosing and were culturally relevant. They planned fund-raisers and with the proceeds contributed to the National Girl Scouts organization and to the local church fund. They also provided candy to be given out to the village children after the Christmas programs at the school and the church.

They used the proceeds to get supplies for their picnics and meeting refreshments. A committee was chosen at each meeting to provide and prepare the next meeting refreshments. They were interested in earning proficiency and merit badges so they engaged in culturally relevant projects, some to bring elders wood, water or help clean the house or yard. The girls wove grass mats and baskets, planted flower and vegetable gardens.

Troop 3 was active until 1955. Momma was not able to continue as troop leader. It seemed that no one was interested to step forward to take her place. She said many years later that being the Girl Scout leader at home was very rewarding and that all of "my Scouts" have done very well in life and "I am very proud of each one of them."

Founders of ANICA, 1947, in White Mountain
L-R: Xavier Pete, Frank Degnan, David Saccheus, Abraham
Lincoln, Simon Bekoalok, Roy Ashenfelter

36. 1950

Momma said that in 1950 the house seemed a lot quieter with the older children gone from home. Poppa was still involved with the projects in the village and the aim was to make sure the benefits would help our people. There still seemed to be confusion among the people about the status of the village government. There was one group that wanted the village to be incorporated as a city of the Territory and abolish the reservation. The other group wanted to retain the Native Village status and carry on their traditional form of government that had always worked.

Momma said, "There was a lot of confusion about reservations and about what they called 'City Two.' My sister Jessie went to all the meetings in the village that were held by those who wanted to abolish the reservation. Poppa and I did not go unless they were village meetings called by our council. After one of the 'Abolish the Reservation' meetings, Jessie came in to tell me about how they were acting. She said that one of the mission workers was explaining that 'to live on a reservation was to be tied up like a dog.' She said he even got on his hands and knees and crawled around the floor until he got to where she was standing. He looked up at her and pointed his finger at her and said, 'But I see I cannot fool this woman.' He then got up and walked out. Jessie said that it was the end of the meeting. To my knowledge that was the end of 'the Abolish the Reservation' open meetings. I am sure that they kept meeting among themselves because the controversy never quit.

"We still had the nutrition program at the school and I was still the cook. We were hearing rumors that I was a slop cook and stealing food from the kids. I told your dad that maybe I should just quit as the principal, R. W. Hamilton did not seem to want me there. Your dad said to me that the health of the children was more important and not to quit. So I listened to him. The reason they may have thought I was stealing was that I would have my helpers open up the Army surplus foods to check for spoilage. The spoiled foods would have to be thrown out.

"Along came the month of April. One morning Chuck and Frances came home from school. I was still at home. Frances was crying and Chuck told me that there were posters on the school building that said something bad about me. Your dad went out and it was a long time before he came back. When he did he told me that he took the posters down and brought them to the principal and asked who put them up there. The principal said that he did not know anything about them. What was on the posters said that: 'Ada Degnan is a slop cook and steals food from the children...'

"I went over to see Hamilton, the principal of the school, and I told him that he was responsible for all of this. I also told him that I would not cook until we found out who wrote those posters. So that is why I took a break as cook in the school lunch program that year."

37. *Poppa Elected to Alaska Territorial Legislature*

The year of 1951 was going to be a new experience for all the family. Poppa was elected to the Twentieth Session of the Alaska Territorial Legislature in the House of Representatives. He was elected in the general election in the Second Division to serve as representative. He ran on the Democratic ticket. Of course he had no budget for campaign but since he had run for the Legislature for so many years he finally made it.

The village had its annual election too and he was elected on January 3, 1951, for another year term as president of the Native Village Council of Unalakleet. The other council members were vice-president Aaron Paneok, treasurer Nick Riley, secretary Myles Gonangnan, and Nils Savetilik. He had the backing of the council and they wished him well as he went to serve in Juneau. It was on January 5 that the school principal closed the Native Store against the wishes of the council.

Poppa left home on January 16, 1951. The Regular Session of the Twentieth Territorial Legislature convened on Monday, January 22, 1951, and adjourned on Thursday, March 22, 1951. Throughout the sessions he served, he had many letters from the local people encouraging him in this endeavor.

Poppa told that when they were sworn in there were other Natives in that group and they were: James K. Wells, Inupiat from Noorvik, Percy Ipalook, Inupiat from Kotzebue, Andrew Hope, Tlinget from Sitka, and Frank

G. Johnson, Tlinget from Kake. Poppa said that when they organized the House he was happy to support a Native-born Alaskan from Valdez as Speaker of the House and that was William A. Egan. Poppa said that Bill Egan was just the kind of man they needed. He had an open mind and listened to all sides. He was fair at all times and a good Democrat. Years later this Speaker of the House was to become Governor of the State of Alaska.

Poppa was able to get several resolutions introduced and passed. Those were for airports for St. Michael, and Shaktoolik, and a road from Unalakleet to Kaltag. In letters to Momma he wrote about the daily and weekly events that were on his mind. Momma kept him abreast of what was happening at home. She wrote and told Poppa that their dear friend Grandma Lena Williams (Kakauraq) had passed away on January 25, 1951. She had been reported to be born about May 9, 1870. She was like Apok and Igailaq. They were about the same age but there was no written records of any of their births, only estimates. Records of births of the Inuit did not happen until much later. They all would miss Kakauraq dearly.

Momma wrote that on February 9, there were several students leaving the village to go to school at Mount Edgecumbe. Some of them were Ada June Degnan, Mathilda Traeger and Beatrice Otton.

On the 12th Momma wrote: "I hope Tiny (Ada June) has arrived by now, I have not heard. You do not know how worried I was the day they left, it was so stormy and Tiny had a cold and it was on the 9th. I felt better when your letter came on the 10th and you had gotten my telegram. The morning on my birthday I woke up and thought, Tiny gone and was kind of blue, just about this time, Chuck from Tiny's bed started to sing Happy Birthday and Fanny by my side joined in singing with him. That gave me courage and drove my sad feeling away. The same evening on my birthday Vernon & Alfred (Ivanoff) invited me and kids for supper. Alfred cooked up a nice supper. Reindeer steaks, mashed potatoes, corn, spinach, gravy. Dessert were ice-cream & cake & jelly rolls. He also had Richard Ivanoff & family & Roland & family. Gertie has not come home from Nome. That was a nice surprise for me. So I tho't I might as well make cake too and in the evening I had a few folks over for coffee. Sam & Jessie(Otton), Martha & Peter (Nanouk,) Nick & Freida (Riley), Frank & Eunice (Ryan). Mother gave me $10.00 & I got 4 more from folks and some other things. And above all I got a nice birthday card from our kids at Edgecumbe." Later in the same letter she continues: "Today the lunch program opens. .... Both mothers are fine."

Momma wrote that Father Jules Convert had held a village meeting on February 16, 1951 promoting a housing program available to the residents through the Alaska Housing Authority. She sent an application for Poppa to handle to apply for loan to build Apok a small house because Apok wanted it. That is how Apok got her new house with a loan of five hundred dollars which paid for lumber. With that lumber Poppa and Momma built a sixteen by twenty-foot frame house for Apok the following summer. Momma said that since there was no insulation she took all of us kids out to the tundra to harvest the tall grass. We made many trips to get enough grass to insulate the whole house. When the house was completed it made a cozy little house that Apok was to enjoy for a little over a year before Poppa had to take her to the Alaska Native Service hospital in Mount Edgecumbe, when she got sick. What kind of sickness that was, Momma did not know. That's why they scraped up enough funds for Poppa to take his dear mother to a hospital so she could get help.

Momma said that Uncle Frank Ryan and Igailaq took advantage of that loan program too. Uncle Frank built the same type of house and when it was finished Igailaq moved in. There she would live until she died. Those houses were tiny but they were special places because that is where our grandmas lived. Those houses were filled with love and many happy memories.

On March 3, 1951, both Momma in Unalakleet and Poppa in Juneau were listening to the same radio station, and heard the news that the James E. Curry contract was okayed by the United States government. This contract with Curry was with the village council to pursue their aboriginal rights claims before the Indian Claims Commission. The attorneys that the council at Unalakleet wanted to work for them were James E. Curry and William Paul Jr.. The council was blocked for many years by the Alaska Native Service in Juneau from retaining those two attorneys which were of their own choosing. This was a momentous time for the council at Unalakleet.

It was finally recognized by the United States government that the Native Village of Unalakleet was legally entitled to retain counsel of their own choosing to represent the local village in matters they deemed necessary. It was very important for this issue to be resolved, and took many years to resolve. It caused much distress and misunderstanding for all parties involved. What it caused was the situation wherein the village could not pay attorneys of their choice out of the federal funds that they borrowed under the federal government loan programs that they qualified for. Now this was resolved and another hurdle out of the way for the council.

The outcome was that the village attorneys filed the Village Council aboriginal claims before the Indian Court of Claims in a timely fashion. This was Docket 285 filed on August 10, 1951, before the Indian Court of Claims by the village attorney James E. Curry in behalf of the Unalakleet and Unaligmiut-Malemiut Eskimos.

Later when the council inquired about the status of this claim they were advised by Robert L. Bennett, Area Director of the Bureau of Indian Affairs in Juneau on August 24, 1962, that their claims under Docket 285 was still before the Indian Court of Claims. In that claim "they had requested payment for damages allegedly sustained due to illegal taking of lands, waters, and property in and about the Village of Unalakleet; breach of fiduciary obligations; and for any amount found due from a general accounting of their funds, property and other assets."

On July 12, 1963, a letter was received from Roy Peratrovich, Area Tribal Operations Officer of the Juneau Bureau of Indian Affairs, saying "Your contract, Contract No. 42619, between the Native Village of Unalakleet, Alaska and Attorney James E. Curry and William L. Paul, Jr., expired March 1, 1961. You still have Docket No. 285 pending..."

Another problem of the village council in 1951 revolved around the operation of the Native Store. The schoolteacher had shut down the store. It would be some time before it was reopened. The council had requested that the loan agreement between the council and the government be enforced in that the council has the right to choose the manager.

Eva was going to get married. Momma wanted Poppa to be sure to make it to Sitka when Eva got married. She was to marry Eldon Ridley on March 3, 1951, but that date was postponed because Eldon's sister Clarissa died in Seattle, Washington. Eva and Eldon were married on March 24, 1951. Eva and Eldon had five children during their marriage. The eldest son was Randolph Eldon Ridley (Inuit name Kiugya meaning "Northern Lights") born on November 18, 1951. Martha Corrine Ridley (Inuit name Apok after Grandma Apok) born on June 2, 1953, and died September 1973 in Anchorage, Alaska. Clarissa Ann Ridley (Inuit name Chinglak) born on June 27, 1954. Maryanne June Ridley (Inuit name Niyaalgak) born on February 20, 1957. Colleen Dorothy Ridley (Inuit name Qikiqtaq) born on March 12, 1961. The children were all born in Sitka. In the 1960's she divorced Eldon and married Ted Mossburg. They had one child, Eva Dian, who was born December 26, 1964, in Juneau. Her Inuit name was Igailaq. The family lived in Pelican until Eva divorced Ted and married George Merrifield. The family moved to Kenai, then Seward, and finally in 1970 they settled in Anchorage.

In her May 18, 1951, letter June wrote home that she, Ida May, Clara Eakon and Henry Otton left on the *M.S. North Star* on May 16th at 7 p.m.. "with about 40 other kids from the school. We are supposed to arrive at home on the 30th of June. .... We are now anchored at Tatitlik. This is our first stop since we left Edgecumbe. Tomorrow we will be at Valdez. .... Jerry sure wanted to go home, he said he always had hard luck, but I told him it won't always be this way, so that cheered him up a little. I left my radio with him, that will be a little better he said. Eva and Eldon went to see us off."

Ida May remembers that trip very well too. She said that the trip was long but it was fun. They were to become well acquainted with all the people on the ship since it took so long to get from Mount Edgecumbe to Unalakleet. The crew included: Captain Selenjius, First Mate Cecil W. Cole, Miss Gaddy, the ship's nurse, Joe Upicksoun, Mr. Cropley, Roger "Sparks" Darby, and others. It did take them a long time to finally arrive at home. The families were happy to be reunited.

Summer flew by fast. The family was busy with the garden and getting ready for the salmon season. This year they would not go to the tundra flats away from the village for that annual egg hunting expedition. They had to be satisfied with looking for eggs on the flats near the village. They were busy helping Igailaq at her fish camp at Mek-kik-lek. Each day Momma would send someone out to the camp to see what her mother needed. On nice days all the family would hike up for the day to have lunch and supper at the camp.

Momma had her own net set at the mouth of the river so that had to be tended. She, Ida and June would cut the fish at the slough to the east of the house. Everyone pitched in to haul the filleted salmon to Momma's fish rack near the cabin. Chuck was the one who used the homemade wheelbarrow that Poppa made to haul the fish. On some fish-cutting days he made many trips.

Momma had a story that she liked to tell about her net-setting on the ocean. She said that she had the little wooden flat-bottomed boat that Poppa built for her to use. She said that she would put on her hip boots and take Frances with her to check the net. She would leave Frances on the beach and then she would wade out pulling the boat in the shallow water. Then she would get into the boat and check the net and put her catch in the boat. Then she would get out of the boat and wade the boat to the beach to cut the fish.

Momma said, "This one day we went to check the net. I left Frances on the beach and I towed the boat out to the net. Then I was going to get into the boat I fell in the water. I felt so silly. Then Frances started crying and hollering, 'Momma is going to ground.' I went right away to her to tell her I was okay. She still wouldn't quit crying because she thought I would drown so we just went home after I put up the boat. I will never forget that day. Later I went back down and that net really had a lot of fresh silvers in it."

Sometimes when a group of people went seining for humpies they would prefer to cut the fish on the gravel beaches and make the load going home in the boat lighter. Those were marvelous outings. The women would take time out to cook the freshly caught fish over the campfire for everyone to enjoy. The children that were taken along were expected to help in all the phases of the fish processing. Those that stayed home had specified chores to do so that the fishermen did not have those chores waiting for them when they came home with their bounty.

After the day's work was done, the children and young adults had their free time for their ball games. Curfew was enforced by the individual families during the summer. For Momma's family all the children knew that if they were not home at her specified hour her loud voice would be heard by everyone in the village when she was calling for her children by name. As a result her children were home at an early hour so that she would not yell for them.

We never knew where Momma got her energy to do all the things in the day that she did. She always replied, "That was what mothers do; when you have children of your own you'll know what I mean." She was such a good cook and would create miracles even if the cupboard looked bare to her husband and children. They all agreed that she made the best doughnuts, coffee-cakes, bread puddings, fried bread, which she called dough fritters, that they could ever eat. Sometimes she made these with the wild eggs that they brought home from their spring camping trips to Canal or Denbigh.

Poppa's comment was that she could make the fastest pot of coffee or tea of anyone he had seen. He would add, "She makes the best cup of coffee in the world." Momma had a thing about coffee. She said, "It should not be strong and it should not be weak. You have to use fresh water from the river or creek in the summer. You could also use fresh rainwater or snow water. It had to be one of these waters that you bring to a rapid rolling boil and then add this to the Hills Brothers coffee in your pot and put back on the flame and bring this back to just the boiling point. Remove immediately from the heat and let the grounds settle. Now that's a good cup of coffee!"

That summer Momma ran out of coffee in her cupboard. That was not good. She sent Frances to the store to get some coffee. Frances checked at the Native Store. They were out of coffee. She went to Traeger's store and asked the clerk for some coffee. The clerk said that they had coffee and how much would you want. Frances replied that her mother wanted only Hills Brothers coffee. The clerk said that he was very sorry but all they had was Gold Shield coffee. Frances knew very well that Momma had no coffee, the neighbors did not have coffee. The other store had no coffee. Traeger's had Gold Shield. What would she do? She had a plan. Momma would have her coffee and it would come in a Hills Brothers can. She brought the coffee home and Momma said that was the best cup of coffee she had in a long time. When she was told what it really was she said that it was okay and that she would order her supply from Nome until the stores got their new stock. After that time she made sure that she never ran out of Hills Brothers coffee at home.

1951 ALASKA TERRITORIAL LEGISLATURE
Frank Degnan, center right

38. 1952--The United States Army Camps at Airport

That year Poppa was re-elected as president of the local Village Council. This position was also for a one-year period. The other seats were for two years. The council included Allen Soosuk, vice-president; Roland Ivanoff, treasurer; Myles Gonangnan, secretary; and Nils Savetilik, councilman. Poppa said that it was a good thing that the president's term was limited to one year. That way the members of the village could choose who they wanted.

That spring the family was expecting Eva and her new baby Randy to come home from Sitka for a visit. The whole family was so excited and it seemed to be such a long time before they arrived on the M. S. North Star. The summer flew by so fast. Apok was glad that she had another boy in the family. Randy had been born on November 18, 1951, at Mount Edgecumbe.

Jerry was in Mount Edgecumbe and told his sisters that he would be going into military service. He had signed up to join the United States Army. He reported for active duty, on November 18, 1952, at Fort Richardson. As it turned out, he was stationed right here in Alaska. That was such a relief to all of us. Poppa said that he was proud of Jerry serving our country and he would learn a lot and that would be equal to a high school education. Jerry did not graduate from Mount Edgecumbe, but he was honorably discharged as a corporal from the Army on November 17,1954. He served in Company A, 53rd Infantry Regiment, 71st Division stationed at Fort Richardson, Alaska.

During his military service he was awarded the Good Conduct medal and National Defense Service medal.

During that summer the U.S. Army 549 Topographic Engineers arrived in Unalakleet. They set up their camp of tents at the north and west edge of the East-West runway with the approval of the village council. Their mission was to do aerial mapping of the area. The village was to find out later that the United States government was planning to set up a distant early warning site near Unalakleet. This was to be known as the D.E.W. line. Poppa said that Colonel Free was in charge of the Army Engineers. Free told Poppa that while they were there they would also survey the Unalakleet to Kaltag road. All that was needed was funding to construct that road.

There were two men that we would especially remember. The first one was Ellsworth Haugen became the husband of Mary Ann Nanouk. Ellsworth was born on December 12, 1927 in Manno, South Dakota. This was his first time in Unalakleet. He met Mary Ann and courted her during his tour here. He said that his job was a driver for the commanding officers at the camp. Mary Ann's Inuit name is Quinigiaq. She was named both the English and Inuit names after her father Peter John Nanouk's mother. Mary Ann's mother was Momma's lifelong friend, Martha Lucy Isaacs Nanouk. Martha and Momma would call Mary Ann an Inuit pet name, "Gu-nooge." After their marriage at a Covenant Church in San Francisco on November 5, 1952, and a short stay at Vermillion, South Dakota, Mary Ann and Ellsworth returned to raise their family here on August 28, 1956.

The other man whom we remember was Lieutenant Bernard Tilton, the camp medic. Momma credited Lieutenant Tilton for saving Poppa's life. Poppa got very sick at the end of June. He went to see the nurse Iris Jette at the local clinic and she said that she wanted him to be seen by the Army doctor. So he went to see Tilton. It was decided that Poppa would go to the Alaska Native Service hospital in Kotzebue. So he left on the next plane on Friday, July 2, 1952. He told us, when he got home several weeks later, on Monday July 28, that Dr. Rabeau took good care of him. The problem he had was a ruptured appendix, but they didn't operate on him until after the Fourth of July holiday. He said: "They opened me up and found that it had been ruptured. Later I told Dr. Rabeau that the Army doctor Tilton had given me a shot of something before I left. Rabeau told me whatever it was, it saved my life." When Poppa got home from the hospital he was well, but very thin. He had lost a lot of weight.

Forty years later, Lieutenant Tilton, who was now Dr. Bernard Tilton, brought his wife Betty on a tour of Alaska. One of their stops was at Unalakleet where they were able to visit Ellsworth and Mary Ann and Momma. Momma was so thrilled. She was able to personally thank Dr. Tilton once again and tell his wife Betty of the incident.

Also that year, the Catholic Church wanted to build a chapel in the village. Tom Powers had willed his property to the church and the diocese approached the village council with their request to build on this property. The council pondered the request and made a proposal. Since the Powers property was in a prime spot for a school they would trade for a like size property at the edge of the village. This was mutually agreeable to all parties and the church was granted a place to build. That is how the town now had two churches. The priest was stationed at St. Michael and made monthly visits to Unalakleet to conduct services for the local Catholics. According to local reports, the Catholic priests had come to Unalakleet since the 1890's to conduct services on special requests by their members.

39. *Apok Leaves Home*

Momma said that they were just worried about Apok. She had not been feeling well. She and Poppa had a conference with Apok and they decided that since there was a hospital at Mount Edgecumbe she should be seen there. She was willing to go as long as her son would take her. They felt that since the older children were there she would not be alone. So Apok would be on her way again to a place she didn't really want to be.

Momma said that she would make a new set of clothes for Apok to wear when she left. "I knew she was very particular about what she wore. She had to wear her parky and mukluks and they were in good shape. So I made her a couple of calico dresses. I made her an underdress of flannel and a couple pairs of bloomers. I went to the store and got her several pairs of long cotton stockings that she liked. I asked her what else she needed." She said: 'You been real good to me. I don't have to worry about my son any more. You brought me to where I belong and I don't need anything any more. Just make sure that you take care of yourself.' I really appreciated what she said to me."

So Poppa took his mother to Sitka and she was admitted to the Mount Edgecumbe Alaska Native Service Hospital in early March. Poppa stayed with Eva and Eldon until he was told by the doctors that he could come home. However, he would not be bringing his mother home with him this time.

After Poppa got home it was not too long that Eva sent a telegram that Apok had died on March 15, 1953. This was such a sad time for all of the family. Since there was no money to bring her home to be buried, Poppa said that there would be a time in the future that we would be bringing her remains home for final burial. That time would not be now. Later Momma told me that Isabelle Tomrun Towarak had passed away at the same hospital and her remains were there along with Apok's remains.

Back at home that year, the main issues facing our village revolved around the management of the Native Store, the status of the reservation versus incorporating as a territorial municipality, the operation of the school, and the lunch program. Many of the people were not satisfied with the operation of the school and were considering the merits of local control of their town, school, and the freedom to do what they wanted with their own land holdings. The council consisted of Frank Degnan, president; Allen Soosuk, vice-president; Nathan Anawrok, secretary; Roland Ivanoff, treasurer; and Nick Riley, councilman.

The village council requested Area Director Hugh J. Wade that he send the officials from the Juneau Area Office of the Alaska Native Service to come and answer questions of the membership relating to important village issues. The village had members who were supporting the establishment of a second-class city, members who were supporting reservation status, and members who wanted establishment of a federal townsite in which title to their own land could be either restricted or unrestricted ownership under a specific federal law.

A special meeting of the village was held on April 10, 1953. Many of the members turned out to hear the federal officials' position on the issues to which they wanted answers. The council had Isaac Eben translate to the membership in the local dialect all that was said and discussed. The members had specific question to the officials. This meeting was actually a hearing. The council wanted to get as much information as they could before the membership could act on the issue of the desired status of their 850-acre Federal Reservation. For the time and place this was a very hot issue.

It was also graduation time for Ida May. The whole family was excited that she would be the first to graduate

from high school in our family. Ida was the class valedictorian and Judy Brown of Juneau was the salutatorian.
That great event happened at Mount Edgecumbe on May
18, 1953. Ida applied for a job at the new Alaska Native
Service Hospital in Anchorage and was hired as the first
clerk-typist for the new facility. She lived at the quarters
at the hospital and June would join her a short time later.
Both girls worked at the hospital until they both got married. Poppa's oldest daughter Kay (Yenney) and her husband Duane Downs were also living in Anchorage. They
would have three sons: Chris, Larry and Mark. So Ida,
June and Jerry had their big sister to keep an eye on them.
Momma was happy about that.

Poppa had a chance to work for the summer again,
resurfacing the runway at the Moses Point airport in 1953.
Momma got the job to be the camp cook. Since there was
only Chuck and Frances at home, they packed up the family and went to Moses Point. The other villagers that went
were Fred Katchatag and Henry Otton. They all lived in a
building near the runway that served as their boarding
house. The contractor was Earl Butcher who was based in
Fairbanks, Alaska. The job lasted from July to September, 1953.

While at Moses Point the children got acquainted with
the other children from the village of Elim. Since it was
summer time all the families were in and out of their summer camps at the mouth of the river. Chuck and Frances
would go to the mouth of the small river and Elsie
McCafferty or Luther Nagaruk would come over in a kayak
and ferry them across to visit. The other children about
their age were Luther Nagaruk, Wilfred Murray, Arnold
Jemewouk, Elsie McCafferty and several others.

Time went by so fast. The fish were plentiful, and
there were all sorts of waterfowl to watch. Momma said
that at the end of the day, Fred Katchatag, Henry Otton
and some of the others would go hunting to have a taste of
their native foods. They would bring their catch to her
and she would prepare it right away for the next dinner.

There was one man by the name of Ed Rice who was
going to show Momma how to pluck the ducks quickly. He
had plucked chickens on a farm so he knew what he was

doing. He sat down next to her to show her. My the feathers did fly! They flew everywhere. Momma told him to stop right there. She did not want to spend her cooking time chasing the feathers. He listened to her. She finished in her own way so the feathers quit flying. We all had such a wonderful dinner. So much good food.

Earl Butcher's son Gary and his Gramps would take Chuck out to catch silver salmon. Momma cleaned the fish and set out to fry the catch for dinner. This same Ed Rice told her that he could not eat fish. She said that it was okay with her as she had leftovers from lunch and he could eat that. When dinner was served everyone at the table ate heartily and it smelled so good. Momma saw that Rice was eating fish just like the others. Later Gramps came to her and said that it was the first time he ever saw Rice eat fish. Momma never replied. So after that, whenever Momma served any kind of fish, Ed Rice never complained.

L-R: *Merlin Oyoumick, Roger Riley, Vernon Auliye,*
Sheldon Ryan, Leonard Brown, Henry Otton, Stanley Ryan,
Chuck Degnan, Jerry Degnan, Jimmy Riley,
Francis Katongan, Gilbert Paniptchuk, Eddie Bradley,
Harris Ivanoff, Alvin Ivanoff

40. Uncle Aaron's Story of Early Contact

It was in 1954 that Aaron Paneok and Poppa talked about the condition of the village. Since they had both served on the village council they were concerned about documentation of events from the indigenous perspective. Poppa asked Aaron to write down what he knew about our history. Aaron was a son of Paneok who was one of Auvnue's brothers. Apok and Aaron were first cousins and both were Unalit. Also on October 16, 1954, Aaron's grand-daughter Ruth Soxie married Gertie Auliye's son Alfred Axel Ivanoff. They were married by Magistrate Mary Bahr. Mary had also been the attending mid-wife at Ruth's birth on August 10, 1936. Ruth was the daughter of Ellen Paneok and Jacob Soxie. Alfred and Ruth's children were: Jacob, Alvin, Judy, Alfred Jr., and Rhonda. Rhonda married Leslie Nashukpuk of Point Hope. Today they all live in Naknek and return to Unalakleet in the summer.

The following is what Aaron Paneok wrote and gave to Poppa.

"The Story of Unalakleet since 1895 until 1954. I should like to write the story of Unalakleet village, the happenings and changes during the past fifty years.

"In these years changes have been taken place, and I will try to write as I know what's going on in the years. First I would like to mention the Missionary, Reverend A. E. Karlson, had been here already. At that time people are living in dug-out houses. Seldom you saw houses on top of the ground and the people are living the way as they know how. The Mission School has been started for the Children: Before I register in the school after new year of 1895. That year was a hard winter, blowing and snowing and everybody have short of food. I might say starving, because the people are live off the country and so they are very little chance to go out hunting in account of the bad weather. At that time I heard of a family of seven divided one candle to eat one evening. I remember Mrs. Karlson brought in pot of cook beans to the schoolhouse and feed the children. I think she did that every day during the famine.

"The year 1898 the big boat arrived here to bring several Lapps families and men to built a station up the river. Lapps are to teach Natives herding reindeer. The herd of Reindeer arrived here next winter from Teller from the north. This is the work of Dr. [Sheldon] Jackson by the Govt. [Government] to the Natives of Alaska.

"Another boat arrived the same year to bring the man to built a railroad between here and Kaltag. Mr. Karlson let them built their station seven miles away from here in order to keep away liquor sale here at the village. The year 1899 there was a big gold strike at Nome and the gold stampede was plenty that winter. You can see strings of dogsleds and some without dogs pulling their sled all day long coming and going and so that those who was going to built the railroad quit the work and left for Nome.

"The year 1900 there was a flu during that summer. Lots of old people died up and down the coast, and my mother died also. My sister and her husband and myself was in the family. I was seventeen years old at that time. I was admitted to the Mission in the fall and have little more school. I have been registered at the school in 1895 but we have been away so many times, and so I have little advance in learning. I stayed at the Mission school three years.

"At that time of 1903 I was permitted to go out to the states have my education but something happen that time three weeks before I could go. My brother-in-law got drowned and I could not leave my older sister with two children alone. In that year of 1903 the school is turned over to the Gov't. I help to built the school house and assist to teaching school even though I was only fourth grade in my schooling.

"I think the people here was told to form a councilmen for the village, assisted by Mr. Karlson and the school-teacher. This is what I should like to write about, our struggle and misunderstanding among our people in so many years now. The school teachers and the Missionaries work together very nicely at that time so the village people follows their example.

"About 1908 or 1909 there was two partners wanted to buy out Stephan Ivanoff store here. They were from St. Michael. They ask permission from Mr. Karlson to buy the business. I heard that they have been told not to mix up their goods with whiskey sale here at the village and so they promise that they will never handle such thing, so they get permit to buy the place. They were Dwyer and Steinhauser. Mr. Karlson died in the 1910 and bury here at Unalakleet. After that Missionaries come and go, same way with school teacher. And we know all people are not alike. We Eskimos are easily to influence by the way they are living because we don't know better.

"The new generation are growing and they hardly don't know who their forefathers are living and so they seem to like to live just like white man. That is good if they could handle rightly but we are lots more to learn so we can handle ourself. Our good Gov't. wanted to teach us still more. After 1910 the village up to this time have struggled to form councilman. One time we had meeting to elect councilman for the village. Both the Gov't. teacher and Missionary was present. One of them says we can handle our affairs here at the village and leave out the white man. I says if that was the case no use to form a committee. Years gone by until 1938 and 1939. Another Gov't. teacher came in by the name E. B. Fisher; he started and form a councilmen. At that time I asked him that we should have a reservation in order to Govern the village. This I understand the only way to keep whiskey sale away from the village. So we apply for permission to grant us or let us have a reservation in order to live and handle our affairs.

"We get a grant. The village of Unalakleet is now a Reserve and have 2 miles square and we have Constitution By-Laws and Cooperate Charter sign by the Assistant Secretary of the Interior, Mr. [Oscar] Chapman, in the year 1939.

"Since 1939 up 'till 1945 we are having same hard time to make our people understand. Up to this time some new residents have moved to the village. They are the ones to start some kind of Society and done away with our reservation. They would like to have "Second [Class] City". They says we are tied up like dogs with chain in the reservation. I cannot understand what they mean, that kind of talking. I know and believe that the Gov't. spend lots of money for us natives in order to help us and gave us good laws to follow. Uncle Sam wanted us to be free and keep up and have a rights in our country. I am very sad to write and ashamed to mention of the ones who are helping those who wanted to have Second Class City here. They are those Missionaries who says we are tied up in the reservation, contrary to what Mr. Karlson, the first Missionary has been working so hard to reserve the native village and taking time to teach how to handle themselves.

"We are learning but slow. But we feel the new generation will know better and we old folks will soon be no more in this world. So we are still wishing our children and grand-children handle fairly by our government in the A. N. S. [Alaska Native Service] for the good work has been doing to us Natives—giving us schools and hospitals and also a freedom to live in our country."

Poppa said that his Uncle Aaron wanted only the best for his people and hometown and was happy to do anything for the betterment of the community. Throughout his life he provided a positive influence in Unalakleet. Aaron passed away in 1963.

41. Local Justice

The village council members elected for the year 1954 were: president, Frank Degnan; vice-president, Allen Soosuk; treasurer, Nick Riley; secretary, Edward Koutchak; and councilman John Auliye. Samuel Nashalook became acting secretary later in the year. An important issue again was the continued operation of the Native Store and the status of the loan management. The council requested the Area Director of the Alaska Native Service in Juneau to handle their ANICA account rather have the account moved to ANICA as a separate entity in Seattle.

Poppa filed for the Territorial Senate from the Second Judicial Division. He had just gone through an incident as a result of a misunderstanding with a local person. Poppa was charged by this individual with "Assault and Battery with intent to do Bodily Harm." Since the complaint was lodged in Unalakleet, the district attorney in Nome ordered the case to be heard before the U.S. Commissioner L.C. Ferguson at Unalakleet. The case was to be heard before a locally selected jury. Poppa could not afford a lawyer so he selected Allen Soosuk as his attorney for the trial.

Momma wanted to have Ida May come home for the trial so that she could take notes for Allen. So Poppa sent for Ida, who took emergency leave from her job as secretary to the hospital administrator (Fred Yenney) of the Alaska Native Service hospital in Anchorage.

The trial was held in a classroom at the elementary school. The case was heard. The opposing party had one witness to testify. Poppa's witness, Archie Wheeler, was in Seward, at that time, and he said that the incident was so minor his presence wouldn't make a difference.

During the course of the trial Momma asked if she could say something about that day since her husband had no witness at the court: "That day and that matter they were having a court on happened when I was not at home.

"That day I left the house to go and see L.C. Ferguson to plan for the Girl Scouts party since he was on our sponsoring committee. I needed to get things to make for refreshments.

"When I left the house my husband was working on his sled in the kitchen. Archie Wheeler was helping him. Frances was on the couch in the other room because she was sick with an earache. Gertie had just come in to bring her some oranges. Chuck had just come home from school.

"I left the house for the store to see Fergie. I don't know anything what happened when I was gone. I was only gone a short while.

"When I got home, as soon as I walked in the door Frank asked me: 'Did you see anybody?' I said, 'No, what's the matter?'

"Frank said: 'Oh, it wasn't very much. A couple of guys were here and when one of them got loud I asked him to leave. He wouldn't leave so I just helped him out the door and they left.'

"So I asked Archie what happened. Archie said that nothing happened.

"So Frances called to me and told me that she started crying when those guys wouldn't leave. She told me that she was crying so they wouldn't hurt her dad.

"Chuck said that dad only let them out of the house.

"I don't know what they mean when they say that Frank had beaten me up and that I was crying in the other room.

"Ferguson here knows that at that very time I was meeting with him to plan for the Girl Scouts party. That's all I can say about those charges against my husband."

The trial lasted for several hours. This created a lot of excitement in the village. There were those that were sure that Poppa would go to jail. And then there were those that were sure he would go free. The jury deliberated. The Judge asked for their findings. The Jury said, "Not Guilty." The Judge dismissed the charges.

The Nome Nugget newspaper in Nome carried a small item about that trial. Peter Nanouk was the marshal for the proceedings and he later told Momma that the emotions were so high after the acquittal one of the spectators was so mad he tried to punch Peter. Peter said, "I am sure glad I didn't strike back otherwise we would have to have another trial." Everyone was glad that Poppa's trial was over and the village could get back to normal. Ida went back to Anchorage.

Momma said that there were some people that still wanted to become a second class city. She said that she read an article in the magazine *The Alaska Sportsman*, Volume XX, May, 1954; Number 5; the editorial page, featured as Main Trails and Bypaths, which stated: "Nine Eskimos of Unalakleet express themselves on freedom and equality, reservations and aboriginal rights." The editorial directly quotes the content of the letter that was sent by the men in Unalakleet who wanted a second class city.

The central issues were finally voiced publicly outside of the confines of the village. The village was attempting to seek information so that they could make up their mind whether to stay a federally recognized tribal entity on a reservation or incorporate as a territorial municipality. That would be put to a vote at a later date.

Earlier in 1954 Hugh J. Wade resigned as Area Director of the Alaska Native Service in Juneau and filed, under the Alaska election laws, for the position of Territorial Treasurer. The primary election was to be held on April 27, 1954.

Poppa ran for the Territorial Senate but he did not get elected. He was a strong believer in voters' rights and would always accept their choice. He decided that he would seek employment in the Territorial Legislature if he could.

Poppa was able to get a job as a messenger that session. He told Momma about his time working in the Legislature; that he enjoyed it and was able to see first-hand what was going on.

That same time Willie Foster of Nome was serving in

the Senate and had his family in Juneau. Poppa said that
he would babysit Willie's and Jane's children when they
wanted him to and he said that he had fun with Jimmy
and Richard. I am sure that he would not be surprised
that that "little" Richard was now serving in our Alaska
State Legislature as our elected Representative, and that,
before that, in the early 1970's, his own son, Chuck
Degnan, would serve two terms in the same seat in the
Legislature from our district.

Both Ida and June were working at the Alaska Native Service Hospital in Anchorage. Their oldest sister Kay
was married to Duane Downs and they were also living in
Anchorage. June had met a young man whose name was
Jim Hartwick. Jim was stationed at Fort Richardson and
was a paratrooper. Jim and June decided to get married
and that they did on November 13, 1954. Poppa made it
for the ceremony at the First Presbyterian Church in downtown Anchorage. Reverend Ralph Walkup performed the
ceremony. Momma did not think that June was old enough
to get married. She always said that seventeen was too
young. Jim met Poppa's approval so Momma conceded,
and finally said that it was all right for June to be married. June had received a dental assistant certificate from
Mount Edgecumbe in 1954.

June and Jim had two children: Matthew James
Hartwick, born at Elmendorf Air Force Base Hospital on
July 21, 1955, in Anchorage, Alaska and his sister, Juliet
Degnan Hartwick, born eight years later in Danville, Pennsylvania on August 23, 1963. Both children were six pounds
thirteen ounces at birth. Matthew's Inuit name was Masu,
and Juliet was named Igailaq as she was born one year
after Grandma's death.

All in all, Momma was glad that her children were
doing just fine. Eva was married. Ida had a good job. June
was married. Jerry was in the Army. Chuck and Frances
were still at home. Momma said that life was good.

Also in 1954 the local Covenant Church transformed
their orphanage into a boarding high school. This was a
big event for the village. Now the local children had the
opportunity to get their high school education without leaving home. This school serviced the entire Northwest re-

gion of Alaska and many students graduated from this school. Since it was a private parochial institution they provided housing for the students from the villages. Most of the teachers and maintenance workers were volunteers from the Covenant Church and its affiliates.

Top L-R: Selma Lockwood, Ada Degnan, Nannie Anawrok, Marion Gonangnan, Frank Degnan
Bottom L-R: Rosie Paneok, Sarah Kotongan, Mrs. Katchatag, Mrs. Nashalook, Igailaq, Mrs. Tomrun

Top L-R: Guerie Towarak, Emily Brown, Amelia Ivanoff, Marion Gonangnan, Eula Traeger, Charlie Traeger, Mabel Fisher, Bessie Smith, Nannie Anawrok, Esther Agibinik, Jessie Paneok
Front L-R: Jennie Toshavik, Clara Oyoumick, Ada Degnan, Ellen Soxie and daughter, Edna Paneok, Ethel Toshavik, Ernest Fisher, Nick Riley, Frieda Riley

189

42. 1955--Alaska Constitutional Convention

Poppa was very much interested in the upcoming Alaska Constitutional Convention that everyone in the territory was so excited about. He and Momma would talk about what a great opportunity it would be to secure a place for the indigenous peoples' rights in the Constitution of Alaska which was to be drafted by Alaska's delegates.

When the time came to file for a seat as delegate, Poppa immediately secured a petition and got it filled out and then notarized by L.C. Ferguson at Traeger's Store in Unalakleet. Poppa then went to Nome to handcarry it to the filing place.

After Poppa got home from Nome Momma got Chuck and Frances busy digging the gardens. She planted the gardens as fast as she could as they planned a boating trip to St. Michael and Canal for egg-hunting. This was to be the last family outing for a long time as Chuck was going to Mount Edgecumbe for high school in the fall. Momma did not want any delay in the trip.

As soon as the ice on the Norton Sound opened, Poppa and Momma loaded up the wooden riverboat and set out on the journey. The trip to Canal was made as fast as the nine-horse-powered outboard motor could handle. The family set up camp at the places that Poppa selected as he knew the whole Canal area like the back of his hand.

The weather was as beautiful as the month of May could produce. All the waterfowl and birds made beautiful music. It was so good to be alive. The daylight was so long that time did not matter, and the family lived off the foods they harvested. Momma knew that this was a special trip because it might the last that they would take as a family unit because she felt that soon her youngest children would be gone like birds from the nest. She would not think about that; she would just enjoy God's great outdoors.

The little family had a glorious time. It was time to go back home. It was to St. Michael for gas and oil for the motor and a little visiting time with friends and catch up on the local news. After the short boat ride to St. Michael, Poppa took the family to see Harry and Ruth Johnson. Ruth was the granddaughter of Kakauraq and she had married Harry who was the son of Alexander and Malorie Johnson. Poppa always stayed with Ruth and Harry whenever he went down to the Canal for hunting. And of course, when the whole family came along they all looked forward to stopping with and visiting with Ruth and Harry.

On this trip Tony and May Joule were teaching at the St. Michael school. They invited the family for supper, and they were going to show a movie for the village in the school that night. After the movie and during their visit, May found the opportunity to ask Poppa if he would allow her to travel with the family back to Unalakleet in the boat. May said that she wanted to see the country and camp out a little bit. It would be no problem for Poppa to take on another rider in his boat. He was used to taking a big load and as many passengers who were willing to ride. May would come home with the family, and after Tony closed the school for the summer, he would fly over, and he and May would travel to their home of Point Hope.

The Yukon River had broken up and the ice on the ocean was moving northward. Poppa said that we would have to be on the move so that we would not be caught in the ice floes that were certain to block our path home. May said many times in later years that she had the best time of her life on that boat trip from St. Michael to Unalakleet.

The trip home was at the usual speed that the motor could muster which was really a leisurely pace compared to the big outboard motors used some forty-one years later.

The current was bringing the Yukon ice on the horizon. The day trip brought the family to the old village of Klikatarek. Poppa beached the boat so that Momma could stretch her legs and make her coffee. It was time for a break.

Klikaterek was once thriving village in the time of Apok and her parents Auvnue and Natigook. Now there were no houses left except those of Sinrock Mary's reindeer operations. Behind the buildings were well-worn trails that led to the corrals that kept many hundreds of reindeer from 1906 to about 1929. There were also the traditional burial places near the houses, and during the many times we visited that place we saw the remains of our ancestors. No person ever bothered the ancestral bones and Mother Nature in her own time buried those remains.

After the short break at Klikaterek the next stretch took the family to Black Point and the twin islands where the family searched for eider duck eggs and sea gull eggs. There were other searching places for eggs, but with the ice closing in Poppa said that we could make it to Golsovia to spend the night.

The herring were in the bay and as we traveled, many seals would pop their heads out of the water to watch us pass by. When you saw the seals up so close you could see that there were herring eggs all over their fur and whiskers. Some of the seals would pop out of the water with herring in their mouths. That was such a wonderful sight. The sound of the herring gulls and arctic terns rang out throughout the Norton Sound.

In Golsovia, Poppa did not have to pitch the tent since there were two buildings left standing, so most of the camping supplies remained in the boat. One of the buildings we spent the night in belonged to Harold Charles. Its former owners had been Edward Bradley and then Edwin Katchatag.

In Apok's time, Golsovia had been a thriving settlement. After the Gold Rush and the decline of the reindeer industry, most of the inhabitants moved to Unalakleet. One of the last to remain in Golsovia was Qaiguq who was also called Golsovia Charlie. When he died in 1940 the place had lost its last year-round resident.

Poppa said that Golsovia was a good harbor. It was sheltered from the storms and had a good fresh water river and plenty of fish and game. We were not to be storm-bound in this harbor. Poppa said in the early morning that the ice pack had moved in, and it would not be safe for the family to travel any further by boat. It was decided that Momma, May and Frances would make their way by foot from Golsovia to Coal Mine, fifteen miles away and wait there for Poppa and Chuck who would take the boat through the ice and meet them there.

Momma said, "The walk from Golsovia to Poker Creek was a good one. We were traveling light so that we would not get tired. May was carrying her small rifle for our protection. We knew that we would have to be on the lookout for bears. Those would be the only animals that could harm us.

"We did not have to carry water because there was plenty of ice and the creeks were all running. When we got to Poker Creek we stayed there and waited for dad and Chuck. When they showed up, I made a pot of coffee right away. We all had a snack. You kids were doing just fine. May said that she was having the time of her life. Dad said that it was time to get going on our way home.

"The next place we would meet would be at Coal Mine, which is fourteen miles South of Unalakleet. We pushed out the boat into the water with dad and Chuck in it. The ice pack was all around the boat. I told dad that he had better be careful. I had such a great fear of the power of the ice and water and what they could do to any kind of boat. I guess that was the reason that May, Frances and I were walking instead of riding.

"Well, we took off again. The walking from Poker Creek was good all the way to Coal Mine. The ice pack did not look good to me. I was worried for the safety of dad and Chuck. I tried not to think of bad things happening. We made it in good time to Coal Mine Creek.

"The ice was a short way off the coast. I knew the boat would be in soon. Even if the sun was shining brightly, I knew that the men would be cold when they made it to us. So I took my time crossing the creek so that I could pick up chunks of coal to put on the campfire so that it could throw off more heat to warm the men.

"I noticed a walrus carcass nearby and little did I know that there was a big grizzly bear feasting on it. Thank God that May and Frances saw the bear. I could hear them yelling, but could not make out what they were saying. Next thing, I see Frank and Chuck coming to shore with the boat. They were all waving for me to come. Next thing, I heard was a low, rumbling growl of a bear. I did not look around. I dropped the coal and started running to my family.

"The next thing I knew I had leaped the creek in one big bound. I did not even get wet. We all hurried into the boat. Dad pushed us out and got hold of his rifle. He shot once at the bear. That bear leaped up and in three long stretches was over the top of the high bluff. We went back to shore and Dad climbed up the bluff to make sure the bear was gone. The bear was gone. What a relief.

"We had a quick lunch and coffee. It was time to be back on our way. There still was a lot of ice so we had to continue our walk home. Dad and Chuck went out in the boat. Dad said not to worry about them. So we all started home.

"As we got to the flats close to the village we saw a flock of white geese on the shoreline. Since May had her gun we decided we would try to sneak them and see if she could get at least one of them for supper. We made our way on the tundra away from the beachline. When we thought we had reached the right spot, May took her gun and went to the beach. She came right back. She said that we had passed the geese by a long way. We did not want to risk seeing another bear so we just kept walking.

"It took us a couple of hours to reach the mouth of the Unalakleet River. Since we were tired we rested in the tall grass. Some of the families were already camping on this side of the river. A group of children were coming our way so we stood up to greet them. Maybe they could help us get a ride to the village. As soon as they saw us they ran away screaming. They were screaming: Indians! We just could not get them to come back.

"When we got to the mouth of the river it was Joe Paniptchuk (Inuit name 'Ku-tee,') that came over in his boat to bring us home. We were so glad to see him. I told him that Frank and Chuck were out in the ice pack on the ocean and should be home before long. We got to the house and I found that I did not have the key to the door. Our neighbor Everett Carr was happy to take out our back window so we could get in the house. It was good to be home. It was early the next morning that Frank and Chuck safely made it home too. They got in on June 18. We had been gone from home for almost three weeks."

The next day Poppa checked at the post office for any mail concerning his filing for the Constitutional Convention. He had a letter from the elections office stating that since there was an erasure on the form he would not be eligible for the Seat Number 9 that he wanted. They would qualify him for Seat Number 7 for which the form was certified for.

This was a problem for Poppa. He wrote several letters to clarify his situation and the reason for his changes on the form. As it ended up, his name was entered as filing for Seat Number 7 and he did not get elected as a delegate for the Alaska State Constitutional Convention from the section he filed. He had thought he had a better chance of being elected if he had filed for Number 9.

Although Poppa was not a delegate to that important convention he made sure that he kept up on the news of the Convention's work. His main concern was to make sure that the Natives of Alaska did not lose any of their aboriginal rights and freedom in their own country. It was our local missionary Maynard D. Londborg that was elected to fill Number 7.

Poppa said that it was not right for the Natives not to be elected as delegates to the Convention. As it turned out there was one Native person that did get elected and that was Frank Peratrovich from Southeastern Alaska.

In August 1955 Chuck left for Mount Edgecumbe with a group of young men on a large Alaska Airlines airplane. The others were Sam Otton Jr., John Akan Jr., and Cornelius Lauredson. That meant that Frances was the last of the children to be home with Momma and Poppa.

Ida contacted the family to let them know that she had met a young man named Jim Bird, who had asked her to marry him. He just happened to come from the same place as Jim Hartwick. Momma and Poppa had no objections but they did not like the idea that she moved to Livonia, Michigan, since it was so far away from home. Ida sent a telegram home and said that she and Jim were married on Saturday, September 24, 1955. In an earlier letter she wrote that she started work in the purchasing department of the Ford Motor Company in Livonia on September 13, 1955. Ida and Jim had only one child, a son, James Cleland Bird Jr., born on October 18, 1956, in Ann Arbor, Michigan. His Inuit names were Apok and Qamuuqin.

Poppa said, "We trained all of you to know right from wrong. You will have to live with your decisions. You all know where you came from and when the time is right you will come back."

Momma agreed with what Poppa had to say. She said, "Both of us loved our parents so very much we could not leave them. So it is pretty hard for us to let you go. We know that we did the very best we could with what we had to make sure you got education so you could compete in this changing world. You all should know what is the right thing to do."

They both agreed that they would not worry about the older children as they still had two younger ones that just might decide to continue living at Unalakleet to carry on the Unalit/Kawerak traditions. There would always be hope that the family would return with many skills to help with the economy of the homeland.

It was also the time that the federal government was in the process of setting up a radar system across the Arctic to provide an early warning defense system to protect the United States from military threats from the Communist block nations on the other side of the world. Actually the perceived threats were just across the Bering Sea from us. To the local village it only meant that the government was going to put some sort of military site at Unalakleet. Maybe some of the people would be able to get some jobs when the construction work started.

43. The Military Moves into Unalakleet

In the early spring of 1956 some of the local men were hired to help with labor and transport of the government contract survey crews. These crews were mapping the areas set aside in the Unalakleet vicinity for the new military radar equipment and site.

Poppa was hired to drive and deliver supplies for the surveyors with his dog team. He had a team of five dogs which were Malemute dogs and some were part husky and bird dog mix. Frank Massey was assigned to help Poppa and the weather was so cold Poppa had to loan some of his clothing on the trail to keep Massey from hypothermia.

With the new people in the area, the government had to build a camp several miles north of the village to house the men and equipment. The villagers took the changes in stride. There was a small opportunity for the men to get jobs as laborers. Since this was a military remote site the amount of aircraft traveling to Unalakleet increased.

Momma still was cooking for the school lunch program. Frances would be finishing the eighth grade in the spring. Momma decided that she would apply for the position of chief cook for the next season, as the Bureau of Indian Affairs had finally adopted the hot lunch program in their school system. This would now be a paying position. Momma was not hired as chief cook. She inquired why not, and was told that she was not qualified for the job. Someone else was hired. Momma said that now was a good time for "retirement.'"

Frances was accepted to attend Mount Edgecumbe High School to join Chuck and the rest of the students from home. Momma said that when all of the children were gone it was hard to accept. She said, "Thank God that you children were faithful in writing home. I was glad I still had my own mother nearby. Now I understood just why a lot of parents did not want their children to leave home for education. With you gone it made us work even harder to get a high school here that parents did not have to pay a tuition for. We all did not have paying jobs so paying tuition for more than one child was still out of the question."

Poppa had filed again for the Territorial Legislature. He was successful in getting the Democratic nomination for the seat. That was good news for the family. However, he did not win the seat in the general election. Poppa took it in his usual stride. He always told his children that it was better to run in an election than to complain. If you were elected you could do what you could. It was the voters who decided who would represent them and that was the best way for government to function. He never felt bad when he lost an election as it was the will of the people.

Apok, Chuck, June, Frances, and Ada Degnan, 1952

44. 1957... and Momma Travels to Sitka

Momma said that the house was so empty without the children. Poppa was busy with short-terms jobs connected with the Air Force site. His aim was to get as many local boys as possible to work on jobs that were coming into the village. It did not seem fair to sit on the side and see strangers taking money out of the area, and not spending it in the village. The village was relatively quiet. The only businesses where money could be spent were at the two retail stores.

Poppa understood that Momma was feeling blue and missing her children. He said, "I figured that it was time to take Momma on a trip and I knew she would not refuse this time. She would go because she would be with her kids for a short time. She did not have an excuse to stay home to take care of 'the kids.' I knew she did not like to travel but she would not be going alone. I thought it would give me a chance to speak with the contractors and unions to see if we could get all of our boys here at home working on the Air Force site they were starting to build.

"We left Unalakleet in early January of 1957 and made a short stop in Anchorage. We stayed with June, Jim and Masu. We could see that they were doing good living in a little house they bought in Abbot Loop. Their closest neighbors were Leonard and Mary Brown and Ralph Katchatag who just happened to be from Unalakleet and living then in Anchorage. I talked with Jim and said he should apply for a job with the contractors since he had heavy duty equipment operator skills. It turned out that if he flew to Unalakleet he would be hired to work on building the road to the proposed sites.

"Momma and I left Anchorage and made our way to Sitka with a stop at Juneau. Momma got to see where I had worked and lived when I was in the Legislature. She was so anxious to see you all in Sitka. When we arrived in Sitka on an Ellis Airlines seaplane, Eva, Eldon, Randy, Martha and Clarissa were at the seaport to greet us. It was such an exciting time for all of us. Chuck and Frances were at the classes at Mount Edgecumbe. The school had such strict rules the kids were not allowed to meet us. We had to go over to the school to see and visit them.

"So Momma and I had a talk with the school superintendent to see when we would be allowed to be with you kids. It turned out that we could check you out on the weekends but could not have you out on school days.

"Eva was living in Sitka and Jerry was working several odd jobs in Edgecumbe. We almost had the whole family in town. Since Eva had such a big family and such a tiny house on Pescharoff Street we took a long term room at the Sitka Hotel on the waterfront. Your Momma never got used to staying in the hotel room. She said it was the noisiest place on Earth with all the stray cats in the world living and screaming under us when we tried to sleep.

"We decided that we would wait for Eva to have her baby before we went back to Unalakleet. It was on February 20, 1957, that I took Eva to the Mount Edgecumbe Hospital and her baby girl was born. They named the baby Maryanne June Ridley. We named the baby the Inuit name of Niyaalgak after Accebuck's wife. Momma said it was time for us to go home. She was satisfied that all of her kids were doing good and now she was lonesome for her mother and her own home.

"We made it home to Unalakleet after a short stop in Anchorage. Jim Hartwick and Jim Bird had been hired to work on the military job at home so we all came home together. The kids decided to stay at my mother Apok's little house. Jerry came home too and when he got hired to work on the road he decided to live near the job site. We pitched him a tent at North River and he used our boat and small motor so he could come to the village whenever he wanted. Momma was so happy about how God brought her children back. We now had babies around us once again.

"The year flew faster than usual it seemed. I was hired as job steward for the Union. When I put our local boys on the job as carpenters my boss told me: Frank, you can't do that, my boys have been sitting on the bench in Fairbanks for months waiting for these jobs. I told him: My boys have been sitting on our beaches for centuries and now it's time for them to have these jobs. So our local boys were hired because they were all qualified. That's how we built the road to White Alice and both the military sites. I was proud of all of the men and the good job they did.

"Ida got a job working for Alaska Airlines at Unalakleet. She worked with Richard Ivanoff, Ralph Ivanoff, Wilfred Ryan and Sig Krogstad. When the Air Force road job was done she and Jim decided that they would return to Michigan to be with his mother Fannie Bird. So they went back in August of 1957."

Ida went back to work for Ford Motor Company in Livonia, Michigan as clerk typist. She worked there at the same Ford Transmission and Chassis plant for thirty years and retired on September 1, 1987, as a program analyst. After her divorce from Jim she married William R. (Bill) Harden on December 20, 1969, at the Presbyterian Church in Livonia. Bill owned his own business and they retired about the same time. They moved to Florida for a few years. Bill asked Ida if she would like to move home to be closer to her mother. They moved to Anchorage on October 5, 1990, and that was one of the happiest times of Momma's life.

June, Jim and Matthew left Unalakleet for his parents home in Belleville, Michigan shortly after Ida, Jim and Tinker went to Ann Arbor, Michigan. June and her family lived in New Jersey, Pennsylvania and Florida. Juliet was born in Danville, Pennsylvania on August 23, 1963. Her Inuit name was 'Igailaq' after her great-grandmother. When June was in Florida she completed her high school education and received her diploma. Then she attended Nova University and received her college diplomas. In April of 1979 she received a Bachelor of Science degree in Psychology, and in 1981 she received a Bachelor of Science degree in Education and a teaching certificate. In 1983 she began graduate studies in Public Administration in Environmental Growth Management.

Jerry moved to Anchorage after his work was done at Unalakleet. He worked on the Alaska Railroad and lived at the railroad camps for about ten years.

Eva, Eldon, and Randy Ridley

Frank and Ada Degnan, Martha Carle, Herman Ridley

45. Changes and More Challenges

Now that the military was moving into the area and there was promise of work for the local people, the village council kept a close eye on what was happening. The people saw that the sites were little closed communities with all the amenities of life provided by the federal government. These simple amenities of electricity, water and sewer, telephones and central heating were not available to the villagers. They were bystanders in their own homeland. They saw changes that affected their lives and values.

Poppa said, "We were glad that some of our boys could work. Some of them got hired to work on the Air Force site permanently. I was still the president of the village council. Whenever any problem or complaint came up about the site or the village the people wanted the council to do something. Those complaints were about the use of alcohol, the gambling that was going on, and the disruption of fishing caused by the increased use of motors on the rivers.

"These incidents were not of a large scale but they did affect all of the community. The people were concerned because they felt that they were bad influences on their way of life. The council kept close contact with all parties involved and somehow we were able to resolve the problems peaceably.

"Positive benefits from having the defense installations in the area were new jobs, telephone service, local access to armed services radio, and improved mail and air service into Unalakleet. We now had a fifteen mile road from the village into the interior where we could go berry and greens picking. We had a few of our people working steady at the Air Force site and they were: Fred Katchatag, Richard Ivanoff, Stanley Ryan, Nathan Anawrok, Harold Charles, Oswald Paneok, Roland Ivanoff, Francis Katongan, Henry Otton, Ellsworth Haugen, and Larry Wilson. Jessie Otton, Elsie Soxie and Frieda Riley also worked at the site as housekeepers."

The United States Air Force radar site was constructed in 1956-57 and operational in 1958. There were one hundred military personnel stationed there of which eight were officers and ninety-two were enlisted men. The site was in operation for ten years until it was shut down in 1968. The site was totally dismantled in 1992 and the land returned to the Unalakleet Native Corporation as part of its land entitlement under the Alaska Native Claims Settlement Act of 1971.

Poppa got the approval of the village council to go into the taxi-cab service in and out of the village in 1958. He applied and received all the necessary licenses to provide service in the area. He bought a 1956 Ford sedan from the contractor Sam Bergesen when the construction of the road was done.

Poppa ran the Unalakleet Cab Company until his death in 1980. His fares were very reasonable and he was available around the clock. During his whole career he was accident-free and enjoyed doing his taxi service. He provided a reliable service and did all of his own maintenance work. Momma said: "Your dad was trying to get me to learn how to drive. I told him that if I started driving I would wind up doing all the calls and would never get my own work done. That is why I would not learn. I learned how to run an outboard motor so I could get my fish and get to camp when he could not take me because he was on cab calls."

46. *College and Airplanes*

Chuck graduated from Mount Edgecumbe High School on May 19, 1959. He was the salutatorian of the graduating class and Vernon Swanson of Koyuk, Alaska was the valedictorian. Chuck told the family that he was accepted at the University of Alaska Fairbanks campus. He was the first one in the family to go to college. He joined Ambrose Towarak and Stanton Oyoumick, both graduates of the local Covenant High School, who had convinced him that it would be good for him to join them at the university.

In the spring of 1959, Eva sent Randy to Unalakleet with Frances so that he could be with the family and experience life at Unalakleet. Randy was six years old and it was agreed that Frances would be in charge of him. The summer flew by so fast. Randy got to help with the gardening and fishing. Momma and Frances took him everywhere they went as Poppa was busy with his taxi service. When it was time for school to start the aunt and nephew went back to Sitka. When they arrived at Sitka Randy was so happy to be back with his parents and family.

Frances graduated on May 17, 1960, from Mount Edgecumbe High School. At that same date, Eva graduated from Sheldon Jackson High School at the same time as Frances. Chuck had convinced Frances to attend the University of Alaska in the fall. The university was relatively close to home so Momma felt good that her youngest children were still reachable. It was just her and Poppa left at Unalakleet.

Poppa was asked by the Wien Consolidated Airlines, Inc. headquarters in Fairbanks to be their station manager at Unalakleet. Poppa accepted the position and Momma said that position would keep her tied to the house. Poppa would be the Wien station agent at Unalakleet until June 1, 1969, when Munz Northern took over the bush route in the Norton Sound area. Many years later Wien provided jet air service in and out of Unalakleet connecting with Nome and Anchorage. This service would end when they went out of business for good.

Frank and Ada Degnan, Frances Degnan,
Eva Merrifield, and Emily Brown
University of Alaska Fairbanks ~ 1964

47. *Aboriginal Rights and Native Affairs*

Momma said, "It was in 1961, that the Village Council and the Mothers Club were concerned about the migratory bird crisis that was going on in our country. The eider duck incident was a protest, by the local Inuit hunters in Barrow, against the Fish and Wildlife Service enforcement of migratory bird hunting regulations. Those regulations prohibited the spring season taking of migratory birds. We all heard reports that the Fish and Wildlife Service was going to do something about the springtime hunting of birds. When the eider duck hunters were arrested in Point Barrow, it made it crystal clear that we all would have to do something to protect the freedom of our land. That freedom to hunt, fish and travel unmolested in our own country. As long as freedom was there, our families were safe and happy because the hunters could provide food for the family, extended family and the community. That was our right, our God-given right. So after the eider duck incident the Mothers Club got right busy and sent a letter. Mrs. Irene Katchatag was our president then.

"Poppa was contacted by Guy Okakok of Point Barrow, Alaska and LaVerne Madigan of the Association on American Indian Affairs in New York about joining a group of Inuit to advocate for Native Rights. They would oppose the upcoming atomic testing at Point Hope called Project Chariot and discuss the Migratory Bird Treaty.

"Poppa did not hesitate and he traveled to Point Hope for the important meeting which was held on August 31,

1961. The group of Inuit decided to organize the Point Barrow Conference on Native Rights and they scheduled a gathering of Inuit delegates to convene in November of 1961 at Point Barrow. [See Appendix A-1]

"Poppa, as president, was to represent the Native Village of Unalakleet at the forthcoming Conference on Native Rights scheduled to be held at Point Barrow during the second week of November. I was selected as one of the delegates to that conference.

"As the committee wanted a record of the proceedings it was necessary to have a recording secretary. Poppa knew that Blanche Sarren had training as a secretary so he recommended to the committee and Laverne Madigan that they hire Blanche for their recorder. Blanche was the daughter of Eugene Sarren (Inuit name Qanaiyaq) and Elizabeth Pazgataagaq Sarren (Inuit name Maasinkaa), both of Unalakleet. Blanche had graduated from Mount Edgecumbe High School on May 17, 1960, along with our daughter Frances. Blanche had all the necessary skills that the conference required. Blanche was willing and available so she traveled with the group from Anchorage to Fairbanks and then on to Barrow. Blanche's Inuit name was Pallah."

Both Chuck and Frances were students at the University of Alaska Fairbanks. They were very excited about the arrival of family and friends to Fairbanks even if it was to be only for one night on the way to Barrow and one night back from Barrow.

That conference was made possible with the financial support of the Association on American Indian Affairs headquartered in New York. This was a private group interested in promoting the welfare of the indigenous peoples in America. Miss Laverne Madigan was the Executive Director, and she set the wheels in motion for the conference. Mr. Guy Okakok, Inupiaq of Barrow was selected as Chairman of that Conference Committee. Frank Degnan, Yup'ik of Unalakleet was named Secretary, and the members who were all Inupiaqs and one Yup'ik rounded out the committee. They were Edward Penatac and Paul Tiulana of King Island Village, Daniel Lisbourne of Point Hope, the Inupiaqs; and Alexander Vaska of Kalskag, a Yup'ik.

This was a challenging undertaking by all the people, villages and delegates involved. The financing was a big hurdle. None of the Native village governments had any money available to them. The delegates had to assume all costs and risks, but they represented their village. Air travel to Barrow was far away and expensive. Anchorage, Bethel, Nome, Kotzebue and Fairbanks were the connecting points on the way to Barrow-the destination.

When the villages selected their delegates to this conference they were not able to give them any money. When the delegates consented to go it was with great hopes for accomplishing good for all their indigenous brothers and sisters. It was time to travel.

Momma said that they all met up in Fairbanks and took a large airplane to Barrow. She said, "I was so excited since it was my first trip to Barrow. I could not get over how long it took us to get there. We did not see too much but the moon was shining so we could see that. I wished that it was summer time so I could get to see how the land looked. Your dad told me, that according to his mother, that this part of the world had been submerged under the ocean. Maybe that is why it is so flat and full of lakes.

"When we arrived in Point Barrow Guy Okakok was there to meet us. He took us right away to the Top of the World Hotel. We did not have much time to look around because we went into our work sessions right away because our aboriginal rights were at stake. LaVerne and Guy had all of our sessions tape-recorded so there could be a record that you could hear in the years to come. [See Appendix A-2]

"Our Conference started on November 14, 1961, and we got right down to business. We called the conference our 'Inupiat Paitot' and to us that meant our aboriginal rights. Each of the delegates had a chance to speak throughout the work sessions and bring their issues to the table. In order to get work done some of the sessions were for delegates only. The meetings were open to all in Barrow who wanted to attend.

"We all supported the Barrow eider duck hunters because we all lived the same kind of life. We were all experiencing the fish and wildlife regulations and enforcements to differing degrees. Each of the delegates told at the conference the specific problems and needs that they had at their homes.

"We talked about hunting, fishing, land rights and title. We talked about the Project Chariot atomic bomb experiments to be held soon at Point Hope, Alaska. We talked about need for housing, airports, high schools at home, water and sewer systems, economic development and just about everything that an Eskimo was concerned about.

"We agreed that our problems were all the same. We lived the same kind of life no matter where we came from. It seemed that the only help we could get to improve our living conditions would come from the federal government. We agreed that the State of Alaska seemed intent only on pushing us out of our own country. It is all there on the tape recording. It really did not make any difference which government we were dealing with they did not seem to want to recognize our way of life. It seemed to be all right for the Outsider to get all the jobs and to take any resource out of our lands and waters and then say that we could not do the same thing.

"We agreed that we would present our concerns to the Department of the Interior representatives that attended our meeting at our request. In our minds we were following the right path to let the Congress of the United States know what we were talking about. We presented our recommendations to John Carver, Assistant Secretary of the Interior and James Hawkins, Area Director of the Bureau of Indian Affairs located in Juneau, Alaska. We delegates found out that we were thinking the same thing.

"The best thing to come out of the sessions was that we agreed that we needed a newspaper that would tell the world about what the Natives in Alaska were doing. We all submitted names for this newspaper and the delegates selected my wording which was "Inupiat Paitot," meaning "our people's heritage." Later when the newspaper was established and Howard Rock was the editor and publisher it was named "Tundra Times." I was happy to see my wording on the masthead."

The delegates and people responsible for the conference were staying at the Top of the World hotel. Momma said that she really enjoyed her stay in Barrow. That was her first time ever visiting that community. She said that the people held on to their native traditions and everyone was fluent in their native language. She said that it really made her feel good to know that our way of life was not lost.

She said that the conference was very good. All the delegates were able to express their need and wishes and that they were all unified.

Momma said, "I was made the treasurer for the conference and I had to keep track of every delegate's expenses and pay them. Laverne (Madigan) told me that I made a very good treasurer, I was accurate to the last penny. You know, of course, that everyone at that conference had no money. It was a big sacrifice to their family that each one of them came. But we all believe in our Maker and everyone knew they had to come to protect our Aboriginal Rights.

"The people in Barrow were so good to me. I will never forget Al Hopson and his wife when they invited us to eat at their restaurant. I still can see Mrs. Hopson using her ulu to expertly cut thick steaks of beef off a hindquarter to cook for us. She was a very good cook too.

"When Guy (Okakok) was going to give John Carver and James Officer from the Interior Department a tour of the village your dad told him to take them to the poorest homes in the village.

"These homes were small and heated with bundles of willows that they gathered for burning in the stove. You know, I am glad we went there and held the conference because now the whole village has natural gas for heating and cooking. Just think, it comes from their own land. We could be doing that right here at home too if people would think right."

After the November conference was over on November 17, 1961, all the delegates went back to their homes and their daily routines. They knew that they would attempt to keep the movement going in order to protect their people's rights to freedom in their own country.

When Poppa and Momma got home from Barrow they found that a petition had circulated and many residents had signed it. The petition requested the village council to explain to its members why the council had formed the Unalakleet Valley Electric Cooperative Association. So a special meeting was held to answer questions.

This was when electricity was introduced into all the individual homes in the village. At that time, and for some years previous, the only places that had electricity were the school and the Federal Aviation Agency. Wayne Eben and his brothers Francis and Isaac had gone into business for themselves to provide a source of electricity for some of the homes, and families were investing in electrical appliances.

People saw how they these innovations could make their lives easier, but when demand was high the power plant was too small to service all the customers so the rest of the village wanted a reliable source of electricity.

The council was glad that the Eben brothers were in business, but the council nevertheless went ahead and looked to REA (Rural Electrification Administration) to see how they could get electricity for all. It turned out that a cooperative, if formed, could be the most cost-effective way for the entire village to have electrical power. After the village council had acquired a reliable source of electricity, they planned to apply for a water and sewer system and new housing for all the villagers and be assured of getting those programs. They were always told by the federal agencies for housing programs that the village had to have a pre-existing utility system in order to be considered eligible for further federal funding.

The Articles of Incorporation for the Unalakleet Valley Electric Cooperative, Incorporated were filed and the State Certificate of Incorporation was issued under the date of November 22, 1961. The names and addresses of the officers and directors elected were as follows: Frank A. Degnan, president, Unalakleet, Alaska; Dale B. Friemering, vice-president, Unalakleet, Alaska; Francis L. Katongan, secretary, Unalakleet, Alaska; F. Sheldon Ryan, treasurer, Unalakleet, Alaska; John A. Moore II, director, Unalakleet, Alaska; Phillip Stainbrook, director,

Unalakleet, Alaska and James O'Sullivan, director, Unalakleet, Alaska.

The Unalakleet Valley Electric Cooperative (UVEC) was organized and directors applied for the Rural Electrification Administration loan at a very low interest rate.

The directors then were fortunate to have the Matanuska Electric Association (MEA) of Palmer, Alaska be willing to be a guiding agency for a new cooperative many hundreds of miles north of Palmer. The cooperative successfully completed their loan application which was then approved. They were ready to go into business.

The men in the community who were willing to work cut down local spruce trees for electrical poles and set them up right away. Momma and Poppa donated the use of their quonset hut for the power generator until the cooperative built their own power generation plant. Richard Ivanoff was the first power generator operator. The cooperative got approval from the village council for a lease of property at the edge of the village for the power generation site.

Some of the men from Palmer MEA who were responsible for the success of the Unalakleet UVEC were Mason Lazelle the General Manager, Phil O'Neill, president of the MEA board of Directors, Willard Johnson and Alex Fuller. John Shaw was the MEA attorney. They were helpful in every aspect of the project.

When the new power plant was built and in operation the coop advertised for Power Plant Manager. Poppa knew that Paul Ivanoff Jr. had the right kind of training for the position and was working in Kotzebue at that time. The cooperative successfully recruited Paul as their manager. Paul Ivanoff Jr. began work on April 22, 1962.

48. Light Bulbs, Telephones and Flush Toilets

Now that the village had the promise of a steady source of electricity the council continued to strive for utilities improvement in the village. In 1960 the council, under president Stanton Katchatag, had been notified about a program under the Indian Health Service concerning water and sewer availability for Indian tribes. The council agreed that this would be good for the health of the people.

At the January 4, 1961, election of the village council, the people had elected Frank Degnan as president, Lowell Anagick as vice-president, Francis L. Kotongan as secretary, Andrew Nashalook as treasurer, and Jack Koutchak as councilman. Jack Koutchak was also the manager of the local Native Store.

On February 24, 1961, the council applied to the Department of Health, Education and Welfare, Public Health Service, Division of Indian Health for a project proposal for provision of Sanitation Facilities under Public Law 86-121. In the application they would adopt a plan, would make a contribution of labor toward the project and they would be willing to assume responsibility for operation and management of sanitary facilities. They stated that the tribe would be willing to adopt laws or regulations that would help in the maintenance of sanitary facilities that would be acquired.

In the remarks section the council stated; "Unalakleet has been a reservation since 1939 under the Wheeler-

Howard Act as extended to Alaska in 1936. It is an ever growing community with a present population approaching 600. Within the community there are 2 B.I.A. (Bureau of Indian Affairs) Schools, a Covenant School, a private store, a Native store, 2 theaters, a Hotel, a Clinic, and an F.A.A. (Federal Aviation Agency) Station. A short distance away there is a White Alice site. ...The Native people of the community are relatively poor and unable to afford the community developments which they desire." This application was sent to the Alaska Native Health Service Area Office, Box 7-741, Anchorage, Alaska.

The council had the greatest faith that their application would be successful. They would be vigilant and make sure they did their part to get the project into reality. They were confident that once there was water and sewer in each home, the health would improve tremendously. That spring, the Indian Health Service, based out of Anchorage, began testing the village area for sources of potable water. The council assisted in the water sampling process. In 1962 the village was approved for a water and sewer system. During that year the engineering studies were completed. In the summer of 1964 the system was constructed using local volunteer labor. Poppa said the project was completed in the fall of 1965. He said that seventy-six homes, agencies and businesses were supplied with running water. The council had selected Allen Soosuk in 1965 to be the acting water commissioner and shortly thereafter had hired Lowell Anagick to be the full-time water commissioner. Lowell said that he connected all the houses to the water system. Each of the houses was connected to septic pits for sewage disposal. However, these pits did not work as well as expected, so sewer lines were installed and a sewage lagoon was built and located east of the village. The entire village helped some way in the installation of water and sewer. Much of the effort was through volunteer work. Everyone was happy that they could run water from the tap and flush a toilet in their own home. They all felt it was a job well done. In January of 1967, a fire destroyed the system's pump house. It was a major setback but with a united effort of the PHS and the village, the system was rebuilt and back in operation that fall. As a result, a new water source was located at a creek several miles away from the village. The water was excellent and the people enjoyed the water. Years later, when the village got larger, a new water source was needed. Today the water source is Powers Creek, located five miles north of the village, and it provides sufficient water for the needs of the people.

Lowell served as water commissioner for eighteen years until he retired about 1983. He was also appointed the magistrate on October 31, 1966. Lowell served in this capacity until his retirement twenty-five years later. He was married to Elizabeth (Betty) Nanouk. Betty was the daughter of Peter and Martha Nanouk. She was born on October 8, 1926, and her Inuit name was Ahneekean. Lowell was born on December 7, 1923, and his Inuit name was Diatweaque. They were married on May 1, 1943, in Unalakleet. They had nine children. Their youngest son, Edgar, born in Anchorage on February 19, 1960, married our sister Eva's daughter, Colleen, on July 1, 1989, in Anchorage.

Edgar and Colleen have two children. Michael was born on November 2, 1988, in Anchorage. Danielle was born on August 14, 1990, in Anchorage. Colleen's eldest son is Bruce Francis Auvnue. Bruce's father is Mike Higa who is from Hawaii. Bruce was born on July 31, 1981, in Anchorage and was named after Poppa.

Another important milestone occurred on April 8, 1961. It was the first birthday of radio broadcasting in Northwest Alaska of Radio Station KICY located in Nome. Arthur R. Zylstra was the general manager of the station that reached all the communities in the Norton Sound area. This station was warmly welcomed because anyone with a radio could receive the station without an elaborate antenna system. This brought instant access to world happenings to each home. A very popular program was the "Eskimo Hour" in which the radio announcer played tape recordings provided by local people speaking and singing in the indigenous languages.

Everyone listened to the "Ptarmigan Telegraph" to find out what messages were sent by and to the listening audience. Since there were no local newspapers except for the *Nome Nugget* out of Nome, we all relied on the messages relayed by the radio station. Poppa said that it was a broadcast of local news. He was always interested in the latest broadcast news and had all of his children trained to tune in the radio at the right time for news and weather. They were happy when the Catholoic Diocese of Fairbanks established their radio station, KNOM, at Nome in 1971. We now had a choice of radio stations to listen to. They were both very welcomed.

The summer of 1962 was busy for the family at home. Momma was occupied with planting and caring for her garden patch. When the king salmon were in, she and Poppa went up the river to seine for the fish. She loved salting the fish bellies and making her traditional smoked fish strips. She enlisted the help of the family in this activity but the finished product was her specialty.

Momma was happy that her two youngest children still lived at home during the summer and that they attended the University of Alaska at Fairbanks. During that summer, they found temporary work at home. Chuck worked on the construction of the new electrical power generation plant and drove Poppa's taxi service. Frances worked as a clerk at the local post office.

Poppa was busy as the Wien Consolidated Airlines bush manager at Unalakleet. He had operated the Unalakleet Cab Company since 1959 and he operated on a twenty-four hour a day call. His rates and fares were very reasonable and many times his passengers said that they did not have any money. That was all right with him for he knew that when they did have the fare they would pay. He did his own car repairs and kept his work vehicle on the road. He was the only private taxi operator in the town then. The rest of the cars and trucks were owned and operated by the military or the federal agencies in the village.

August was a busy fishing time for Momma. She loved to spend days and nights at the fish camp at Tirakpak. Her favorite method of catching the silver salmon was using a cottonwood sapling cut down to her size and attaching linen twine and tying on a large treble hook. When the silvers were running, she would wrap fresh salmon roe on the hook and cast the baited hook into the water while standing on the riverbank. She said that fishing this way was so enjoyable, especially when the silver (salmon) attacked the bait. When this happened she would land the fish with a loud "Whoop" and immediately get ready for the next strike.

On August 21, that year, Momma and Poppa were at Tirakpak to put up the winter supply of silver salmon. That morning Max Mixsooke went over to Igailaq's to see if she had any work for him to do. Max had worked for Uncle Frank and one of his chores was to check on Igailaq. He said that he knocked on her door. She did not answer. That was very unusual for her since she was an early riser. He said that he opened the door and peeked in. She was still sleeping. Max called to her and she did not respond. This was not like her. He said that he went over to her and said that she was dead. This is the story that he reported to Frances at the post office.

Frances went over to her grandmother's house and found out that Max's story was true. What was she going to do? She knew that her own mother's heart would be broken.

Chuck was at work so Frances went to tell him the sad news. She and Chuck took leave from their work and hurried up to Tirakpak in a boat to tell of Igailaq's death. When they arrived at the camp she ran to Poppa to tell him the news as she could not bear to tell her mother that grandma had died.

Later Momma told her children that the death of her mother was one of the most difficult times she had to face in her life. Momma said, "I did not mind that I was not living with my father. He had claimed me as his own. I knew that he had his own family. I had my husband and my children and I also had my mother, my brother and two sisters. I considered myself to be blessed. But that day, when mother died, it felt that my best friend in this world was gone forever. But I thank God to this day that we had the love of my dear mother. I always miss her coming over to check on us. I only hope that I can be a little like her to my family."

It was not long after Igailaq's death that Poppa received a letter, dated September 10, 1962, from Mr. Oliver

La Farge, President of the Association on American Indian Affairs in New York stating that he wanted to explain his telegram advising of the tragic death of La Verne Madigan. "LaVerne was killed suddenly when she was thrown from a horse. She was then in Vermont, taking a brief and long overdue vacation from her unflagging labors for the first Americans. In private life she was Mrs. Harold Bordewich. Our profound sympathy goes to her husband and to her 14-year old son Fergus."

It was a difficult time as the Inupiat Paitot had scheduled another conference on Native Rights to be held in October of that year. Mr. La Farge stated, "Her cooperation with the Eskimos of Alaska was authorized by our Board of Directors, highly approved by us, and she had kept us informed about it. We shall continue what she started. ..."

Poppa said that the people of the North would dearly miss La Verne Madigan as she had the energy, imagination and dedication to the task before her. She had a great deal of empathy for our people. He also said that the Inupiat Paitot meeting would still be held as planned in Kotzebue that October. [See Appendix A-3 for meeting record.]

Poppa said that the Inupiat Paitot meeting was held as scheduled. The delegation felt the absence of Miss Madigan. He said that they reviewed the progress of Native rights since their last meeting. They felt as a group that it was time to have their voice heard. They had great faith in the ability and energy of Howard Rock to make the newspaper Tundra Times the voice to let the world know what was happening to the Inupiat. Guy Okakok continued to give his reports on native affairs to the Fairbanks Daily News-Miner and to the Tundra Times newspapers in Fairbanks.

The Kotzebue meeting was the last official meeting of the Inupiat Paitot group but they were confident that Howard Rock would keep the world informed on the events that affected all their lives. Howard ran the newspaper from his offices in Fairbanks and his reach was worldwide.

Back in the village, the council was successful in their

goal of electricity for each home. They had the help of the Matanuska Electric Association (MEA) of Palmer. Mason LaZelle was the General Manager of MEA and Willard Johnson was the Chief Engineer. They were able to assist the local Unalakleet Valley Electric Cooperative (UVEC) in all the phases of providing electric generation in the village.

The local cooperative had all local men to build the new generation plant located at the north-east corner of the village. In the first months of operation, it was Richard Ivanoff who was hired as the first power plant operator. The plant that he ran was in the quonset hut building provided by Poppa.

Momma told of the time that Mason LaZelle asked Poppa to be present at the annual meeting of the members of the Matanuska Electric Association that was held in mid-April of 1962. He also invited Momma to attend. Momma said: "We were happy to go to Palmer so that we could thank the people there for taking a chance on helping our village get electrified. Your dad and I did not know that there were members there that were unhappy that they were helping us get our plant in operation since we were only a little village a long way from Palmer. We went to the meeting. Diane Carpenter from Stony River was also a guest there. When it came time for your dad to talk the auditorium was noisy. Your dad took the microphone and he said that he was happy to be with them. He said that we were coming out of the Stone-Age. He said, when we get our electricity we will then be able to get our flush-toilets next. Then we will be able to pull a chain and the lights will go on and the toilet will flush. He got a big applause. Mason was relieved. We were happy when the people told us that they were glad we came to talk with them and now they understand why their manager and workers were so busy up North. I was glad to meet the people who helped our village get our electricity. Poppa and I enjoyed our short visit to Palmer. We met many good people."

When the new building was completed at Unalakleet and the generators installed, the cooperative looked for a permanent plant operator. They had offered the job to Ri-

chard but he turned it down. He had done a good job providing reliable electric service to the village. He said that
he wanted to do other things. When all the applications
were reviewed, it was decided to offer the position to Paul
Ivanoff Jr.. Paul accepted the challenge and began his work
on April 22, 1962.   Paul is still employed as the power
plant manager. Paul was the son of Paul Ivanoff Sr. and
May Tetpon. He was the grandson of Stephan and Amelia
Ivanoff. Paul and his wife Lizzie Nels moved to Unalakleet.
Paul's Inuit name was Dungaq and Lizzie's Inuit was
Abizgunaq.

The cooperative hired Harry Johnson Sr. in 1964 to
work at the power plant. He had many years of experience of engine repair and expertise. Harry was originally
from the village of St. Michael. He was the son of Alexander
Johnson and Malorie Jacob. His Inuit name was Siqulgeq.
Harry married Ruth Ivanoff. Ruth was the daughter of
Henry Ivanoff and Laura Williams. Laura's mother was
Kakauraq (Lena Williams) of Unalakleet and her father
was Frank Williams, the trader at St. Michael. Henry's
parents were Stephan and Amelia Ivanoff. After living
many years in St. Michael, Harry told Momma and Poppa
that it was time that Ruth raised the family in Unalakleet.

Poppa said the village was able to get a telephone
company into the village about 1962. The Tundra Telephone company leased a small site in the village to install
telephone equipment. It was now possible to have a direct
dial telephone in each home. In earlier years, the
Unalakleet Lodge had the only telephone connecting
Unalakleet with the outside world. The ability to use a
telephone was made possible by the microwave transmit-
ting site a short distance from the village that was operated by the federal government and was connected with
the radar site. Tundra Telephone later filed bankruptcy.

General Telephone took over the telephone exchange
in Unalakleet on January 1, 1966.

Poppa filed again for a seat in the Alaska State Legislature. He did not get elected. He said that it was up to
the voters to select whom they wanted to represent them.
He continued filing for the legislature when that time
rolled around again. He said that he was satisfied that

the people in the village wanted him to be on the local council and he would do his best to serve them.

After the state election in 1962, Governor William A. (Bill) Egan appointed Poppa to fill a vacancy on the state Fish and Game Board. Poppa was now a member of a state board. There was no salary attached to the job. He got his transportation and living expenses reimbursed for every meeting he attended.

He was pleased to be serving on the board since there were few indigenous persons appointed to any state boards. He mentioned that in their meetings they considered many issues and decided on what regulations must be adopted. He had to read many reports and recommendations made by state employees. When they held their meetings the public had the opportunity to express their views on the issues. Poppa said that at one time it was recommended that Besboro Island, between Unalakleet and Shaktoolik, be made into a marine wildlife sanctuary. He said he objected because this island was used for subsistence by the Norton Sound people and should not be put off limits "just because one walrus was seen to be taking a rest on the rocks there." Besboro was not made a refuge. He served one term on the Board. On February 7, 1966, Governor William A. Egan reappointed him, subject to legislative confirmation to the board for a term expiring January 31, 1970. On February 20, 1967, Governor Walter J. Hickel wrote to thank Poppa for his service and advised him another person was to be appointed to that board. That was the end of his appointment.

The village council met regularly to work on the projects they felt were needed in the community. They looked at the economy of the vicinity. They were happy that some of the local people had year round employment at the nearby Air Force and White Alice sites. Their goal was to have all the households having family members hold jobs that would make their lives easier. They identified that the seasonal activities of subsistence and commercial fishing were the mainstay for a majority of the local households. The fish buyers were interested in the salmon fishery and several individuals came back each year to buy fish from the commercial fish permit holders.

The early fish buyers were Ralph Griswold, Jack Most, Jack Logan, and William McBride. The fishermen were happy to sell their salmon to the buyers as the money they earned helped them in their daily subsistence activities. There was interest shown in developing the herring roe as a fishery that year also by outside Japanese interests. Poppa said that he had a commercial fishing permit since 1952 and he did not make much money off the effort as it was dependent on the availability of commercial air transport to Nome and Fairbanks. He said it would make more sense if it were a community effort to bring a quality product to the consumer. In 1964 the council organized the Unalakleet Fisheries, Incorporated and got in the business of fishery products. They initiated a small scale fish buying and processing operation and operated the business through a lease with an outside operator. They secured a Small Business Administration (SBA) loan and constructed a fish plant in 1965. The ultimate goal of the council was to have all phases of the business managed and operated by tribal members. It was in the mid-70's that the tribal council fishery operations were turned over to the Unalakleet Native Corporation in order to repay the SBA loan. Today, the tribal council has a new fish processing facility to produce value-added fish products for sale to outside markets.

Another important issue was the safety and protection of the community from the forces of Nature. Since Unalakleet was located at the mouth of a river and on the shores of the sea, the lands were subjected to constant erosion. This erosion came from the forces of the river and the summer and fall sea surges from severe storms. There were times that the villagers were forced from their homes to seek shelter on higher grounds. The most severe storms occurred in 1961, 1965, 1968 and 1974. After each event, the council sought federal help. Several survey studies were made by the federal government's U. S. Corps of Engineers and the results were always the same. It was not cost effective to build a breakwater for the tiny village. Poppa said that he told the officials: "Our homes are our castles. Every life is worth protecting." It would not be until many years later that city of Unalakleet would get a project to build a retaining dike built on the north-east side of the village that would protect homes if there is severe sea storm flooding.

Momma and Poppa were very proud to travel to Fairbanks in the spring of 1964. They attended the graduation of Emily Ivanoff Brown and their youngest daughter Frances from the University of Alaska that was on May 25, 1964. Emily had been the second grade teacher of Frances at Unalakleet. Emily was the eldest graduate and Frances was one of the youngest of the graduating class of 1964. Eva flew up from Sitka for the event. Mr. Jake Tansy and his wife Lily came up from Cantwell to be there. Their own daughter Louise Tansy had graduated from the University the previous year. Their other daughter Ruby would be graduating with Chuck the next year. It was a happy time for all. Rod Moore, his wife Margaret Anawrok Moore and her mother Nannie Anawrok hosted a reception for the graduates at their home in College to celebrate the event.

A month later Poppa and Frances traveled to Fairbanks, Alaska to attend the Conference of Villages that was organized for native groups to discuss mutual problems and solutions pertaining to Native Rights across the state of Alaska. The three day meeting, June 26, 27, and 28, 1964, was held at the Fairbanks Chamber of Commerce building located on the bank of the Chena River. (See Appendix B for report.)

Poppa was very concerned about the status of the aboriginal land claims that the Village Council of Unalakleet had filed in behalf of the Unaliq-Malemuit tribes of Unalakleet, St. Michael, Stebbins, Shaktoolik and Koyuk on the shores of the Norton Sound. This claim was filed timely before the Indian Court of Claims as Docket 285 on August 10, 1951. This was the only opportunity for Indian tribes in Alaska to seek compensation for lands lost to them. Poppa said that we needed to make sure that our aboriginal rights were protected and recognized by the federal and state governments. The village of Unalakleet was part of a federal reserve but the reserve was so small it did not encompass all the territory used by the Inuit since time immemorial.

The council members in 1965 were: president Frank Degnan, vice president and ANICA director Nick Riley, secretary Sheldon Ryan, treasurer Andrew Nashalook and councilman Harry D. Johnson. Poppa said that we would have to present our case to the government and get recognition for our tribal boundaries. Poppa said that it could not come soon enough now that Alaska had become a state and the state government was opening up the lands for development. Soon there would be "No Trespassing" signs posted where we have continuously hunted, fished and gathered since the time of our ancestors. Poppa spoke with Arthur Lazarus, who was affiliated with Association on American Indian Affairs. He also spoke with Fred Paul, brother of William Paul, Jr.. He wanted to know if they would be willing to assist the Village Council on the claims before the Indian Claims Commission.

After the conference at Fairbanks, Poppa reported to the council at Unalakleet. They agreed with him that it was important to pursue the issue of land claims. They asserted their traditional boundaries, which went to Pastolik in the South and Koyuk to the North. This included the villages of Stebbins, St. Michael, Unalakleet, Shaktoolik and Koyuk. Poppa told the council that he applied for a vacation pass with Wien (Airlines) so that he could travel on his own expense to Washington, D. C. to meet with our congressional delegation. The council agreed and passed resolutions for Poppa to carry with him as authorization to do business for the village. Momma went with him on the trip.

Momma had many stories to tell on their return home. She said that they traveled to Washington, D. C. and they happened to be traveling with Dr. Mick. They had met him when they were in Palmer in 1962. He helped them find a hotel, The Burlington Hotel, that was close to the Capitol. She said: "This was my first time to Washington so I left it up to dad to lead the way. We were there from July 6 to July 9. We had such a nice time there. The people in Senator Bartlett's office were so good to us. Your dad went to see all the officials and let them know that it was time for the water and sewer project to start. He told them about our aboriginal rights and all the land we, as villages, have use and occupied since time immemorial. We were assured that we would get our water and sewer for Unalakleet. We were very happy. It was dad's birthday on July 7, and Bartlett brought us to the Senate restaurant for lunch. We had a delicious fresh strawberry shortcake to celebrate dad's sixty-third birthday. Dad said that it was time for us to go. So we left D. C. I will never forget that trip because it was a good trip."

They went to visit June, Jim, Matthew and Juliet in Pattenburg, New Jersey. June had driven over to Washington, D. C. and picked up Momma and brought her to Pattenburg. Two days later Poppa arrived on a bus to join the family. The World's Fair was held in New York so June and the children drove them to visit the Fair. June took the family on a helicopter tour of New York City that excited them all. Momma said that she really liked the Alaska Exhibit at the Fair because their good friends Robert Mayokuk and Pearl Johnson of Nome worked there and did a fine job of representing Alaska. They went and visited Ida, Jim and Jimmy in Livonia, Michigan. There they met Jim's mother Fannie Bird and his brother Fred and Fred's wife Marilyn. After a short visit, it was time to return home and normal routine. Momma said that she was happy that she got to see where her family worked and lived. It was worth the trip, but "there is no place like home."

That summer Frances moved to Nome to work as employment counselor. She started work on July 23, 1964, at the just-opened William E. Beltz vocational school. Momma said that she was glad that Frances boarded with Mrs. Helen Fagerstrom during her stay in Nome. Helen was a dear friend of the family and was the widow of Charlie Fagerstrom. Charlie had served in the Territorial House of Representatives and served the district he represented well. Charlie and Helen had always opened their home whenever our family traveled to Nome for a few days or longer. The entire Fagerstrom family opened their homes to all who needed a place to stay while in Nome. Momma said that now she could go to Nome for a visit anytime she wanted. Poppa always stayed with Chuck and Peggy Fagerstrom. They took such good care of him. Years later, when Peggy attended the University of Las Vegas, she painted a huge portrait of Poppa which she gave to Momma as a birthday present. Momma was so proud of that beautiful work of art.

Poppa got sick that fall, and had to be hospitalized in Anchorage. Chuck made the decision to remain home to take care of the Wien bush flights and operate the taxi service. It was then that he met Virginia Breedlove. Virginia was the daughter of Henry and Agnes Breedlove and she had a younger sister named Nancy. The Breedloves were teachers at the local Bureau of Indian Affairs school for many years. After Henry retired from teaching, they opened the "Breedlove's Retreat on the Unalakleet" in 1969. Agnes kept teaching until 1976 and in 1976 they sold the summer fishing lodge they operated for many years to Dr. Gary Archer. Later Archer sold the property and business to Lynn Castle. Many years later the Unalakleet Native Corporation bought the property. It is currently being operated as the Unalakleet River Lodge.

Chuck and Virginia were married, on September 10, 1965, at Unalakleet. Frances came home for the wedding. She decided to stay at home to help Poppa while Chuck and Virginia attended the University of Alaska. Chuck graduated from the University of Alaska Fairbanks campus, on May 23, 1966, with a Bachelor of Education Degree. Chuck and Virginia moved to Bethel as he was hired by Governor William A. Egan to be in charge of the Neighborhood Youth Corps program for that area. Since Chuck was a Second Lieutenant in the United States Army ROTC in college he was required to report to active duty. He was assigned to report for duty in Berlin, Germany in the fall of 1966. They remained in Berlin until September, 1968, when Chuck was honorably discharged from service as a First Lieutenant. They returned to Juneau for Chuck to report to the Office of Governor to return to his job. He was assigned as the Neighborhood Youth Corps Director stationed in Nome. They had three children: Jennifer Audrey born on June 27, 1969, (Inuit name is Apok), Laura Leann born on September 26, 1970, (Inuit name U-gu), and John Martin born on December 22, 1973, (Inuit name Ganagzagak), and he died on September 7, 1978, in

Unalakleet. They were all born in Nome. Chuck received a Master of Education degree with a major in Educational Administration from Texas A & M, Commerce in Commerce, Texas on August 14, 1987. Virginia had taken a break from school to raise her children. When they were old enough she went back to college. She received her Bachelor of Arts degree in 1978, a Master of Education in Reading in 1981, a Master of Education in Educational Administration in 1983, and in December of 1985 she received an Ed.D. in Educational Administration. All these she completed at Texas A&M University Commerce.

In the late summer of 1966, Bunny Huffer, the daughter of Charlie and Helen Fagerstrom, sent word to Momma that Eric Johnsson was not well. He was at the Everett General Hospital in Everett, Washington. Chuck and Virginia planned to drive from Fairbanks to the Army reporting station in Fort Gordon, Georgia in early September of 1966. Frances asked to join them on their trip if they stopped in Everett to see grandpa so that Momma would know what happened to him. That was the plan. So, on September 15, 1966, the trio arrived in Everett and telephoned Margaret Johnsson to see if they could visit grandpa. She told them that he was in a coma but they could visit him. They went to the hospital and met Margaret and her granddaughter there. Margaret took them to grandpa's room right away. Grandpa did not respond to his family. It was a sad time, sad to see such a giant of a man not reacting to his family. Grandpa was ninety-one years of age. Margaret said: "Dad's doctor told me that his heart was strong but the will to live was weak." The family left the room. After Margaret left the hospital grounds, Frances said she wanted to go back for one more look at Grandpa so they went back up to his room. When they got in the door he woke up and looked at them. Frances ran to his side and said in a loud voice: "I am Frances Ann Degnan. This is my brother Chuck and his wife Virginia. Momma told us to come to see you. She sends you all of her love. She is fine. Do you know who I am?" Grandpa answered: "Yes, tell her I love her. I always loved her." When they left the hospital they found a telephone and called home. They reported to their mother the event that just transpired. Momma said: "I could not believe a miracle had happened. My dad knew who you were. I am so glad you made it in time. Later she said: "My dad died the next day on September 16, l966. After his death was when Margaret started to become close to me. After that, she would make visits to Unalakleet to see her relatives. Your dad and I would make sure she had enough Native foods that she liked. I really liked it when my sister Ann (Phillips) would come here with her mother Margaret. It was good to be with my other family because we all loved our dad dearly."

UNALAKLEET VALLEY ELECTRIC COOPERATIVE
L-R: Dale Friemering, not identified, John Moore, Frank Degnan,
Phil Stainbrook, Jack Koutchak, Lowell Anagick
in front of Degnan's quonset hut.

1964 ~ ALASKA FISH & GAME BOARD:
Frank Degnan, end right

229

49. Land Claims

Poppa and the other council members were very much interested in protecting the land base for the indigenous members of the tribe. With the State of Alaska, the federal government and a few private individuals having the only recognized land title in the village, they felt it was very important to have the small reservation enlarged to encompass the nine million acres they and their ancestors occupied to survive. This land needed to be in their possession.

On January 12, 1966, the village elections were held. Poppa was not re-elected to the council but the members elected Ada Degnan as treasurer. She was the first woman to served on the elected tribal council. Lowell Anagick was elected president, Nick Riley was elected vice-president, Allen Soosuk was elected secretary and Harry Johnson continued as councilman.

One of the first actions the newly elected council took was to set up the Unalakleet Land Claims Commission. They appointed Frank Degnan as chairman and Nick Riley and Allen Soosuk to serve the Commission to protect the village land base. At this time the native organizations throughout the State of Alaska were attempting to unify. The council and the commission were agreeable to these efforts. They would do their part to retain their ancestral grounds. This commission reported to the village council, which in turn passed resolutions authorizing Poppa and the other members to represent the Native Village of Unalakleet in matters dealing with aboriginal rights and land title to protect the land base. The council retained the services of a law firm in Anchorage. The council did not have excess capital in their meager treasury so the attorneys worked on the promise that they would be paid for their work sometime in the future or earlier if funds were available.

It was on February 7, 1966, that Jessie Otton died. Momma said that she felt so sad when their oldest sister died. She had been sick for some time. Momma and her sisters always had a strong bond throughout their lives. When Jessie died, her husband Sam remained in the family home. Their daughter Millie moved home to Unalakleet in 1962 to be with and care for her parents. Millie was following true Inuit tradition: "Respect your elders and provide help to your elderly parents." Jessie's husband Sam had suffered a series of strokes that left him partially paralyzed. Sam managed well with the aid of a wheelchair and the daily assistance of his children. Sam died at home on July 20, 1970. Momma said: "When your family members, relatives and close friends die, it leaves a big empty feeling in your heart. It feels like you lost a part of yourself and you will never find it again. I will never forget my big sister and how good she was to me. Sam was the one who saved Chuck's life. It was in the spring-time when Chuck was a big boy that our dog attacked him, back of the house. From by his house, Sam saw it happen and he came running over the snow bank to our house with a shovel. We saw him from the window and wondered what was happening. We ran out and saw the dog biting Chuck. Your dad had to shoot the dog to save Chuck. Chuck was sick from the bites for a long time. Mrs. Lorraine Londborg had to give Chuck medicine some days later and he finally got well. We were very thankful for Sam and Mrs. Londborg."

Momma told of how Poppa got involved in helping the Alaska Federation of Natives get organized. She said: "You know that your dad has always fought for native rights and he believed in them. Anyway, it was during the summer of 1966 that two men came in an airplane to pick dad up to bring him to an important meeting in Anchorage. It was king salmon season and we had a net set in the ocean so I could get some fish to strip and smoke. Anyway those men, I believe they were Fred Notti and Jules

Wright, came to the house and said they were here to pick up Frank. Your dad told them that he had to get his net and fish before they left. So he and Fred went out in the boat to get the net. The pilot (Jules) looked so tired I told him to take a nap. I fixed a quick meal for all of them. I was happy that dad and Fred brought home the net and a bunch of kings. After I fed them lunch, they left in a little plane. When dad got home he said that we would now have a state-wide organization to fight for our land claims. It was the Alaska Federation of Natives.

"It was a good thing that we started our own land claims commission here too. We were very confident that the new AFN organization would be successful. Anyway, we would do our part and keep working until the day that the state government and Congress would recognize our aboriginal rights and title to our lands. We knew it would not be easy to do just from our own experiences here in the village. Our village was just a small reservation. Our tribal council tried for many years to expand our reserve to include the traditional lands our people used since time immemorial. The council was still was not successful in getting it expanded. Your dad and the village council made sure that they had representation at the statewide meetings. The council sent Frank (Degnan), Adeline Katongan (Hopson), and Frances (Degnan) to attend meetings and to testify before congressional hearings on land claims for our village. You know it was not easy for any of us since it takes money to travel. The village council did not have much money so we all had to sacrifice to send our representatives on these trips. You can read the congressional hearing records on Alaska native land claims to see what all of our people said in their testimony."

The first state-wide convention had been held in Anchorage in October 1966. The newly formed AFN organization adopted a constitution and by-laws during their April 8 and 9, 1967, meeting. They elected officers, which included: Emil Notti as president, Don Wright as first vice-president, Byron Mallott as second vice-president, Elva Nannes as secretary, Seraphrim Stephan as treasurer, and Oscar Craig as sergeant-at-arms. Nineteen directors elected were: Cecil Barnes, John Borbridge Jr., Frank

Degnan, Andrew Demoski, Charles Franz, Tom Gregoroff, William Hensley, Eben Hopson, Axel Johnson, Flore Lekanof, Tony Lewis, Emil McCord, Hugh Nicholls, George Olson, John Sackett, Harvey Samuelson, Reverend Walter Soboleff, Jerome Trigg, and Jules Wright. The new board planned to meet quarterly each year as long as there were sufficient funds. Stanley J. McCutcheon and Clifford Groh, Anchorage attorneys, and Tom Pillifant, a B.I.A. officer in Anchorage, were made "Honorary Chiefs." These men were honored for their contributions to the Natives.

Poppa said: "We had a good group of people from all over the state and I knew that we would work real hard to get our land claims settled. We were lucky to have the Tyonek native village get a settlement from the government. The Tyoneks were very generous in the funding of the AFN to help get it started. Then the Yakima Indian Nation, under their chief Robert 'Bob' Jim, very willingly gave us a loan to help us in our fight. Also the Tlinget and Haida Central Council stepped in to help us too. You know, without their help I don't know how it would have been. I can say that all the villages and groups did their part in making the AFN work. It was not an easy time, but the spirit of the people made it work. We were unified in our effort and I believed each one of the AFN members made it work to get our land claims." Poppa was elected to the AFN Board of Directors as Sergeant at Arms at the annual conventions of 1968, 1969, and 1970. He remained at this post until the time in the fall 1972 when the organization was restructured to follow the regional corporations as set forth by the Claims Act.

Poppa was elected president of the village council on January 9, 1967. Nick Riley was continued as vice-president. Allen Soosuk was elected as secretary, and Guerie Towarak replaced Ada Degnan as treasurer as it was the rule that no two people from the same family could serve on the council at the same time. Nils Savetilik was elected as council member. The council worked on getting the water system replaced after the pump house burned down on January 12, 1967. They worked to get the fisheries' plant upgraded so that the local fishermen could have a market for their product. They continued to assert their land claims and made sure that their interests were known in hearings before Congress. They invited congressmen and their delegations traveling to Alaska to come and visit Unalakleet. The council made sure that they protected the tribal rights of their members. They knew that they were in control of their country. They were recognized by the federal government.

The village council retained the services of the law firm of McCutcheon, Groh and Benkert in Anchorage. Shortly after that they retained John (Jack) Hendrickson as their attorney. Poppa said that the law firm was retained and they would be paid when the land claims were settled. Each time there was a congressional hearing on land claims, the council sent their authorized delegates to present their position. The position presented was always that of securing title to the claimed area outlined in Docket 285. The council never changed their position that the land, sea, and air space were critical to their way of life. They knew that their federal reservation lands were too small to support their way of life and had moved on several occasions to enlarge the reservation to encompass nine million acres of their territory but the people in the federal agencies never responded to their initiative.

It was in 1968 that the federal government closed down the Air Force site that affected the economy of the community. Those people who were working at the site had the option of relocating to similar jobs connected with the military sites. Some of the workers left the community to continue their employment. Those who remained at home joined the ranks of the unemployed. The White Alice site was still operational. The crew that maintained that site came from different parts of the country. With the site still operational the village was able to enjoy radio and telephone communications with the outside world. The government still continued the air subsidy support and the community enjoyed continued jet service into the village. Another benefit provided by the workers at the site was that they kept the fifteen mile road well maintained to the village and airport. When the site was shut down in 1972, the community had no funds to maintain the roadways away from the village. To this day, the roads are used by trucks, cars, all-terrain vehicles and snowmobiles, at the risk of the driver. The buildings at both sites were sealed and abandoned. After the passage of the land claims act the village was eligible to select the land these sites occupied. The village corporation selected the land and asked that these sites be returned to the same condition they were in before the sites were constructed and used. It was some years later that Congress appropriated funds to clean up the abandoned military sites in Alaska. The sites at Unalakleet were included in the program. As a result, there were many local residents trained and hired by the contractors to clean up the sites. Today the sites are clear of building and structures but the contours of the land show where structures once existed.

In 1968, the council members were president Frank Degnan, vice-president Francis Soxie, secretary Allan Soosuk, treasurer Adeline Katongan, and councilman Nils Savetilik. When the village council learned of the planned closure of the military sites, they immediately requested the sites to be used for educational and health facilities to serve the village and possibly the region. As a result of their efforts a task force from the federal and state governments traveled to the village to consider the feasibility of using the military sites to the benefit of the village residents. In 1969, the council members were president Frank Degnan, vice-president Francis Soxie, secretary Helen Lockwood, treasurer Adeline Katongan, and councilman Alfred Nanouk. In 1970, the council consisted of Francis Soxie as president, Frank Degnan as vice-president, Helen Lockwood as secretary, Adeline Katongan as treasurer, and Alfred Nanouk as councilman.

Momma said that the governmental task force visited Unalakleet on July 2 to 4, 1970. She said, "That day the task force was due in, Francis Soxie told dad that he would have to take care of the visitors as Francis had to take care of his fishing. So when dad told me that, I said that Frances and I would help him. So we went over to the hearing at the BIA school on their last day. There were twenty-five men that came from all over the country. We told them about the need for high school, perhaps a hospital, and vocational school. We hated to see those expensive buildings and such go to waste by being vacant. Some of the people were worried about bussing their children up to the hill to go to school. I thought that we had a good chance of getting funding and the council would be in charge. Anyway, your dad had to leave the meeting to check his king salmon net. I knew that he would catch at least one king so I took a chance and invited any of the task force to come to our house to have a snack. I left Frances at the meeting and hurried home. Your dad arrived with one big king and I hurriedly butchered it. I found out I only had a couple of spuds left so I ran over to my sister Gertie's house to borrow some spuds. She had just received a whole bag of them from Anchorage and she gave me ten pounds. I ran home and started cooking. I figured that maybe one or two of the men would come to eat. Anyway I fried the fish on the Coleman gas stove and worked on the potato salad. I got it done in a hurry and the next thing I know was that your dad brought in all of the task force. When it was all over and everyone was fed I saw that they had finished the fish and all the salad. I sure was glad that they enjoyed the meal. When it was all over and the task force finished their job I found out that they would not give the site to us because it would cost too much to run. I guess it was not too expensive when it was for the military and the good of all the country but it was too expensive for a small village's use."

In the fall of 1970 the Alaska Federation of Natives had their convention in Anchorage. Poppa said that we were getting close to having something done because the oil companies were wanting to produce oil from the Arctic. He said, "We Natives did not have a problem of working together to help our people. We were united. If Congress would listen to us and work directly with us, we could settle this issue. The problem was that we had too many outside interests trying to get their way too. Our village did the best we could. We had our position. It was that of our claims that were filed when the President of the United States issued a proclamation for us to file now and forever after shut up. We believed that we filed in time, in 1951, and that we could get our nine million acres for our five villages. We were happy to join the AFN and stand united to get the best deal for our people. You know, if we had done this before statehood, they would gladly give us our own state. But that was not the case in this day and age when they found out that we were sitting on all the gas, oil, and minerals you could think of. Once they pumped the land dry and taken the minerals they will be very happy to give it all back to the Natives. But you know what? We Natives are a very peaceful and patriotic bunch of people. We have a lot of love in our hearts. We greet a stranger with a smile, invite him to our home, and share our food with him. We have always done that. That's the way our ancestors done it and that's the way we do it. If you don't have love for your fellowman, you got nothing. Anyhow, that's the way it is. We don't have all the answers, but what we do know is, is that this is our land. God gave it to our ancestors and we never left it. We greeted everyone who came in and made a place for them in our home. Now they are aiming to take it all. It is about time we say, 'Enough is enough.' Anyway, everybody did their best to do the right thing for the people. Our own thought was to divide the land in three parts. One part for the federal government, one part to the state government and one part to be kept by the Natives. What happened was that we wound up with forty million acres in the end. We were not in control. This was just a land transaction. This was a law passed by Congress and signed by President Richard Nixon on December 18, 1971. We still had our federal charter recognized by the federal government. Well, our village was a reservation, just a small one. So it was only fair that the village take title as a corporation and that's what the village did. I was not on the council any more. I figured that it was up to the people to get who they wanted, and they did. They organized as a second-class city in 1974. The village corporation was organized in 1973. We have title to a part of our ancestral lands. It is up to the next generations to do the best they can for our people. They are college-educated and got a lot of modern conveniences to work with to keep our young people at home and coming back home to work and live. I don't worry about them too much anymore."

Chuck ran for the Alaska State Legislature in 1970.

He was elected to the House of Representatives that fall. He served two terms representing our district. He served on the Finance and Natural Resources committees in the House. During the sessions the family lived in Juneau. Chuck ran for the Senate seat the next election, but it was Frank Ferguson of Kotzebue who was elected.

Chuck, Virginia, Jennifer, and Laura returned home to live. The girls graduated from Frank A. Degnan High School. They both attended Harding University in Searcy, Arkansas. Jennifer received her Bachelor of Arts in Education degree in May of 1991. She married John W. (Jack) Davis Jr. on May 27, 1989. They were both teachers and had their first assignment in Golovin. Then in 1993 they were transferred to teach in Unalakleet. Momma was delighted that they were home to stay. Their first child, John Charles, was born on November 13, 1994, in Anchorage. Momma named him Auvnue after Poppa, Iyaqungaq after Nick Riley, Bugleq after Simon Bekoalok, and Aagulgaluq after Henry Nashalook. Joy Marie was born on December 22, 1996, after Momma died. Frances named Joy all of Momma's names which were Quyan, Sapsugaq, Ah-wah-lik, and Kaalatuq. Joanna Audrey was born December 28, 1998, in Anchorage. Frances named her Nataguq after Poppa's grandmother; Killaun after Momma's grandmother; Bitcheu after Virginia Agibinik, and Anikan after Jessie Paniptchuk. Laura received her Bachelor of Arts degree in English in 1992. She married Robert (Bob) T. Lawrence on May 23, 1992. Laura received her Master of Education degree in 1993. After teaching in Arkansas they moved to Anchorage where she taught at East High School. Bob was a minister at Turnagain Church of Christ. Their son, Degnan William, was born on March 14, 1998, in Anchorage. Ruth Johnson named him Siqulgeq after her husband Harry Johnson who had died on March 29, 1998, in Unalakleet. Degnan was also named Auvnue after Poppa.

50. Senior Citizens

Although Poppa was not on the village council he remained very supportive of the council and their continued efforts to serve their membership. His last term was in 1971 as vice-president. Poppa served the village as ANICA director representing the native store for many years until the corporation withdrew their membership in March of 1979. He also represented the village on the Kotzebue Area Health Board for many years. He served on the Unalakleet Valley Electric Cooperative board until his death. He was willing to represent the village at any public law hearing that the different Congressional committees held in Alaska. One law that was critical to the village existence was the Sea Mammal Protection Act. A hearing was scheduled in Nome on May 9, 1972, and the council sent Poppa to testify. As he recalled: "I went to that hearing and Senator Ted Stevens and Senator Mike Gravel were in charge. When it was time for me to speak, I answered all the questions. I gave them our position on how the sea mammals were a part of our way of life. When Ted asked me how do I spell walrus hide (Qouq), I told him, 'We don't spell it, we eat it.' That seemed to tickle everyone."

Momma said, "Now that the land claims act passed and we had three different groups recognized in the village it meant that we had more work to do to keep our lands and rights. Those groups were the IRA, the city, and the corporation. We all had to elect our representatives to each of those groups. Somehow it just seemed to make things more complicated. We were really lucky to have a lot of our own people willing to serve. So your dad and I were real proud of our people. We all wanted to make sure that everyone was enrolled into the corporation. Our local people did the job. I think that each of the families did their part. We did not know what to expect. I think that we were glad that we got some of our lands but we wished that we could have gotten all the lands we claimed in 1951. That would have made it nine million acres."

On the statewide level, the Alaska Federation of Natives, Incorporated was set up in 1972 recognizing the corporate boundaries of the Claims Act. Poppa was surprised when the AFN selected him as their first recipient of their Citizen of the Year Award at their 1974 convention in Anchorage. He was considered as one of the original founders of that organization.

Momma said that they were both so surprised and proud of that honor because it came from our own. The following year Poppa received another unexpected honor. The University of Alaska at Fairbanks advised Poppa that he would be conferred an honorary doctorate and invited both he and Momma to the 1975 Commencement in Fairbanks. Momma said, "Your dad and I went to Fairbanks to attend the graduation at the University of Alaska. They were real good to us. Mary Jane Fate and Sam Kito were on the Board of Regents and Poppa was glad to see them at the dinner they held. Mary Jane had been a classmate of our daughter Ida May at Mount Edgecumbe. We will never forget the graduation because you kids were there with us. I can still see Eva, Chuck, Frances sitting by me. You know, it was the year that Annabelle Towarak graduated from there. I was so proud of her. Anyway, Chuck Imig was there to video the whole program for Poppa and me to have. Well, Poppa got his honorary doctorate, with his cap and gown and it was a beautiful sight to see. We will never forget that day. After it was all over and it was time to go home I wanted to see some of the country. We decided to send the kids to Anchorage on the plane. We would take the ride down the highway with Eva. That we did. It was such beautiful country. Eva and Chuck Imig took turns driving so Poppa and I were really tourists. I will never forget that trip for the rest of my life. But we were so glad to get back home to Unalakleet. I told your dad that there's no place like home. That is how he became Frank Auvnue Degnan, Doctor of Public Service on May 18, 1975."

Momma said that now that dad was not on the council he was traveling for them even more. Especially after the land claims was passed. He represented the village at the White House Conferences on Health and on Aging which were held in Washington D.C.. He made it a point to stop off and visit his daughter Ida and her husband Bill and grandson Jim in Northville, Michigan and also flew down to Florida to visit his daughter June and her children, Matthew and Juliet. Eva and her children were living in Anchorage so Poppa stayed with them on each of his trips. Momma said that she would rather remain at home than to travel. She knew her children would visit her once a year, and that they all did. She was satisfied with that.

Poppa maintained his commercial fishing license and was fishing until the limited entry permit program was introduced and enforced in the Norton Sound fishery. He applied for his limited entry permit and was denied a permit for lack of fishing in 1971. Poppa appealed the ruling up until he died. He had been holding a commercial fishing permit for Unalakleet fishery since 1952. He paid and fished each year's license, excepting for no fish sales in 1971 and he did not understand why he was denied. After his death, Frances pursued the appeal but was told you could not get a permit posthumously. So the family let the issue go.

In 1977, Poppa was contacted by Eben Hopson of Barrow about a new organization that he was spearheading. It was the Inuit Circumpolar Conference. Poppa was very glad to help out. He traveled to Barrow and helped in the formation. This conference would encompass all the Inuit and their homelands in the world. The first conference was held in June of 1977. Fred Katchatag, Anna Riley McAlear, and Poppa took part in this new beginning. The highlights were documented on film by Bo Boudart and it was entitled *Inuit* and in the fall of 1977 Poppa flew down to Oakland, California to do a part of the narration for

Boudart. He was confident that this new organization would be a successful voice for the united Inuit of the world. He was very proud of all the people involved.

Momma and Poppa loved their outdoor activities. In the spring they would be out every day to greet the incoming birds, waterfowl and rejoice to see the seagulls and arctic terns return to the country. Momma said that the last boat trip she and Poppa took to Golsovia and the twin islands was in the spring of 1979. Poppa had a new twenty-foot aluminum boat with a thirty-five horse-powered outboard motor. He wanted to take a trip to St. Michael. So she packed a lunch and they hurried off. She said: "It was a beautiful day. The sea was calm so I wasn't going to be scared. Your dad went as fast as the motor would let him. It wasn't long we were at Golsovia. We decided to check the twin islands. Maybe we could find some eggs. When we got to the rocks I jumped out. There were no eggs. Your dad said we would go to St. Michael. I looked up in the sky to check the clouds. They looked okay. I checked the water for waves. They looked okay. Then dad decided to get out of the boat. He had a tough time to get out. I had to help him over the rocks. I knew right there and then that we should turn around and go home. I said to him that we should have our lunch. He agreed and that's what we did. It was so good to be out in the clean air. I said to Dad that I really thought we had better head home. St. Michael was really too far away. He looked at me and then said, 'You're right, we go home.' That made me the happiest person on earth. On the way home the waves kept getting bigger. I tell you, I was really happy when we entered the mouth of the Unalakleet river. If your dad was going to St. Michael, he was going by plane, if I had anything to say about it. But we sure enjoyed our outing. The new boat and motor proved to be worth their price. And I still thank God for taking good care of us."

They continued to camp at Tirakpak, up the Unalakleet river, for fish and possibly a moose, if they were lucky. All of their children would visit them and the joy was to spend time fishing, berry-picking and eating from Momma's garden. They were happy when Margaret Johnsson and daughter Ann came to spend time with them at the camp. Every summer they knew that their grand-children would come to live and learn with them. Poppa's last trip as captain of his boat was in September of 1980. Momma said, "Your dad and I had good time at camp. Somehow or another I had a feeling this might be our last time up here together. We hoped a moose would come out. I caught a few silvers. Dad sat on the bank and watched me. We went home the next day. That day, Chuck had to take him to the hospital in Anchorage. What a terrible day for us all. I thank God for the good doctors and nurses at the Native hospital. All of you children came to be with us. Dad died on Thanksgiving day, November 27, 1980, at 2:30 p.m.. We took his remains home after a memorial service in Anchorage. Father Endal took care of the ser-vices at home. We buried Dad on December 2, 1980 at home. I didn't know how life would be without him. Some-how we made it. We will never forget him. We talk about him every day. That's how life is. The Bering Strait School District named the local school after him. The city council named the old city hall after him. The electric cooperative named the wind generators after him. I did not expect that, but it was nice of them to do that."

When Momma talked about her life she would say that she would not change anything about it. She said that we were all placed where God wanted us to be. She said: "I loved my family and I know they loved me. We all had to work together and we learned a lot from our moth-ers. When I got married and had my own home I knew just what to do. We were no different from our neighbors. We were all cash poor. We had to hustle to get the food we needed. Our parents showed us how to survive by using natural resources around us. This was a healthy life. We all worked hard and I can say I did not know one lazy person. We had a lot of fun too. Everyone visited each other and worked together. It was a good life, we had lot of love for each other. What more could you ask for?"

Momma was proud of her involvement with the Es-kimo Mothers Club and the nutrition program in the school. She said: "We had a good group of mothers. We were all interested in making this a good place to live. Whenever a baby was born we would present the new mother with a complete handmade layette for the new-born. We also had a small revolving loan fund for the members. This was from monies we made at our annual auctions. Those auctions were fun times. We had all kinds of baked goods, and handmade items and local crafts. The whole town would turn out for the auction. We set aside some of the money for a building fund. Our goal was to get our own building to hold our meetings and events. On our loan fund, the members could borrow with the promise to pay as soon as they could. This worked real well. When the members borrowed they always paid back. It was a good program. Anyway, the club started in 1945 and carried on until the late 70's. After that it kind of died out. I was sorry to see that happen. Maybe someday it will be started again. We always backed our IRA council and sent letters to help them get improvements in the village. We were always willing to sing at special events. We had a good group of singers. We all loved to sing and our theme song was "Home Sweet Home." When Alaska became a state we sang for the television special which was done by Martin Agronsky on July 13, 1958, which was aired on national TV. We didn't have TV so we never got to see that show. We got letters congratulating us for our excellent singing. Anyway when Wally Hickel was Secretary of Interior he sent me a letter thanking me for my services as volunteer cook for ten years at our school. That was pay enough for me. Also the mothers nominated me for State Mother of the Year in 1974 and I thank Yvonne Sarren for that. Her nomination was accepted by Mrs. Paul B. Haggland, Chairman in Fairbanks and I was recognized on March 1, 1974 as Mother of the Year. I didn't travel anywhere or read about it in any papers but since my mothers nominated me that was the real honor."

After Poppa died Momma said that she continued to take life one day at a time. That was what her mother taught her. Her brother Frank died a year before Poppa. He and Eunice were living at their camp upriver when he got sick. After some time he was admitted to the hospital in Anchorage. He died on January 1, 1979. Then in 1983 Momma's sister Gertie was admitted to the hospital in Anchorage and died there on July 18, 1983. A month later

Momma's sister Ann Johnsson Phillips died on August 7, 1983, in Olympia, Washington. She said that she felt so alone now that the older members of her family were gone. She never lost interest in her daily activities. She continued to go camping, fishing, berry-picking, and enjoying the spring and fall migration of all the birds. She kept her flower and vegetable gardens blooming each summer. All of her children and their children continued to visit her at her home. Her daughter June returned to work for the corporation as land planner in 1983 and stayed in Unalakleet until 1987. She went to Anchorage and became a teacher at Service High. Ida and Bill retired in 1987 and moved to Florida. Then in 1990 it was Bill who decided to move to Alaska. They settled in Anchorage on October 5, 1990, to be closer to Momma and their son Jim Bird and his family at North Pole. Eva was living in Anchorage and was able to visit anytime she wanted. Chuck and Virginia and their children lived in Unalakleet. Frances lived with Momma and they considered themselves as "constant companions."

It was in 1992 that Linda Larson and her son Eric paid a visit to their Aunt Ada. Linda was the daughter of Momma's sister Ann. It was a joyful event for all of us. Also the man, Dr. Bernard Tilton, whom Momma credited for saving Poppa's life in 1952, brought his wife Betty to meet Momma. She was thankful she was able to see him once again.

Momma was such a nature lover. She loved to fish for silver salmon. When the local Alaska Commercial Company store sponsored a silver salmon derby she made sure she was entered. When she was eighty years old she won the senior section of the derby by entering the biggest fish. Her prize was a recliner chair. She said it was too big for her little house and could she get another item? She selected a large canvas tarp to shelter her fish rack. She said that was a worthy prize.

Momma believed in education. She said that she never stopped learning. Her saying was, "You can always learn something new everyday if you just set your mind to do it." She loved to see the children in the village succeed in getting their formal education and encouraged all that came to her home. She said that if we take one challenge at a time we could do anything. She loved her family, she loved her village and she said that she and Poppa loved their life under the Arctic sun. That is the story of Frank and Ada Degnan.

Ada Degnan ~ 1992

Frank Auvnue Degnan ~ 1974

Photographs

1913 ~ St. Michael School: Frank Degnan holding flag

1924 ~ Unalakleet School with Momma in the back row

1926 ~ Silent picture "The Heart of the Yukon"...
Frank Degnan in parka...filmed in Washington at Mount Rainier
by H.C. Weaver Productions, 1926

1926 ~ Silent picture "The Heart of the Yukon"
...center in parka is Frank Degnan

1934 ~ Apok   *1934 ~ Frank and Ada Degnan*

1934 ~ X shows Eva and Jerry

*1939 ~ Camp Creek gold prospectors
Sam Otton and Frank Degnan*

*1941 ~ Spring camp at Ching-iat
Momma, June, Eva, and Ida*

1943 ~ Unalakleet Alaska Territorial Guard
Lt. Frank Degnan, front left

1944 ~ Chuck, June, Ida, Jerry, Eva, and Frances Degnan

1945 ~ Back Row: Apok, Eva, Jerry, Ida, and Frank Degnan
Front Row: June, Chuck, and Frances

1945 ~ Apok, Eva, Jerry, Ida, Momma
June, Chuck, and Frances

1947 ~ Gertie Auliye, Shafter Toshavik, and Ada Degnan

1947 ~ Chuck, June, Jerry, Ada and Maurice,
Frank, Frances, and Ida Degnan

1948 ~ Three sisters: Jessie Otton, Gertie Auliye, and Ada Degnan
(Photo by Charlie Williams)

1948 ~ Lena Williams, Agnes Ryan, and Martha Degnan
Kukaruq   Igailaq   Apok
(Photo by Charlie Williams)

1949 ~ Unalakleet
Back Row: Poppa, Ida, Momma, Eva
Front: Chuck, June, Frances

1949 ~ Back L-R: Gertie Auliye, Kay Downs, Ida Degnan
Front L-R: Chuck, June, Apok, Frances, and Eva Degnan

1949 ~ Back L-R: Eula Trager, Ada Degnan,
Eva Degnan, Mary Asicksik
Front L-R; Chuck, June, Frances Degnan,
Clarabelle and Thora Katchatag

1950 ~ Jessie, Sam, Ruth, Susie, Lois, and Beatrice Otton

*Myrtle, Sophie, Eva
Mildred, and Henry Otton*

Lois, Beatrice, and Sam Otton, Jr.

1952 ~ Back L-R: Ada, Eva, Ida
Front: June and Jerry Degnan

1952 ~ Frieda Riley, Nick Riley, Esther Agibinik, Nathan Anawrok,
Alice Anagick, Ada Degnan

*September 17, 1952 ~ H. May Iuier, Frank, Eunice, and Tim Ryan
at Grand Coulee Dam*

1953 ~ Chuck, Frank, and Jerry Degnan in Unalakleet

1955 ~ Ada Degnan, cook at the elementary school, Unalakleet

1959 ~ Mother's Day Picnic at North River
Eva Ryan, Marjorie Ivanoff, May Ivanoff, Gertie Auliye, Alma
Ivanoff, Roland Ivanoff, Pat Auliye, Vernon Auliye, Richard Ivanoff
with their children

1961 ~ Jim and Ida Bird with Jimmy

1960's ~ Momma's favorite activity in the winter

262

November, 1961 ~ Barrow Inupiat Paitot Conference
Frank Degnan, LaVerne Madigan, and Ada Degnan

1962 ~ Agnes Ryan and daughter Ada

1962 ~ John, Linda, and Gertie Auliye; Ada Degnan in background

1964 ~ June and Jim Hartwick with Juliet and Matthew

1964 ~ Conference of Native Organizations, Fairbanks Front Row L-R: Alfred Grant, Tanana; Bernard Nash, president, Pt. Hope; Guy Okakok, chairman, Inupiat Paitot; John Hope, president, Alaska Native Brotherhood; Tony Joule, council member, Kotzebue; Howard Rock, executive secretary, Inupiat Paitot; Robert Newlin, president, Noorvik; Archie Moses, Fairbanks.

Second Row: Mardow Solomon, Ft. Yukon; Ed Lutsen, representative, Fairbanks Native Association; Frances Degnan, Unalakleet; Frank Degnan, mayor, Unalakleet; Roy Peratrovich, BIA, Juneau; Peter Simple, Ft. Yukon; Alfred Ketzler, Nenana; Nick Gray, Anchorage; and Barbara Trigg, Nome.

*L-R: Janie and Jim Bird, Jr.; Frank Degnan;
Ida and Bill Harden, Unalakleet*

*1973 ~ Frank visited Chuck in Juneau during the time Chuck
served in the Alaska Legislature*

May 18, 1975 ~ Dr. Frank Auvnue Degnan
Honorary Doctor of Public Service, University of Alaska, Fairbanks

Clockwise: Ada and Frank Degnan, Jennifer Degnan, Agnes and
Henry Breedlove, Virginia, Chuck, John, and Laura Degnan

267

1978 ~ Frances, Ida, June, Frank, and Ada Degnan

Appendices

Appendix A-1

"Record of August 31, 1961, meeting of Native Rights planning meeting for The Point Barrow Conference on Native Rights November 15-17, 1961."

"Meeting held August 31, 1961 in Pt. Hope, Alaska. Committees as seated, Chairman Guy Okakok of Barrow; Secretary Frank Degnan, Daniel Lisborne of Pt. Hope, Alexander Vaska of Kalskag, and Edward Penatac of Nome. Chairman Guy Okakok open the floor, and have started the meeting. He said, men you all know, why we are here to attend the meeting. Meeting where no one will disturb us in our speech. First, I would like each one of you to know, we Eskimos who have been taking birds for food since time immemorial have not violated the migratory birds treaties. Right now lies the solution of the war or fight between we Eskimos and the Fish and Wildlife Agents. Yet we Eskimos have been living on ducks from generations to generations, taking the ducks with slings and other implements of our own devising before the white man ever lay his on Alaska. And I will be asking any of you committees to stand up. And probably will have further more speech about our ducks. Mr. [Frank] Degnan stood up and said, Mr. Chairman, I have heard lots about you Eskimos up at Barrow, it's not only in your place Barrow but we have same problems like you have. Since then as you mention about migratory birds, I further more will say that this treaty between United States, Canada, and Mexico be changed right away. [Frank] Degnan sat down and Mr. Chairman [Guy Okakok] thank him for having felt the same thought. Chairman asked any more objection? No one stood up and Chairman said to the committees this is one of the problems we to discuss about in the November meeting.

"Mr. Chairman [Guy Okakok] asked the committees about housing that's one of our problems. Mr. [Frank] Degnan stood up and said, "Mr. Chairman I have studied this for years and we have children, our children's children needs a modern homes, and I am asking or would like to have revolving funds for $50,000,000.00. This is a lot of money but I know our fund committee and our community can both help on this. This can go from Barrow to Hooper Bay. When Indians could have modern homes to live in, I'm sure we too Eskimos could get them. Because our children needs better education.

"Thank you Mr. [Frank] Degnan, Chairman Guy [Okakok] said, that we could get help for this and will furthermore relay this in our November meeting. Chairman asked the committees if they agreed. All agreed.

"Third. Dan [Daniel Lisburne]? have you any problems you wish to speak about? [Daniel Lisburne speaks] Mr. Chairman few years ago the atomic have placed a sign up. The Atomic [Energy] Commission have planned to blow a Nuclear Explosives. And I was not around when they held a meeting here in Pt. Hope. I myself as a citizen is against it, not me alone, but the rest of the residents of Pt. Hope. They told me, the measurement that they to blast is 40 X 60 miles. That means our hunting ground will be destroyed. If they do where are we going to hunt the games, and how are we to find food for our families. Our people of Pt. Hope don't want to move or leave their ground. I know this blaze will be so strong and dangerous, probably will effect on our own people. Dan [Lisburne] also said that why they have to draw out money from A.E.C. [Atomic Energy Commission] and not from universities. Mr. Chairman, Dan [Lisburne] asked, you better have to talk about this and explain it in the meeting this coming November. Mr. Chairman said, Dan, you have a very good speech, and will mention on this in our conference Inupiat meeting in Barrow. (No objection.)

"Fifth: Mr. Chairman, Dan [Lisburne] said, I made a motion the Assistance [Assistant] Secretary [of Interior] John Carver, Commissioner Philleo Nash, [Bureau of Indian Affairs Juneau, Alaska] Area Director James Hawkins and Executive [Director of Association on American Indian Affairs, New York] LaVerne Madigan be invited to this November meeting at Pt. Barrow, Alaska. As James Hawkins knows more about Eskimos problems. Mr. Hawkins said, we should try; to have meeting in our own village to save and vote for the delegates from each districts. He said Alaskan are so many and Alaska itself is so large we can't have just only one meeting. Frank [Degnan] said, we committees should select a good persons as soon as possible. Chairman Guy [Okakok] said there are several good and honest persons in every districts. So men, choose a right man, man who is interested in this meeting. You men are the ones to choose for delegates from your own sections or districts. It's got to be an honest person. Mr. [James] Hawkins said, he also would like to see the Arctic Brotherhood and Association on American Indian Affairs Inc. be connected together. Mr. Chairman [Guy Okakok] said they should not be two party. Mr. [James] Hawkins also said to be sure send where we choose the delegates from. The location we are going to take care of. Guy [Okakok] from Pt. Lay to Demarcation Pt.

Dan [Lisburne] from Pt. Hope to Shishmaref.

Edward [Penatac] from Wales to Golovin also two Islands [Diomede and St. Lawrence].

[Frank] Degnan from Elim to Hooper Bay.

Big problem is to solve of finance about $5,000.00 for fare and expense. Meeting was closed. President of the [Point Hope] village council Mr. David Frankson invited the committees for a good supper at Pt. Hope Lodge."

Appendix A-2

(Tape Number One of Three of Inupiat Paitot Conference held in Barrow, Alaska, November 1961, entitled Reports of Delegates and Committee Members, Side A.)

"November 14 through 17, 1961; Inupiat Paitot Conference on Aboriginal Rights held in Barrow, Alaska. The sponsoring agency was the Association on American Indian Affairs Association which was headquartered in New York. LaVerne Madigan, Executive Director helped coordinate the conference. The conference committee was composed of Guy Okakok, chairman from Barrow, Frank Degnan, secretary from Unalakleet, Daniel Lisbourne of Point Hope, Alexander Vaska of Kalskag, Paul Tiulana and Edward Penatac of King Island Village. Regional representatives were: Simon Paneok of Anaktuvak Pass, David A. Kagak of Wainwright, Herbert Konooyak of Point Hope, Mrs. Ada Degnan of Unalakleet, David Saccheus of Elim, Raymond Adam of Stebbins, Tim Kameroff of Aniak, Frank Kialook of Buckland, Tony Joule of Kotzebue, Herbert Onalik of Noatak, Willis Walunga of Gambell, Jonah Tokienna of Wales, Howard Rock of Point Hope, David Frankson of Point Hope, and Carl Kawagley of Bethel."

(Note: Much of the dialogue is in the Inupiat and Yupik languages with each of the different dialects being used. For the main part much of the dialogue is translated for those who listen to the tape and do not speak those languages could understand the content of the dialogue. The main emphasis of the conference was the affirmation of the Aboriginal Rights of the Indigenous Peoples inhabiting the Arctic. There were delegates from all the Eskimo groups in Alaska along with LaVerne Madigan, representing the Association on American Indian affairs and Assistant Secretary John Carver representing the Department of Interior of the United States government. The tape is of poor quality but is still audible.)

Chairman Guy Okakok of Barrow, Alaska: "Even though I'm president I'm asking David Frankson."

Voice: "He's not in."

Chairman Guy Okakok: "Oh. We might just as well go ahead. I would like to bring to your attention while we are here now together in an assembly of Eskimos from different outlying villages. We are here to organize to have the opportunity together and discuss our common problems. Each of us has some problems. Why can't you sit over here Frank (Degnan), you might want to speak too. This is our own conference. It is just not anyone's. It's Inupiat's own conference today. It is important to all of us because it deals with our Natives aboriginal rights. (He speaks in Inupiat.) Hunting and fishing rights and how these rights could be protected, can be protected. We have to talk over these some time today. Of development of natural resources of Natives areas for the benefit of the Natives. Such included business in every villages. So that it could run by some of you Natives. Like look as some of the Natives Arts and Crafts plans. For development of Natives retail outlets for sale of Arts and Crafts. Special problems deal with birds here in the Arctic around on this coast here. And also housing. This housing means lots to us and it seems, it would be, ah, long term loans to us, to the Natives. Program, this program will mean better health for all of us, for Inupiats, that's Eskimos.

What we need, not we alone, what every Eskimo's need is modern homes. Long terms money for relending to Eskimos to go into business. We should talk about that too. There is only one way we can to repay that service. How? How? That is to be a better citizens. Men, with God's help, I am sure we could do it. I am going to ask Frank Degnan here, our secretary, committee secretary to stand and make a speech."

Frank Degnan of Unalakleet, Alaska: "Thank you, ah, Mr. President and all of the delegates, Inupiat and Yup'iit. Tim Kameroff. [Speaks in Yup'ik to Mr. Kameroff.] I asked Tim Kameroff, he's from the Kuskokwim district, he speaks a little different dialects than some of our delegates here. I spoke in his dialect. I asked him if he understood what our President has said in English. As Inupiats, we must get together, and unify ourselves for one purpose. Our aboriginal rights. When the United States bought Alaska, they bought Alaska, not from the Eskimos. But it was just a business transaction that they made because of certain things at that time back in eighteen-sixty-seven. They had problems then. The Whiteman had problems. They were out to colonize the World. They were pretty smart. When they come to our country we welcomed them. It didn't make any difference whether they were Russians or any man that was created with a smile on his face. He was our friend. We never thought for one moment that the Russians would come in and put a flag in the ground and claim it for the Czar of All Russia. We figured when a man come to our country we went out and met him with a pleasant smile and a place to eat and a place to sleep. That was our religion. We loved our God and we feared him. If we did something wrong we were punished by the Great Spirit. Today we have what we call Christianity. All people were born equally. But we have not been treated equally. You know, last spring many things happened, up here someone was arrested by the Fish and Wildlife (agents). It was a mystery to our people why an Eskimo should be persecuted for shooting the birds or getting the bird that came in here that was sent by God up here to feed our children. It mystified us. We thought that we were free. They tell us democracy is free. I believe that democracy is the best thing in the world, when you are treated equally. We have certain rights and our aboriginal rights go back over seven thousand years. That was before, that was B.C. They claim, they tried to trace our antediluvian ancestors and said that we were Mongolian race. I don't believe we're Mongolian race. I believe the Mongolian come from us because we are at the top of the world. It is also important at this time we have no fear of anyone but God. Our aboriginal rights go back; we should have our mineral rights. We should have our gas and oil rights. We should have the right to go out and get the birds that is sent in by God not the game wardens. The birds that come in up here have been coming in for centuries. You will not deplete them. There is only one that will deplete them and protect them and that is God. Now at this meeting we are Inupiats, Yup'iit, [speaks in Yup'ik,] the Christian world recognizes that we have aboriginal rights. It makes no difference which country you come from, aboriginal means 'where you come from.' There is two people according to the Christian world aboriginally come from the Garden of Eden. Whoever put us out of there I don't know. But today we have over three billion people in the world. How did they get there? From the seed of two. We have many religions in this world. They claim Unity will win. I think the Christian world is somewhat confused sometimes. We have the Seventh Day Adventist, we have the Protestants, we have the Catholics but they have one goal, and that's Heaven. We have a goal too but we must keep our body and soul together to get to Heaven safely. Love thy neighbor as thyself for the love of God. How can you love your neighbor when he's got everything and taking it away from you. But we want to do what we are going to do peacefully through love. We hate no one but we like to be treated fairly and squarely. Thank You." (Applause.)

Chairman Guy Okakak: "Mineral Rights."

Paul Tiulana of King Island: "Our problem at King Island is our hunting rights on walrus. The Fish and Game, ah, Department gave us only five female to kill for the one year. And that isn't provide us to ah, to meet our, ah, expenses for the winter because we are, ah, living on Arts and Crafts. Mostly at King Island that is our most economy over at King Island. When we don't have any way to, ah, to support our families...another problem that we have is at King Island: we want education for our children. They go back to the island even if they don't have school there. That isn't right. Nowadays Eskimos must have more education to apply for better jobs to make it better for himself. We have been fighting out here to reopen the school on King Island...we have been trying for many years to relocate our village on the mainland. This last year I have been trying to work with Bob Grant...to get housings from the BIA. And there about is twenty-one families that would like to go to mainland to relocate. If we relocate to mainland we would have better chance to make better living in our future. We would have our school. We would have berries we could find. There is to medical and we would have post office, airfield, cold storage, a lot of things. It would be better for us. If we were to stay on the Island our children would have no education, there would be hardly any income. And we are applying for reservation now. But before that we are trying to apply for the reservation but somebody told us if we get reservation we won't have any votes, no voice, no way to get up on the land. And after I talk with Mrs. Madigan, she told me that isn't the truth. I think that covers all our problems at King Island. Thank you." (Applause.)

Simon Paneok: "Mrs. LaVerne Madigan, Guy Okakok, the chairman of the conference. But I need the help on interpreting because I have never been educated. Maybe lot of words, I would miss it, but, ah, I'll try by, and up here in my country our problem is, it is not very easy one time and after Fish and Wildlife they is trying hard to stop the caribou killing. They say we are handling too many dogs and feed with the caribou meat. But, and right now, situation is we need the dogs not like old timer.

Nobody like to pull their sled when we move around like Negro. Right now all these White people go all over the world they go by like airplane, cars and railroads and all that things. Nobody like to go move around by foot. Same thing, we like to ride on the sled a little more easy. Lot of trouble on feeding those dogs. But they, we got to have them here. We don't have any cars, and no roads and we are pretty poor and have to get the money so we could get the money on wages. Now, and all the Eskimos, what I understand, everywhere they have a one problem. I living all my life out in the bush and I am going to eat my food, I am a living on hunting. Right. Right now I would be all the Eskimos together and use their heads like and if we are believing in truth and God maybe it might come the right thing to do. All over in Alaska. So the all Eskimos can prove that they own the animals. Problems during all my life they seem to know that before my time. But if the students as we learn it from our parents, then all over inland they're in Alaska lot of Eskimos that have a animals no Whiteman people even have got time to buy...in life. Before a lot of people have going up to the east to the Canadian border. They have enough of animal. And right now, and listen from Anaktuvuk Pass up in the Brooks Range just like I was on top of the road and watching out of sight and side. Now we got to get the information and we believe the Indian Affair handling all the Eskimo problems. Sure I hope they get it better. But I believing all the Eskimos and over in the nearest Indian people in the Koyukuk. They are like a Eskimos, living too. But Fish and Wildlife Service watch them pretty close over there not like us. Ah, the Indian Affairs or the Alaska Native Service should take care of it too there; they're good people over in, in Koyukuk. Then, I say, we come together here from all of the villages from out about, its very easy together right now but, ah, thankfully all these...in one place, sure we can do what the Alaska Native Service do, we have to run together...I think that is all I can say right now, maybe a little later too. Thank You." (Applause.)

Tony Joule: "It is good that we can come together here and talk over our common problems we have in our villages. Mr. and Mrs. Frank Degnan, whenever we get together here and there around the state when we are traveling. And, ah, when we talk together, I mean stop talking together, ah, I don't think we ever got away from rights, talking about this. That's our usual favorite subject to talk about when we get together. Well, I think that 'Rights,' is really international, it's all over. The rights all over the world want to be practiced. Equal rights all over the United States, among all people. They talk about equal rights. Everybody wants it. We want it. Our Native people want it. White people wanted it. But there is always a catch to that equal rights. Even the Whites themselves, even if all they talking about equal rights. Everybody is created equal, of course. That's their favorite subjects. Why should the Eskimos and Natives have the special, the villages. Whenever we get a little headway of obtaining some help there's always some little interference that interferes if we want to get our rights. When a person becomes domineering, our neighbor become domineering among our own people. Becomes a bully. Becomes selfish. Greedy. That neighbor, whose neighbor who isn't able speak for himself suffers it, dominated. Well, we won't take it anymore. When it come to that stage, when a person has been dominated for so long he's gonna have to explode sometimes. I think that's where we are coming to. We've got to stand up for our own rights and we can't always be dominated. We don't have to. Nobody likes it. We lose our rights that way. Anybody. The Eskimo is meat eating, his diet is composed mostly of meat. One season we have seal meat. We have seal meat for so long we get tired of it. Nothing but seal meat sometimes tough and have manage to top it off with cup of tea. Am I right? Sometimes, ah, those who are fortunate enough they have well, well balanced meals. But not all of them, very few. So we are live on seal meat. We get tired of it, and we turn to walrus. We try to alternate them so that they, we wouldn't get tired of them. And we eat caribou and we get tired of it. We eat it alright even though we really don't have nothing. We have reindeer and we have fish. We get tired of that. Well. Its pretty hard. And we call, it's really slim diet. Then in springtime comes what all of us want to have little more change. The ducks come. We'd hunt. We want to eat some ducks because we have been eating meat, different kind of meat all, all winter long. That season, that spring, we want to eat ducks. What's wrong with that? If each one of you have a little garden and your back garden, pig, chickens, that would change all your diet. That might be different. I think we can see some justification there if the bird season is, is placed here and there for open season, and it might be alright. It is really pretty hard and we can't help breaking law, I mean, so we catch ducks lots of ducks so I can use this spring. I had, somebody had to say something. We got to get out and have something to eat. now in the Kotzebue area...there are men from different places from about nine villages that are always needing jobs. To supplement, something else to supplement their food, the meats they eat...just a small, small percentage of those men have jobs. When they do have a little job, its seasonal. Some of them are fortunate...a large percentage of those people have to live on the meat and fish. Now somebody can't talk to them and we all know we don't like to let our children get too far away. Kotzebue is the distributing place for boats and for airlines and ships. It really is, all the villages, up the river villages are being served through Kotzebue, even by air or boat. Like Point Hope get their freight direct. Still the airlines, they are being served from Kotzebue. And a lot of all those outlying villages. What I am about to come to is that we, this rural high schools. Since Kotzebue is center, I think Kotzebue would be ideal place to establish school."

Ada Degnan: "There's only a Mount Edgecumbe; parents don't like to have their childrens, poor substitute, we send our children too far away from us, and they get homesick and they get out of control. But if they..."

Tony Joule: "There could be a school established at Kotzebue if, we say, there is a lot of money, especially transportation money. Many of those villages here can reach Kotzebue by boat. Because it is not too far away except for Point Hope and Shishmaref, the two villages that are really...but still transportation is not too bad. So, ah, that's one of those things that we should have is high school at Kotzebue. And I also so glad to hear about the housing situation. I think that is one of the things that we really need up here. Housing. Housings are already pre-built will really help in our villages. As the houses are being built maybe somewhat easier to heat, they won't take much fuel. That will help us a great deal. Because many of those villages got a fuel situation which is very critical. It is pretty hard, it is pretty hard for a hunter to get fuel at the same time. So I think that housing is one of the biggest items we need up here. Course I wasn't planning about this ah, development of economy. That's I think there several things that would help us obtain year round economy, year-round jobs. That is the main thing we need in our villages. Because in order, well its we'd have more food, we'd save on wood, and we'd have some Whiteman's grub to supplement our food, main diet. Main diet, well balanced diet is what we need in order to be healthy. As it is even though our diet is on meat, nothing but meat...but I think it is wonderful. So...babies is strong. So I'm sure if we get that, we obtain jobs and we go through, Eskimo would be more healthy. It is too expensive to go to hospital. It's really, it's too expensive to be sick. I am pretty sure that it would help Eskimos a great deal. I have some letters here that you might like to read in regard to the council to the Governor of Alaska. Regarding to the drinking situation there in Kotzebue. Of course you know Kotzebue it's a, you know, lot of our boys and girls get together and affording liquor through out the stores it's not so good for the community. I don't know for some reason we Natives, the Eskimos have not learned how to use liquor. It don't matter which we drink, one drink or two drinks it probably would not affect but if we don't stop it becomes an item we are not able to control very much. That is one of the things, of course that I have deal with equal rights too. With equal rights involved. Why, a few drinks I don't think we have much trouble...that's all I have to say. (Applause.) I have here a letter I am going to read. A letter from The common council of the city of Kotzebue. Names as follows Mrs. Elizabeth Kost; president, Tony Joule; vice-president, Mary Goodwin; councilman, Henry Harris; councilman, Donald Mogg: councilman, James H. Hayes; councilman. Dear Governor Egan: In January nineteen-fifty-nine the results of anti-liquor election held by the city of Kotzebue is the city would remain dry in so far as the sale of alcoholic beverage is concerned. Prior to and after that time alcoholic beverages being shipped from liquor dealers in Nome to persons in Kotzebue by mail order methods. Some time later liquor shipments began to arrive in Kotzebue on a cost basis through the airlines serving this area. Through this medium of purchases many thousands of dollars have been sent annually to Nome by people of Kotzebue and many thousands of dollars have been spent by the city of Kotzebue and the State of Alaska for law enforcement. Violations resulting from this business. In September of this year a memorandum opinion was given by the Honorable Ken Gilbert, Superior Court Judge for the Second District confirming the State Liquor statute; A-five-four-one-one; ATLA 1949 as amended; Regulating the Sale of Intoxicating Liquors by Retail Liquor Dealers. In his opinion, Judge Gilbert, tells that it is unlawful for a liquor dealer to sell any liquors in any manner other than by direct sale to the buyer for cash within the premises of his establishment. The Judge listening to the rules for the sale of this product purchased within the city of Kotzebue by mail order caught or any other means than that provided by the law is a violation and would be subject to the full extent of the law. On evidence of this opinion all liquor shipments to Kotzebue seized for a period of a week or so. The liquor dealers and the two airlines serving this area were notified by the district attorney's office in Nome of the Superior Court ruling and advised that the law would be upheld. Shortly thereafter, shipments of liquor again begin to arrive in Kotzebue from liquor dealers in Nome. On the direction of the district attorney office, the office of state police in Kotzebue immediately seized the shipments as evidence as being used in action against the dealer in violation of the law. After several such seizures the Police departments were advised to discontinue this procedure and delay any further actions because the district attorney had been advised not to prosecute the violations before...could meet and set the policy regarding this type of methods. As a result...the shipments of liquor to Kotzebue by mail order has renewed as before. During this time the legal laws were being enforced in Kotzebue a pronounced improvement was noticed in the behavior of the town in general. And only a slight amount of law enforcement was necessary by the local agencies in this regard. The local merchants have stated that a noticeable decrease in business has resulted from that time which appeared to have gone out of town for liquor is now being used to purchase locally. This council is really concerned that the state law regulating this business. We have been...by the Superior Court and which is now being violated, by right and must be enforced by the law enforcement agencies. We cannot understand why the State Department of Law should find it necessary to throw away action pending decisions of the Alcoholic Beverage Control Board which in this case acted 'No Sale...we realize that this business is profitable and also deal in the sale of liquor and the upholding of the law be determined. However, we also realize that the intent of the legislature in passing the law was not that violations should go...the legislature has decided that the citizens determine by local election whether or not liquor will be sold. If it is decided by the people of Kotzebue that they desire liquor to be sold in Kotzebue now this will be indicated in local election in as much as they had decided. Until this time it should be not until we feel it is the responsibility of the state to see that state laws are enforced and that liquor be kept out of the city until the people decide and indicated by their vote. It is our request that proper actions be taken by the state immediately to enforce...as amended, to its fullest extent. Then it will have the utmost cooperation of this city that passed the law. Respectfully."

Tim Kameroff of Aniak, Alaska: "I am Tim Kameroff from the Kuskokwim River." (Tim Kameroff speaks in Yup'ik about their current life.)

Alexander Vaska of Kalskag, Alaska: "I am from the villages of Kuskokwim. These two villages...our young men go down to Bethel to work for wages whenever there is work. They earn a little money, that way they help the family with their old people and the children. Buy the clothes when they need...in a good year a family will have two hundred dollars in cash and live on that and what they get by fishing and hunting. All this our problem from the day we are born until the day we die. The people that don't live in this country don't know how to find food to people like us who live by hunting and fishing. We are not asking anything from anybody. We do not want anything from anybody. All we want is..."

Chairman Guy Okakok: "We have heard reports from Kalskag and Aniak from Alexander Vaska and Tim Kameroff. Continuation. We will talk about these problems that our people have, One: about restricted on the hunting of migrating birds. Two: State game rules. Third: White hunters. Fourth: Stumpage fees on timbers. Five: Housing. Six: Aboriginal rights to land. Generations of our people had the right to hunt these birds long before any Whiteman ever came into the land. These birds are not only for, they had to feed their animals in the spring. It has always been that way. There was no closed season for any bird or animal in other days. And a man could take care of himself without breaking the law. Now there are game laws and a man has to break the law to live. There is great hunger and hardship especially in the spring on the tundra. On the Kuskokwim (River) and on the Lower Yukon (River), but the Fish and Wildlife Service say it is against the law to shoot the birds we need for food. That makes life very hard for us. We had no money to buy food from stores because there are no jobs in our country. We catch, of course, a few muskrat but we can't eat rat every day. The law is long and cruel and is not necessary. When the birds come, they cover the sky and every man went out with his gun the sky would still be clouded. We do not waste any part of the birds we shoot. We eat every bit of the meat. We use every feather for blankets, clothes and mattresses. All we throw away is the bones. If we are going to go on living we have to be able to hunt migrating birds in the month of May until the fish start running in the river. The law must be changed to allow that. Otherwise we will go ahead and shoot the birds anyway. That is that. The government should not make us break the law. There are two open seasons. One in September and one starting on the tenth of November. Each man is only allowed one bull moose a year. If we get one moose in the first open season we are not allowed to get one in the second open season. One moose is too much for a rich sportsman who wants a head to nail or...." (End of Tape One Of Three, Side A.)

(Beginning of Tape One of Three Side B,) "but one moose is not enough for a hungry family that has no money to buy food in the store. We never hunt the moose when the fish are running. Only in the winter when there are no bears or anything else to eat. One handle to the problem would be to let us take a moose in each open season, two a year. That is still not, but that is not a real hunt answer. The real answer is that the government should say that it is our aboriginal right and land and on that land we have our aboriginal rights to hunt for food whenever we need them. Rich people should not be allowed to herd, that's white hunters. Rich people should not be allowed to come in planes and shoot the animals on our land. These people do not need the animals, they are not hungry. But they come with airplanes and catch all the animals or drive them away. We have heard that this happens up in this Arctic region too. That rich hunters in planes shoot down the polar bears and just take the skin and leave the meat out on the ice. The answer is that the land around our villages should be a Native reserve, ah, reservation that we could hunt and fish there for food and animals would be protected from the sportsman in planes who do not need food. There it could be kept up. Four: Timber agents came to our village last summer. We do not know whether they came from the federal government or the state. No one bothered to tell us. These men told the people they would not have to pay stumpage fees for timber they cut for their own use. But they would have to pay for any wood they cut for commercial use. This regulation will cause our people great hardship. Wood is like the animals to us. It is like money, we never have to buy anything with the money we can't get selling a little wood. We need this money to buy the clothes we cannot make from fur and hides and the food we can't get. We have our aboriginal rights to our land and the animals and wood on our land. We should make regulations to protect the supply of animals and these wood for the future generations but our right to these things must be recognized. Five: Housing: Food is a terrible problem our people think about all of the time. If we knew that we had enough to eat, if our food supply was safe, then we would move on to our next problem. That's housing. Our villages need new housing on the little children's sake. These little ones need decent homes. They need to know what sanitation means. There are no houses for the young married couples. They have to live their parents or their parents have to live on their parents houses. Outsiders may say we want to live like that but they do not know us. They do not understand. We have heard about public housing and government programs built houses that poor people can rent for thirty-five or forty dollars a month. And these poor people can't pay that rent in some places. In our villages a man would have to be rich to pay that much, and nobody is rich. We are hunters and fishermen, we do not earn salaries so we could never be sure that we could pay rent every month. We need a special kind of housing program. Maybe it should be called 'Ask Him Self Help Housing Program.' We need a twelve by twenty-four log house and each family should have one, we could cut our own logs in our own forests. Pick, peel few logs for our own houses. We could built the houses with our own hands. All we would need from the government would be, ah, three or four Hundred dollars. For the flooring, the windows, the roof and a little tar paper for keeping the house from leaking. Number Six: Aboriginal rights; We have talked about the problems of hunting and fishing and timber but these are not really separate they are all the same problems, all the same problems off our aboriginal rights as a people who were here before any one else came. When Alaska was purchased from Russia the United States recognized that we Natives have rights and said that some day Congress would say what those rights are. Then when Alaska became a State then the United States recognized our rights and said again that some day Congress would say what our land and hunting rights are. And that Some Day never come. Now that Alaska is a state we Natives can homestead but so can Outsiders come in and homestead on the same land that is on our aboriginal rights. Also if there is gas or oil or minerals in the land they will not belong to us. How can we be homesteaders on the land when we lose, when we have no special rights to our aboriginal rights, land when the Alaska Purchase Act and the Alaska Statehood Act said that we do have special rights. There are some white people who try to tell us that this can not be equal citizens that we have aboriginal rights that anyone have. That does not make sense. The Natives and the Whiteman are not different politically because they are all American citizens. But that political equal has nothing to do with our lands and hunting rights. We are our aboriginal rights. Now we know who has the percentage to be an aboriginal and they cannot be aboriginal too no matter how hard they tried. We think that Congress is serious in the Alaska Purchase Act and the Alaska Statehood Act and give us Native people the land and hunting rights that we have. We think the Interior Department should tell the State of Alaska until the Congress passes a law the state will stop. The Department of Interior should withdraw tracts of land around the villages and reserve this land and its minerals for the Natives and stop Outsiders from staking this land until the Congress passes a law. Maybe the Department of Interior could withdraw these tracts in the villages and then give all Native people the right to hunt and fish freely anywhere on this withdrawn land. Now that is our Recommendations. We have the delegates here at the Point Barrow Conference on Native Rights to join us in that Recommendation and make it better and stronger." (Applause.)

David Saccheus of Elim, Alaska: "I am very glad to be here and I have been called by the Committee to attend a meeting. We also have problems. The hunting and fishing problem we have down there too. We are living off the center and we do not live like these people down there at Kotzebue. We are living off game, seals and all kind of animal what you can get. And so are the other neighbor villages like Norton Bay. And this game law hurt us a lot last spring. We have had been duck hunting before. We can get all the ducks we want before and we were doing very good. But this last spring, that hurts us a lot. We can't buy no canned goods from the store and we don't carry a lot of money in our pockets and very few people do, alright. But most of us doesn't carry checkbooks like those people. When hunting season comes along last spring when game warden flies along and where we used to hunt, on the flat, hunt ducks. We like to eat ducks. We like to eat fresh meat. We like to eat whatever we used to eat before when our fathers, our ancestors that used to get before. Now that hurts us, our livelihood. And last fall we were doing pretty good when September came and we were allowed to hunt few ducks and geese. And we were getting some moose too. You know we get tired of seal meat whenever there is no fresh meat of other kind. We don't eat seal meat all of the time. We get seals alright, we get some oogruk alright. We get walrus. However we don't get any whales like Point Barrow people does.

But we should have and use or whatever we can the game we have been using before. Those people out there make laws and have no representatives from up here. They just made laws down there and don't know what they are doing down there. After they know, they would, they would make a laws better as laws. However, without no representation up here, it does hurts a lot of people, it hurts us, hurts, it hurts down right in our country, down in Norton Bay, Kotzebue, Point Barrow and all those that live in Bristol Bay area and Kuskokwim area. What we need is have better laws and better leading for the poor Eskimos like us. And that is why I am very glad to be here with meeting. That we accomplish something before we go home so we can have better time and better living. While I was around there, one time, about a couple of years ago while I was out hunting, there's a sports hunter come along, a sports hunter come along and shot the ducks, and he shot them and shoot them ducks that he shot and just look at them and leave them right out in the country. Well, he was just sports hunting. Wasting ducks. Waste, waste the good meat for us. Now I always thought about that before I'm after. Sports hunting is what I don't agree with because we don't hunt like for sport. We hunt for our life. We hunt for, what? For our children! And we should have better rules for our children. And that's all I can say." (Applause.)

Voice: "What is your name?"

David Saccheus: "This is David Saccheus from Elim."

Chairman Guy Okakok: "Before I call this man's name I had a letter from Lloyd Avakanna from Anchorage. And Lloyd Avakanna from Anchorage says that Carl is a full time member of the National Guard and an active member of the Alaska Native Brotherhood of Alaska. And I did not know him until now. Carl."

Carl Kawagley of Bethel, Alaska: "Carl Kawagley from Lower Kuskokwim. And we have similar problems as the people who has already talked ahead of me. We have same kind of troubles. The hunting problems are the same as the Elim boy just said. And last spring, last spring was a shock to us when the game wardens arresting our people. Why they arrest these people? Cause, just because they went out to get something to eat. Well, I got a letter here from Emmonak, that's lower part of Yukon. It says the feeling of the Eskimos on the Lower Yukon and coast about hunting of ducks and geese and all birds in the spring for livelihood was last spring putting a hardship on the people. Since man was able to shoot and set snares or traps for birds has been done regardless of what the law says. It was 'Live or Starve.' And therefore we dare anyone if he's in our shoes and living as we do to try and go without getting birds to eat for food in the spring. It has been our way since God knows when. And when someone tries to change our way of living overnight has got a real problem. We know now that the people in Siberia do hunt and eat birds in the spring. And these days the people do not use many birds as they used to. We have not, we get bird in the spring. But we use the feathers, use the feathers for blankets, pillows. They use the feathers for their jackets. They don't waste food, all they throw away is bones. Now why who make these laws saying that we, we the people cannot hunt in the spring-time? Who has made these laws? Has the people of Alaska them-selves make these laws? By getting together here at Point Bar-row Conference our purpose is to help each other. Our purpose here is to find out our problems and to help each fellow Alaskan to live a better way of life. Well that's all I have to say for now. Thank You." (Applause.)

Chairman Guy Okakok: "Let's hear from Onalik, ka-nook-at-tah..."

Herbert Onalik of Noatak: (Speaks in Inupiat.) (Continues in English.) "Well I get nothing much to say, see I didn't have no reports to take along with me so I think that that's just about all. Thanks a lot."

Chairman Guy Okakok: "Point Hope."

Howard Rock: "Mr. Chairman, Miss Madigan, ladies and gentlemen. I am very happy that I was also invited to this meet-ing and I think you can never stress too much the importance of this gathering in Barrow. This is, ah, primarily I think this or-ganization should hear all of us, should think about very, very seriously and really make it work. Because I've heard requests from different areas that some attempts have been made to try something like this. For some reason they haven't worked, you know, to what they are supposed to do. So I think all of us should realize how important this is and really make it work. Cause that way we could much better fight, ah, the problems we are talking about now. And unification of all the Natives up here we could use our unity, our hopes and anything like that whatever problems that are facing us. And another thing I would like to stress here is education...I think that the best way to do that is through proper education of our young people starting now. I keep hearing reports, remarks here and there that the standard of education of Natives, Eskimos, is somewhat below average. I do not know if it is true or not but I keep hearing it today. And to get proper education I think we might find out the standards of education of other areas like Fairbanks area, An-chorage area so our young people could be graduated from high schools followed by working in the universities. And I keep hear-ing this that our young people graduated from high schools are not too well qualified. That could be due to well below average education and they are not well prepared to enter our university or college and to compete with other students you know who are much more qualified than they are. So I think something like that should be corrected through something like this conference. Because, like I say, civilization is right upon us, we cannot escape it and we might as well do what we can to live with it. And we could do it by proper education. And we have another problem that I have in mind that we at Point Hope are very much concerned. And that's Project Chariot. I understand that this is just an experiment. An experiment just to see how if atomic power could be used to move or dig or excavate land. And there is and I understand too that it is just an experiment and after they are through with it. Well they would be through there they would go somewhere else after they found out what that atomic power could do to excavate mountains and things like that. Well, that Project Chariot is only thirty miles from Point Hope. And we had a meeting with AEC (Atomic Energy Commission), officials up there at Point Hope this summer. And it was a long meeting about four and one-half hours. And all through that meeting that we noticed, lots of us up there we noticed it. What they talked about, when they were talking about it, there was always 'if,' 'maybe,' 'perhaps,' 'possible,' words like that. And they are not sure. And they will and they admit it. You know, if that thing is set off, they admit it they will be some radiation. And they don't know how much will escape. And then, ah, there's a chance there'd be, well, miscalculation in the explosion where a great deal of radiation could escape. In that case, a lot of land around the explosion area would be contaminated with radiation. And lots of you know that we have caribou, we pick berries there. We hunt seals, whales, walruses, all the sea animals. Well all those people and animals in that area can be affected by this radiation. And there is another thing, if they explode that device up there, a lot of times our wind is southwest up there and sometimes the wind blows from the southwest and that would be going to Wainwright that is towards inland. And that wind blows from one direction for days, I guess. That's the ideal time to would take it up there. The wind could shear. It could shear toward Noatak not very far from the explosion area. And then shear towards Kotzebue then the winds change toward Wainwright. Then somewhere indirectly to Fairbanks. Indirectly all these areas would get some contamination from this explosion. And it's a scientific fact that I learned sometime last year, sometime during the year. In the Point Hope area around Cape Thompson there was some two hundred thousand caribou grazing there. That would include the herd from Point Barrow and from Canada this way. Caribou migrate from up all those back there up to Point Hope to graze around in here. And this is something that takes place. Where this caribou is grazing a lot of that would be contaminated. The caribou eats mosses, grasses and from what I understand that grasses and mosses soak in radiation like a sponge. And that is the favorite food of the grazing caribou. And if that happened the people in Wainwright and Point Hope, Noatak and Kotzebue, some of those animals they kill might be contaminated. So this Point Hope meeting we had was very much needed for us. So some of you who come from the northern part of Alaska should know that there might be some contamination of these animals. Of course we are trying to stop it. I think we have made some little progress on this from what I understand and wishing there would be more. So I think that is about all I can say about it. Thank you very much." (Applause.)

Chairman Guy Okakok: "Thank you Howard. We have heard the report Point Hope people. I would call on David Frankson from Point Hope."

David Frankson: "Ladies and Gentlemen, I am very happy to be with you all. I have to say sometimes I have a little trouble with my English language. I am President of Point Hope Native Council for the past several years. Our main problem at Point Hope is Project Chariot. I would like to talk about it. At the time when the Project Chariot was started at Cape Thompson. We don't quite understand what it is all about at Point Hope for several months and finally we got the point what they are at. Cause first when we heard it, there was going to be a project up on that. We thought it was for a government work that they are planning to make a harbor for all the boats under government control Then later on we heard it just experiment. It is going to be just experiment. Because we, I don't understand too much about radiation. How the radiation works. After the bomb explodes, but the radiation is pretty bad for all the living creatures. So after the day after we find out we at Point Hope don't want that Project Chariot. This Project Chariot it is going to be exploded underground. Where underground I don't know. I do not know too much about that. So I want you people to know the people at Point Hope that I represent right now are against this Project Chariot at Cape Thompson up to this day. Even though they say that they are doing some findings about before whether they explode that nuclear there or not. Until they find out whether this bomb won't affect any creatures or humans. They told us that they won't do it if they think that it will affect the people and the animals. We believe them but even though they say all the Point Hope feels, after they had noticed this all the Eskimos at Point Hope how they feel about it. Maybe all scared. I know for sure. And we are all objecting very much about this what is going on. Most of the Point Hope people would like to have all of Russians know that they are objecting to Russian tests. All the Russians tests. What we are understood about that, I do not know. To our understanding at Point Hope, the testing, the Russian testing in the air. And the United States are planning to test maybe some places under the ground. And our government say the tests that they will make will all be exploded under the ground and the radiation will come up. And it will be decayed before it come up on the surface. Well, I'm so stupid about that I guess, I don't take not too much interest in what they are saying about it. But what I think today is this way. The United States is testing nuclears underground. The Russians is testing in the air. After ten or twenty years are these radiation from the above and under the ground are being worse. What they gonna be? Probably after we all dead. They never do care. I can't tell, I don't know. That's what I thought about. So that's why I tell you about it. Now about the ducks season. The duck season in Point Hope, we take the duck season for this area is upside down. It should be straightened up so the people can have the ducks for their food at the time when they can get it. For at the time when the ducks is plentiful. Now in fall at Point Hope when the duck season is open we don't pay any attention to the ducks that fly. We have some other Native products, some other animals to hunt all at that time And in the springtime that's the time at Point Hope that we hunt ducks. And they're real important in the coming days. Lots of you all understand all of the schools, their educations and all that we would like to talk about. We are all in favor of our Eskimo kids to get as good education as possible like Whiteman's land. I did not show this morning because I didn't get this paper I didn't go around to Na-lug-gu-tak (dance) last night. I went over to that hall where the time is. There's nobody there. So I attend this morning meeting. So for the time being that's all I have." (Applause.)

Voice: (Speaks in Inupiat about Cape Thompson.) "Ducks and game warden. They hunt the ducks for food for the kids...depend on land and sea for food." (Applause.)

Jonah Tokienna: "Fellow Inupiaqs, when I first got the notice that I was selected, nominated to attend the Point Barrow Conference on Native Rights by Mr. Edward Penatac I was in doubt. But now after hearing the speeches that was presented it is my desire to assess and point out as best as I can what has been presented. I am with the Native Village of Wales Council and a member. Before I attended the Wales Council has presented me and desired me to present problems that are affecting everyone, Inupiaq, all over Alaska. Studies in Alaska villages, in outlying villages area. Number One: Migratory birds; Fish and Wildlife Service, the greatest harm to the Natives when they went past their rights and arrested Natives in Point Barrow last Spring. Everything, to my community, was wrong. They were aware, they written several letters to the people there that represented Alaska in Congress. Saying that the treaty between the three nations, the United States, Mexico and Canada, get them together and rearrange and get the Natives the benefit in getting the migratory birds. That is the healthiest things...before the Whiteman's rules...they were the general diet, they cannot live, they want certain things...it is a gift. We are aware of that, it is not a sport. These people, from the lower forty-eight...with aircraft, these thing, when they get, they just leave it, they forget about it...the same thing with the polar bear...they leave the polar bear...they hunt, they fly around, they scare off the polar bear. The Native by that, they get deeper in poverty. Walrus hunt, for one...they hunt for ivory to help their families out...when Fish and Wildlife stops...They waste the food, the Natives good food...the people from the Lower Forty-Eight come up, they want to take over...we want the opportunity to develop...the Natives should have the facilities...they have a hard time...why? Because the Natives are...they are building up in their Store. Then there is that resupply to that question. Because they do not have the money to get the resupply...we get deeper, how are we going to help our people...they are taking our walrus, they are coming in by air. They are coming in and leaving the animals. Therefore we should have some action on that. Now in hunting, why do they want to make such laws. What is the problem, before they have to understand the Natives, that's their way of life...in the outlying areas, in Wales, lot of times, in springtime, when the current switches you see a lot of headless walrus laying on top of the ice. That's not right. Those people out there are hunting just for the ivory. Maybe when they are hunting...they do not take everything like the Natives do...the Natives get for food; they do not waste what they get. They use them all. And in the springtime lot of the people already used their winter supply. And then the fish along the coastline and all the way to Wales, they want their fresh meats, fresh food. The first means for getting away for fresh foods from what they have been eating all winter. And in the springtime always there's a lot of ducks when they migrate past the Natives don't have airplane or anything for that matter to get them because they are flying too high. This is the wrong time. The Fish and Wildlife Service have set...." (End of Tape One of Three, Side B.)

(Beginning of Tape Two of Three, Side A.) Secretary **Frank Degnan**: "This committee and delegates, the problems for discussion and recommendations. Number One; Aboriginal rights. That means, you gone through that. And that's the most important one of all. It concerns our land. It concerns our hunting. It concerns the fish and wildlife. It concerns, it means more to us than all the money in the world. Our land rights. You can spend all your money but they can't move the land. So hold on to your lands. It's important. Out of this land you can collect royalties. Out of this land you can take care of your families. That comes first. Suggestion and Solutions: Interior Department withdraw tracts around villages pending Congressional action to settle Native claims and to allow all Natives to hunt and fish on withdrawal lands without restrictions. That means if you can get your aboriginal claims and the Secretary of Interior can withdraw portions big enough so that you can hunt, fish without being molested by the game wardens. That is very important to all of us. Interior Department prevents Project Chariot on the grounds that the lands claimed by the Natives cannot be legally given to AEC (Atomic Energy Commission) by Bureau of Land Management. That's very true. You got to get that down on record. We should have been working on this last night. Time is pressing. It is important that we get together and get these resolutions in. Two: Housing; Suggested solutions. Federal Housing programs. Eskimos Self-Help housing. You know, we need homes. Some areas are hard to get to. Some are easy. Some may have modern homes. Some may be self-built with the help of the government. They claim that the government's got to help you. It is true. With their help we can do a lot. But if we get our aboriginal claims we can help ourselves. But right at the present time we will have the federal government, ask the federal government for help. Three: Arts and Crafts; Discussion was in Eskimo. You remember that come on our tape recorder. Four: Tourist Business; The reason why we have tourist business because we got to bring them in and get all the money we can out of them. If everything concerns the Whiteman, is money. And he wants the tourists to come in with their money. They don't care for the tourist but they like to get their money. But we need them. The airplane companies gets their money on their airplane tickets. All the merchants gets their money through their business. And you know how people are, they have to take souvenirs home. And I think our Eskimos are tops in Alaska where they can do great business. Let's get some of that money going into our Eskimo peoples' pockets so we can buy something. Discussion was in Eskimo. Five: Landing Strips for Villages; We have villages in the outlying districts that have strips that are not safe to land on...Six: Minerals;...Seward Peninsula get employment for mining camps. That's very good. If they could raise the standard, the price of gold. That means more work for our people. Not only for our people but others as well. Seven: Education; There was unanimous opinion the Eskimo children should be encouraged to continue education. That is very true. The reason why we never send our children to school long before now because our family ties was so strong. We love our children. We hated to send them away because we was afraid they may never come back. Today we are not afraid anymore. Let them get their education wherever they can get it and go any part of the world. We have transportation. We have airplanes. We have communications. Its modern today, not like in the olden days. Education is very important. After few, children should not have to go far away from home to attend schools. There were special requests for high school at Kotzebue and a high school near Teller Mission. That is very true. In my community I tried to, I'm from Unalakleet, we tried for that school that was passed through legislation. A boarding school, to create employment and educate our children. We tried very hard to get it in Unalakleet. Because we thought that it was centrally located. We could have created employment for our community but the Chamber of Commerce went to work and they got it in Nome. So it's okay. We will still use it. Eight: ANICA; ANICA is Alaska Natives Industries Co-operative Association. That's your Native Store business. Nine: Election of Eskimos to State Legislature and Congress: That was brought up at our meeting and it is important to think about and campaign for our people to fight for us. Ten: Organization to continue the work of Point Barrow Conference on Native Rights; There is nobody can work better than the Natives for their own rights. That is very true. The following problems of special villages were mentioned. These problems were not common to all villages. One: Natural Gas, Barrow; this is also question of aboriginal rights. You people here in Barrow, if you had your aboriginal claim, you would have gas today. And you would be collecting royalty from the people that come here. Standard Oil, the Army or Navy or whoever came. We were asleep when this happened. But today we are awake. Let's get the Secretary of Interior, if they withdrew this, if we have certain portion of our land withdrawn for our people as a reserve to be taken care of through Congress in a future date. Let's make a request that when the Navy turns back this land, not to give it back to the state. But give it back to the Natives so that they can collect royalties, have their lights and gas like the rest of the people. They can do that in foreign countries, they can do it here. This is democracy. They'll do it for you. But you have to work for it. Faith without works is dead. You've got to work for it. You got to ask for it. Now is the time to do it. We're pressed for time. Maybe I am talking too much. The following problems for specified villages were mentioned. One: Natural Gas for Barrow; This also a question of aboriginal rights. Two: New King Island Village; There's an island out in the Bering Sea called King Island. Its got a wonderful name and wonderful people lived on it. They would like to get a reservation and I believe they have that program already set up and that also can be on aboriginal claims. Maybe move in from the island on the mainland they'll have a better living. They could start a new city of their own. Not second class but first class. Three: Violation of Liquor Laws at Kotzebue: You heard that mentioned yesterday. Four: Project Chariot, Point Hope; This is also a question of aboriginal rights to land. That is very true. And it come up at the right time. When the world is confused. Atomic bomb, the hydrogen bomb, the atom bomb. You had very good members here explaining this in your own dialects and in English. I was very proud of them. Five: Need for water system at Stebbins; for health and sanitation that is very important. Because the waters close. It's only two and a half miles away. All they have to do is get a pipeline in there and siphon it and it will run itself downhill. It don't cost too much. Those things we can do. It takes too long to go through legislation. We are Inupiaqs. We have to ask for these things. This is what we are doing today. Need for sanitation program at Unalakleet: Unalakleet is not the only one that needs sanitation, we need sanitation right here in at your back door. That concerns everybody, Eskimos, Indians, and Whiteman alike. Seven: Needs following at Teller Mission; Salmon cannery, post office, Native store, high school. There is more work to be done. This is just an outline of what we are supposed to do. This is what we are going to work on this morning. Let's all get our heads together and get this program a going. We've very short time. It is now a quarter to ten (a.m .). Eleven-thirty (a.m.), if the plane comes on schedule, the people that we have to present it to, will be here. We have time. But not much. Thank you." (Applause.)

Jonah Tokienna: "There is one other thing that I would like to bring up before we actually get into the discussion. That is the mail service with our own people up here. King Island, St. Lawrence, Diomede Island all the ones that are not getting enough cooperation under the mail system now. In many cases, the most important things, the letters concerning the store, the schools are delayed. In fact, in some cases, the letters that have to be on time to be received by the NCIOC's of the National Guard. They are the ones that are going to be protecting us if anything happens. Our Natives across there, if they get over here, and if the military keeps its at the rate at it is now our lives are at stake. So we must stress this farther and get some improvements on the mail service on the outlying districts of the United States in our State. I Thank you." (Applause.)

Chairman Guy Okakok: "Thank you. You've heard most everything what we are going to discuss this morning. And our secretary Frank (Degnan) here mentioned most everything. How about this one here? Would you read that? People. We haven't got very much time. Now as is we only have two days ahead. I am sure you hear I had to cancel the meeting last night. Which we could have done more. Especially to the committees, it never mind much to the delegates. We would have bring everything last night and then get it over with. I noticed that some of you, you never, you didn't go to the services last night. If I could have hold some of you here, in this building, and work on our programs. I am sorry I had to say this. But anyway we gonna do the best we can. It is important. Let's do it. From all sincerely heart. I know we can do it. It is the time now to work on our problems. Well, I have challenged myself, I have lived here in Barrow for several years, fifty-four years, over fifty years now. So I never did notice that we had this gas all the time. Not until several years ago. I found that out. And now it is right under our houses. And I think we have to discuss on this first thing of all. Whether it be a right for you people or not. I know you more could help us on this. I need this gas very well to myself, especially to our children. Just look at that family over there, over on the other side, it is not shown here. See this house. A poor family like me. No dogs, they don't have any dogs. They don't have any vehicles, anything like this. They go along through these streets here and get their materials, woods and things like that. And their children's are starving. Not really starving. But they come to school without anything in their stomachs. Empty. No heat. They know that this gas is here. And they could use it. And I am gonna ask Frank (Degnan) here. He can give you more information than I could. Whether we would speak about it first and discuss. It's up to you people to discuss, you know, and work on these problems. Frank."

Frank Degnan: "Delegates, committee. It is important. We know. Our aboriginal claims covers that. So if we can get started on this. We have our gas and oil rights. And it is on the headlines. We got to stress on that in Point Barrow Conference required something for us here. What we did here today. Get it on record. It will help all of us. We got to get started somewhere. It is important in Point Barrow and Point Hope, Chariot. Its a headliner. And if we could put it in words before our Secretary of Interior, the rest of the committee. We have no time to argue or discuss about the other problems right at the present time. Let's get to work and get this on record. We have less than two hours. But your aboriginal claims will cover your ducks, your land and your housing in your community. The most important thing now is get this gas and oil and the land reserved. When you got that you won. That takes care of the Chariot, the atomic bombs and the rest of the housing and schooling. We have to choose the voice on the committee to help all of us. We'll help. Howard (Rock) should be working on the committee. Howard Rock. And (David) Frankson of Point Hope. And the rest of the committee get together now and draft. We have a pattern to go by. And I am sure that will take care of our problems from Point Barrow to Hooper Bay. What do you think?"

Howard Rock: "Mr. Chairman, as I understood it, this report to the Assistant Secretary (of Department of Interior) is to be drafted tonight. And I think we should discuss what we should say in it here at this moment. And some questions to, well perhaps, to ask Assistant Secretary today. If he is going to be in the meeting. Some questions we want to ask him and get those straightened out so we know what we will say. And that way we won't have to grope around for anything you see. If we have those things beforehand we can work so much smoother you know."

Frank Degnan: "That's very true."

Chairman Guy Okakok: "But I don't think the Secretary Carver will come into this building. That's why I would like. Between nine and twelve he will arrive."

Howard Rock: "Well anytime, you know, that way we'll have some few questions ready. That's good. We'll do it."

Voice: "How we discuss it, each subject at a time?"

Chairman Guy Okakok: "Each subject at a time. Oh yes. I think it will be better that way, committees, delegates?"

Voice: "Yes. When we get through with this one we go on to the next."

Voices: "Yah. Yah. That's it."

Howard Rock: "You can tell us what to discuss and then we will try discuss it. And get more information on it and move on to the next one. That way we can do more."

Chairman Guy Okakok: "You've been on this for quite a while. Why don't you all sit down and quiet down. I think that Frank [Degnan] got more experience on how to make drafts and it's important to be getting in our best to help. Cause we don't have much time now. Yah, that's good. Let's go ahead and start off this right away now."

Howard Rock: "I think like I said about discussions on each problem what a lot of you presented to the meeting here. Discuss each problem that well that some of these villages presented to the meeting and we need to fill in a little more what you want to say in it and you know recommendations and something for what you want to say in this, on that subject. And then we can hash that over tonight and whenever we are going to write what we say and decide what's important and be through."

Chairman Guy Okakok: "Thank you, Howard."

Frank Degnan: "Committeemen, we get together to table the area papers and we'll draft to the best of our knowledge what we should do. Each one spoke, remember, yesterday,"

Howard Rock: "Yes, on their problems."

Frank Degnan: "And all problems concerned aboriginal claims. And that covers everything. And if we keep a talking, and explaining each one, each community, it's going to be a long dragged out session. So, at this time, we will make it as a committee as a whole. We get together and get our ideas together and draft, an honorary draft, it would take in everything from each IRA (Indian Reorganization Act tribal council) and in the meantime from this draft we. automatically put it into words for it to be presentable. You know Inupiaq, he puts everything in. Sometimes there are twenty-two things that are very important, it covers most of everything. And this time we should tell the committee as a whole, what I mean, the committee and the delegates. We all get together and get it into writing and go to work. We have here a program. We need papers?"

Tony Joule: "I got papers here."

Frank Degnan: "Tony Joule, could you help us out on the draft?"

Tony Joule: "On our aboriginal rights and the other on economics. So I'll ask our man here, Howard Rock, to read this. I can't get the writing."

Howard Rock: "This is the outline with what we intend to do to work out the final report on aboriginal rights and economics and social development. The group should write a statement of policy and recommendations. And resolutions should be passed adopting the policies as the official policies of the Inupiat at the Point Barrow Conference on Native Rights. The policy statement should say that there are two types of problems. Aboriginal rights and economic and social development. The statement should then discuss both problems. The aboriginal rights section should tell what aboriginal rights are. And it will include Purchase Act, Statehood Act. Second, what aboriginal rights will include: hunting and fishing, timber, mineral rights. Examples; Kalskag—timber, Barrow—gas. Third; probabilities where, this is found about these rights and...Four; Recommendations: Congress should settle Alaskan aboriginal claims. All villages should be truthfully informed about issue and be permitted to apply for a Reservation or to sue U.S. (United States) for land or place they were defrauded. Interior Department should withdraw tracts of land around villages that applied for settlement of land claims pending action by Congress. And we suggest to the chairman. And there's more positions. Here's the issue; migratory birds, Project Chariot, economic and social development section should include; housing, education, liquor law, airstrips, water supply, reindeer herds, arts and crafts, ANICA and tourist business. Sewer systems et cetera. A little more here. The concluding statement should say that each village should discuss and understand and Inupiat should try to meet in permanent Conference on Native Lands. That's is the future you should try to work out plans so that we can meet and decide on it once a year or something like that. So we can think about that and we be ready to say something on that. So what we are trying to say here is that we are going to write a final statement on what we have been doing. And that is to be presented to the public. And John Carver and others. And then we have listed two committees. One's our chairman and our other committees to approve. We sent that to the chairman and he form two committees. Each one to write a section on aboriginal rights and the other on economics. And here's a list for aboriginal rights: Jonah Tokienna, Frank Degnan, Paul Tiulana, Howard Rock, Hank Kanayurak. And on economics and social development: Tony Joule, Edward Penatac, Willis Walunga, Daniel Lisbourne. Oh. David Frankson on economics."

LaVerne Madigan: "And then there is one thing we talked about and that is the committee on economic development can take care of the papers that were written today and they can go over that and take out the problems of the different villages that were mentioned there. Which ones that want airstrips and so on and incorporate into that section of the statement. The people working on the text on aboriginal rights won't need the report because this is more of an idea. We don't need all those little facts there. This whole principle of aboriginal rights. So I would think that all this papers should probably be turned over to Mr. Joule's committee. Don't you think?"

Tony Joule: "Yeah. Mr. Chairman. I agree.... As we form this, as we write on this, we can help in to the attention of matters that count on the Indian Rights. We have to catch up on those things too. Under our subjects, our main subject, it seems to me. Do you understand what I mean there."

LaVerne Madigan: "We thought after the two committees worked real hard drafting the statements if they can have them ready later this evening and we could put the two of them together. And take things out of one and set in the other."

Chairman Guy Okakok: "We have to come back."

LaVerne Madigan: "The committees have to work until it's done."

Chairman Guy Okakok: "It would take a couple of days. We will have to work on this all night long."

Frank Degnan: "Mr. Chairman."

Chairman Guy Okakok: "Frank."

Frank Degnan: "At this time when you get your committees formed I think it would be proper that the committees are not too large and we go to our Top of the World Hotel and we have a room in there for ourselves and we talk about our problems and make up our minds what we are going to do. Now each committee should have a room there too. Rather than just sitting here in mixed groups and the balance of the delegates would be at liberty till the call of the chair. We could set a time."

LaVerne Madigan: "When would that be approximately? Because we have to be done."

Frank Degnan: "We don't know now how long it will take us now. It is a big job. It is very important. We have got a long line of things on aborigines and the rest of the things. We have got a lot of things that will go into our report. The committees will be busy. The committee will have to meet right after supper and you have your rooms and you set your time and then you report back. What is your telephone number, Mr. President?"

LaVerne Madigan: "The two committees will work. But the chairman, he will call the whole group together again. This is important."

Chairman Guy Okakok: "We gonna have supper around six o'clock tonight. So we committees will have to discuss on this we have to work on these aboriginal rights and economics. We may have to work on these for hours and hours. I do not know. But anyway around ten or ten-thirty we are gonna call up those delegates. I will now as the whole committees, the delegates to come back at ten (o'clock) at the hotel, the whole group. Will it be possible to have a full agenda for each committee? It's four o'clock right now. The committees would like to have a full agenda, program so that will know just what to talk about...be at the hotel ten o'clock sharp tonight." (End of day's taping.)

(Beginning of following day taping.) **Chairman Guy Okakok**: "The meeting we have will come to order now. It is a pleasure to have these men from far off country who could be with us this morning. Honorable John Carver, Assistant Secretary of the Interior, Washington, D. C.. (Applause.) Mr. James Hawkins, Area Director of Bureau of Indian Affairs. (Applause.) Also Mr. Larry...from Juneau. (Applause.) These people that have visit us to see the Eskimos, especially you people who runs this Inupiat Conference here in Barrow. We have here a statement of policy and recommendations adopted by the Point Barrow Conference on Inupiat...a Statement of Policy and Recommendations adopted by the Point Barrow Conference on Native Rights, Barrow, Alaska November 17, 1961. We the people here have come together for the first time ever in all the years of our history. In order to come together in meeting from all the villages from Lower Kuskokwim to Point Barrow. We had to come from so far together for this reason. We always thought our Inupiat Paitot was safe to be passed down to our future generations as our fathers passed down to us. Our Inupiat Paitot is our land around the whole Arctic world where we the Inupiat live, our right to hunt our food in anyplace, any time of year as it always had been, our right to be great hunters and brave independent people like our grandfathers. Our rights to the minerals that belong to us in the land we claim. Today our Inupiat Paitot is called by the Whiteman as aboriginal rights. We were quiet and happy because we always thought that we had these aboriginal rights until last year when agents of Fish and Wildlife Service last year arrested two Inupiat hunters from Barrow. They arrested these Natives because they shot eider ducks for food. They told these Natives they could not hunt the eider ducks in 1960 because of Migratory Bird Treaty with Canada and Mexico. The other men of Barrow, one hundred and thirty-eight hunters, all walked up to Fish and Wildlife Service agents to be arrested too. Each man had an eider duck in his hand. Each man said, 'We are all hunters. It is our right to hunt birds. But if you arrest two, you must arrest all of us.' When Barrow Natives did this bravely and honestly, Inupiat everywhere started to tell how game laws and other laws take away Inupiat Paitot. Inupiat of King Island and St. Lawrence Island said Fish and Wildlife agents restricted also hunting of walrus, for ivory and food, even if these walrus were many more than before passing north. Inupiat of Kalskag and Aniak on

Kuskokwim (River) said agents let them take only one moose a year even if the moose were in large numbers on Inupiat land and the children hungry. Now that we have come together, we found that we have hunting and all other problems together. We Inupiat have the same problems in all areas of Alaska. Now we know this, we have joined together to solve these problems. People have thought we did not have problems because we did not say something. But when we came together we found we Inupiat all share the same problems. Our problems are two kinds: Aboriginal land, and hunting rights. Economic and social developments. Aboriginal rights: The rights of us Inupiat have never been explained truthfully and properly to us. They have even been confused to us, which we Inupiat were entitled to understand. We were told that if the government reserved our aboriginal land for us, we could not be citizens of United States, could not vote, we would be tied a reservation like a dog and could not have businesses come on our land or sell products of our land. That was a lie told to us Inupiat to take away our aboriginal lands and mineral rights. Talking here at this meeting, about what we were told about aboriginal rights and reservations, we found that each one of our villages were told the same lies. But we never knew that, because we never before had the chance to talk to each other. We did not know before what our aboriginal rights are, but now we know. They are our Inupait Paitot. Our Inupiat Right to own the land and minerals of our ancestors, to hunt and fish without restrictions over this (land) and the sea. Example; At Kalskag on Lower Kuskokwim (River), agents told Natives to pay stumpage fee on timber cut for sale and not for own use. The Kalskag Natives are very poor and they need cash from timber they sell to buy clothes they cannot make from fur and hides. The right to cut timber for sales on their own land is an aboriginal right, part of Inupiat Paitot. Example; At Barrow, the poor families cannot afford to buy fuel to heat their homes, and there is hardship. Yet Barrow village sits on top of a great resource of fuel, a great resource of natural gas. The cold people cannot use this natural gas, because Barrow is in the Naval Petroleum Reserve. If the Barrow Natives had known about their rights long ago and their aboriginal land was a reservation, then the people could use the fuel, the natural gas. Then someday in the future, they could have it developed and have income from it. The natural gas at Barrow is part of our Inupiat Paitot. Congress should not pass a law to take this gas and give it to private business to develop. The Natives would not get benefit that way. The Interior Department should say that the gas belongs to Barrow Natives and should be given back to them when the Navy is through. The Interior Department should arrange with the Navy for the Barrow Native to use some of the natural gas now to heat their homes, immediately. These are examples of things from which we could get income and royalties. We could use these to develop our people; to improve our education, housing and sanitation; to make employment; to get better transportation for our villages. We could use this income to keep the independence we the Inupiat have always had and want to pass on to our children. Recommendations on aboriginal rights: Number One; When Alaska was purchased, when Alaska became a State, the United States said in the Acts that the Natives have aboriginal land and hunting rights. The United States said Congress would define these rights some day. The Alaska Statehood Act also says that the state may take nearly two hundred million acres from the public domain in twenty-five years. If Congress does not define our rights soon, the twenty-five years will be up and our Inupiat Paitot will be gone. Congress should act now to settle our Alaska Native claims. All villages should be, that's Number Two; All villages should be truthfully informed how aboriginal land and hunting rights can be protected by the Interior Department without restricting the Natives' freedom as citizens, and all villages should be allowed to apply for a reservation with full mineral and hunting rights. All villages if they want reservations or not they should be told about claims in the U. S. Court of Claims for lands...Number Three: The Interior Department should immediately withdraw, from the public domain in Alaska, tracts of land around all Native villages, pending the establishment of reservations or other settlement of Alaska Native claims. Natives should be free to hunt on all withdrawn land and on the sea. We found that we have two problems of our rights, which are special. One is the Migratory Bird Treaty with Canada and Mexico. One is Project Chariot, the proposed nuclear explosion at Point Hope. Number One: Migratory Bird treaty; Our right to hunt should not be subject to any international treaty without our consent. We ask the Interior Department to exempt us from this Treaty and save us from the need to be lawbreakers. Number Two: Project Chariot; The Bureau of Land Management has licensed the Atomic Energy Commission to do research on Cape Thompson, near Point Hope village, leading to an experimental nuclear explosion. The result of the explosion will be very dangerous to Natives' health because of the effect of radiation on the animals hunted by the people for food. The site of this experiment is located on lands claimed by the Point Hope Natives. We deny the right of the Bureau of Land

Management to dispose of land claimed by a Native Village, and urge the Interior Department to revoke the permit before the experiment is allowed to go any further. We, the Inupiat, strongly protest and request of the President of the United States that the experiments of the Russians on the nuclear explosions be discontinued."

Jonah Tokienna: "Mr. Chairman, Honorable John Carver, Mr. (James) Hawkins,...delegates and fellow Inupiats. We are now under Point Number Two: Economic and Social Development. Number One; Migratory Fowl. The people that I'm representing stated as follows: The primary purpose of the treaty, that was established in that treaty was intended for the preservation of the game from the sportsman. Eskimos and Whites should have equal rights under the treaty. Those who are below a certain economic level should have a right to take the wild fowl. The action of Fish and Wildlife Service was unfair to those who are below the economic level. The open season regulated by the Fish and Game Commission do not apply for this area. The water fowl that we sorely needed are already on their way to south. The open season for Inupiat should be at such a time that the game is still available and needed. The kill taken by hunters amounts to a good many for necessity, but it does not anywhere near compare to the kill taken by sportsmen in the Lower Forty-eight, whose livelihood does not depend on living off the land but whose livelihood depends on farming and definite industrial enterprises that provide steady employment. As they expressed it what water fowl that we take for food is like a drop in the bucket in comparison with what is being taken in the lower forty-eight, that is taken by sportsmen. In regard to conservation, man is not responsible. Land animals and birds destroy tremendous number of our game birds. Foxes destroy because at that time they are raising their young. Jaegers, hawks, owls, seagull kill tremendous numbers. These predators again far exceeds the number that are taken by Natives. The Kotzebue area recommended that some bounty be provided for these mentioned predators. Our problem is based on the problem of those whose economic level is low. Employment: very small percentage of men enjoy year round employment. Out of this small percentage few jobs they are able to obtain on seasonal longshoring, on construction. There again employment is limited to fill-in jobs by Native members of the Union. In these construction jobs many of the men are imported from the States, when many of our men are just as capable and qualified. During the last half of the winter there are as many as thirty or forty light planes that hunt polar bear and lined up on ice in front of the town on ice. These sports hunters cover a large area around the of the vicinity southwest, west and north of Kotzebue, Kivalena and Point Hope. These planes land on ice to make their kills. These planes make their kills shooting from planes while flying. These hunters make their kill, take the skin and leave the carcass. Some planes take home sometimes a small portion of the meat. These hunters, as one person said, that finding their kill not of right size, leave it untouched. The indications is when dead bears comes up to shore with bullet holes. Some are found dead untouched on ice with bullet holes Three: These sport hunters do not kill for eating purposes. As long as planes are being used they prevent the bears from getting close enough to mainland for Natives who need the skin for sale to supplement their meager income and for food. The sports hunters deprive Natives of their rights. A man who is hunting for sport is depriving the less fortunate man, Inupiat. This sportsman is also demanding equal rights, is domineering, selfish and therefore far exceeds his rights that he becomes inconsiderate and also is not practicing equal rights. Four: While all Natives appreciate the boarding school at Mt. Edgecumbe, which is being provided for them, more and more they have come to realize their loved ones get too far away from them and lose control of their ways when they return home. Kotzebue is a terminal for two big airlines, a distributing center for the outlying areas along the Kobuk River, Noatak River and the villages around Kotzebue Sound. All the surrounding area villages are being served commercially by freight lines by air and sea. Kotzebue is easily accessible by traveling in boats and dogteams, without too much being affected by unknown weather conditions. It is good hunting and fishing around this vicinity. The transportation that consume a large portion of appropriations has come to a quite an expenditures of sums...In the parents opinion the students' morale would improve knowing that they are not too far away from home. If emergency arises in a matter of few hours parents of students would be contacted. This area is also aware of the fact that adult education is a necessity. The people realize that the time is speeding up so much they are not able to keep up. Everything in that is without a foundation when it becomes so complex in many circumstances. Education, this item is pretty well covered under high school and adult education. However from time to time we have had teachers whose interest only in making money and they had no interest in the Natives, who do not care whether or not Natives learn. We got quite a desire that Mr. Hawkins, our Area Director, Bureau of Indian Affairs, Juneau to retain his position. If we are not able to hold him in this position that he be transferred to Washington, D. C. under the Assistant Secretary of Interior, and be given a promotion that deals with Bureau of Indian Affairs. Mr. Hawkins has done so much to promote what we are at present, present time trying to help others on expenses on American Indian affairs. Recommendation for Housing: Housing should be made available under the program that is being worked out under the Economic Redevelopment Plan by the State of Alaska. We understand this program will be worked out with those who need housing on long term low interest basis. We suggest that such houses be made available according to the sizes of the families and newly married couples. And that it be built suitable to withstand severe weather conditions. Many of the Native people cannot afford to buy housing in one lump sum payment. King Island have been requesting approval to relocate themselves on mainland. Many of the localities on coast from Demarcation Point to Lower Kuskokwim are the ones that are severely affected housing shortage. Many of the homes are inadequate and overcrowded which are detrimental to health. Poor material or insufficiently supplied is not the answer. In other words, poorly constructed homes that fail to meet severe weather conditions are detrimental to health. Under this housing project, materials from timber areas could be worked out to supply the areas which are affected by housing shortages. Employment: Some small percentage of men from each village have been able to obtain employment. Very few men in these villages enjoy year round employment. Many of the men from each village have to seek jobs during the summer. Few of them have been fortunate enough to find jobs only work for few weeks in longshoring and in odds and ends jobs. A few of our men who are members of the Union get fill-in jobs that were available under construction projects. Contractors of construction projects import many of their workers from the lower forty-eight. This practice, to us, discriminates men who are available for jobs. Men who are just as capable and qualified. Men who can skillfully operate heavy-duty equipment, Men who are carpenters and can work willingly under proper supervision. We would like to see road building projects. Roads could possibly make some industries and resources open up the Natives. Reports from Noatak indicate the villagers there would like to have a road built from Noatak to the mouth. The river is low at the time when the yearly store supplies are transported by barge. During the summer the Native Store has to ship the main staples by air from Kotzebue to landing strip at Noatak. The freight rate is five cents per pound. From their strip to the community store the cost of longshoring is a dollar, seventy-five cents an hour. There are other possibilities like sawmills and in order to transport cheapest sawmill ever will have to be made available. That road building would also provide local employment. Reports from Gambell, St. Lawrence Island also indicated that roads are a necessity. Roads can always be used when traveling by boats is impossible and travel by air caused by weather conditions. This roads would aid dogteam travel. Many times the sea ice for traveling is rough and impossible to get through. In many instances our natural resources are inaccessible because of lack of better means of travel. High grade coal is in different localities, such as Kaparuk, Corvin. The coal mines are pretty much inaccessible because of no roads around these areas. Getting fuel our people have to use much time they could be using to do other things for their living. Fuel being so important, hunting time is lost because there are no roads. Sawmills should be provided in timber areas. Canneries should be established where fish is plentiful. New air land strips should be built and maintaining air strips should be stressed for safety sake. At present there are no air strips at Savoonga, Stebbins and at Buckland. Air strips at Gambell, Wales and Noatak need maintenance. Maintaining these air strips is necessary for those who ship reindeer for sale, for better mail service and for emergencies. These projects, however small, will help provide short term employment that are sorely needed by those who are not able to seek employment elsewhere. Health: Under the Sanitation Department the State of Alaska should promote better water systems. This is a specific need at Stebbins, St. Lawrence Island, and most other villages. A hospital is needed at Unalakleet, a population center in an area which needs such service very much. A hospital is also needed at St. Lawrence Island. The only medical help now available is through a clinic inadequate to meet the need. Arts and Crafts: In many villages Native arts are the most important source of cash. It is recommended that there be a survey of the operations of ANAC (Alaska Native Arts and Crafts) with the emphasis on the development of new outlets and on an alternative to sale by consignment. The latter constitutes a grave and inexcusable hardship to Natives who have to wait many months for compensation for work done. Arts and crafts outlets, operated by Natives, should be established in the villages in connection with the tourist industry. ANICA (Alaska Native Industries Cooperatives Association): ANICA should encourage the employment of qualified Natives in its headquarters whenever possible. Village councils should exercise great care in the selection of the managers of local stores. It is recommended that stores be established in villages where needed, as for example, Barter Island and Teller Mission. Migratory Birds and Game: Walrus; Alaska Natives are being blamed for killing walrus for tusks by taking off their heads and leaving the carcass exposed on the ice or on the beach. These walrus have been wantonly killed by Siberians and the Fish and Wildlife Service should retract its accusation. Alaska Natives do not wantonly kill for tusk purposes. They kill for food also. Organization: Organization should be established. Truthfully, the Association on American Indian Affairs should not pay the expenses each time. It is suggested that a self-supporting organization be recognized by this Conference by paying small fees toward another conference. It is also suggested that a bulletin or newsletter be published and circulated every so often to villages about what is being done within the Inupiat organization. This organization should be well established, not be allowed to fade as other organizations have done in the past. All the Native villages should be informed what has been accomplished for the good of those villages." (Applause.)

John Carver, Assistant Secretary of Interior: "I am very delighted to be here today and have this opportunity to visit with you. That is quite an encyclopedic, rather an encyclopedia of work. Apparently your long night last night and your long day yesterday and your long night the night before has been very successful where you have very well summarized your problems. You have stated them very eloquently and very well. I was particularly pleased to hear your resolution in favor of our Area Director Mr. Hawkins. Because I feel that everything that you have, because I know that the things you have told me, in your words, are things which he has known, and does know, of course, your needs. He has told these same things. And the fact that we haven't been able to do all of the things that ought to be done. In fact we haven't been able to take care of the recognition of your place in the North lands when it comes to the actions of the other Government agencies. It is no reflection on the Native people from the Bureau of Indian Affairs working here. They are dedicated and devoted people as you know as I try to assure you that Mr. Hawkins all his experience with you. He served down in Dillingham, in the South. That experience will not be lost. He'll still be able to help out I am sure. He has the welfare of the Indian people in Alaska at heart. (Applause.) And your suggestion as to his getting a promotion in Washington, D. C. .... (Laughter.) I am like Guy (Okakok) I have to get pretty close to my work to see it here. I'll step down the step here. I want to talk about two or three of the problems here. The problem that is closest to the hearts of all of you. I know it's closest to my heart. It's not really the matter of the ducks, it's not the walrus, it's not even the jobs. Most of all I think we should really should choose just one from this long list. It should be the matter of the education of your children. Now what you said about education is that you want to have good teachers and you would like to keep your children close to their family ties. You said you would like them to get the skills which would enable them to compete with the imported labor. And you have said you wanted to have educational opportunities for the older people in the village. And these are all objectives that all of us, all of us have. Mr. (James) Hawkins, Mr...and I spent many hours yesterday in the school here at Barrow. And that school, the school which you have in Barrow is probably typical of the good and the bad...the good is the dedication of the teachers...the bad is that the teachers don't have always the kind of materials that are applicable for teaching the Eskimo children...we teach them in buildings which are old and cold. And we are a little slow in improving some of these conditions. But I am sure that all of you feel in visiting the schools the good outweighs the bad. But you also feel that we must keep on trying to improve. Particularly when you get into smaller villages. It is very very important for us to get good teachers and schools. I hope that you don't think that you have the only problem of this kind. I ran into the same kind of problem ten thousand, twelve thousand, ten thousand miles away. That's not that far in a direct line, but by the way you have to go. And the islands in the Pacific they have the Samoan children, they are Americans just as your children are Americans. Who grow up with their own language. Who've never seen a train or a big building. And who have to learn their lessons either from locally trained people who,...or they have to learn from people brought in from many miles...we have this problem right in the heart of the lower forty-eight...I come to Barrow and find the problems of education that you have listed...even as far away from Washington, D. C. and Juneau as you are. We are not dealing with one government, we are dealing with many governments. We are dealing with Indian Affairs, we are dealing with military departments and you know something of the Weather Bureau, Commerce Department, Federal Aviation Administration. These are only a few. You know about the State of Alaska, the Commissioner of Education. You know about the courts. You know you have to go as far away as Nome from Barrow, probating in the state. You know that things are not all central and I suppose this is difficult to deal with...the first time all the Eskimos people have met through their representatives to talk about common problems, are the same. It's as far from here to Kuskokwim I guess it is as it is from Washington to Chicago maybe even farther than that. Certainly costs more to get to Kotzebue to Barrow than it is from New York to San Francisco...how much does it cost to go from Kotzebue to Barrow...one hundred seventy-six with tax. And yet when you come together from towns, your problems are all very similar. I was down at the Alaska Native Brotherhood meeting at Klukwan and I talked individually with representatives there. They are close together, they're all in a handful. And they can visit back and forth and they see each other in the streets of Juneau often. And yet even as close as they are each of them thinks that his problem is the most serious. It is the only one of its kind till they get together. Each problem is a little different but all their worrying about the same things. ...those things are for education. Preservation of their own, preserving or saving for themselves the integrity of their own culture. Their own good things which has kept them as a self-sufficient group through some very dark days. And it was the maintenance of their own base of land and water for their own living. They could not see themselves pushed into the time frame of working for wages or an employer. They wanted the job opportunities. They wanted to have the choice as to whether they should work for a contractor or work for...also they wanted to maintain in their Native groups a real choice. They wanted to be able to think about it and make their own choice. Not to have it pushed upon them. Now I think that's what you had here because there is a very interesting...in your various resolutions. ...fix the airport, you want jobs, you want roads built...and yet you also insist...hunting and the Eskimos not leaving the carcasses. You feel the Fish and Wildlife Service owes you an apology. And so do I. And in the hunting of ducks you do not desire to poach or to steal. You are not asking for any favors. You are not asking for any exceptions...yet when you get to talking about your rights you say in another resolution that you want Congress to spell out what kind they are, to make more definite, make more understandable. Not for you cause you understand it. But for you to be able to say, here is where that, what they are. You can turn around and say you can't do this, it is mine...the Bureau of Land Management comes and patents the land to someone else that you know is yours without proving it is yours. Because it is all tied up in a very general a very difficult term called aboriginal rights. The very term aboriginal is a kind of offensive term. Your aboriginal ancestors are no older than mine or Miss Madigan's. In other words, if you have rights, you have rights. And I can't help but thinking that we recognize...stretching all the way from Greenland clear around down into the southwest Alaska and over into Siberia. The maintenance of life through the years in the most difficult and forbidding circumstances meant that you had to bring in to subjugation you had to bring in control of your land of every resource that was there. ...Spain and Mexico, like California before it come into the Union under the old land grant system.... At any rate the Government thinks about you...because they regard you as different. They say anyone who would even be in Barrow is different. Because they say it is impossible for civilized...to live in such environments...I can assure you, under President Kennedy, under Secretary Udall, have had, have emphasize...is we care. I don't know when the last any representative of the Secretary's office was in Barrow. Do you know Guy (Okakok)? Probably never. And I did not come here to preach to you. And I am telling you I learned a great deal and I'll learn some more before this day is over. I feel if I come to preach to you, or to talk to you or to lecture to you I could stay in Washington and write letters to you how you should obey the law and be good citizens and it wouldn't mean anything because I wouldn't have any concept. By coming up here I can say better than in a letter...It's up to you to teach me. So if you have a little time why don't we start right now. Let me point to some of these recommendation you might like to emphasize. Mr.([Frank) Degnan. First I'll tell you a little of what I understand. The general framework of it and then you tell me your ideas. When the Territory (of Alaska) was purchased. I'll go back a little ways. When the Russians had the Territory (of Alaska) the governmental functions were given by the Russians to a couple of companies, trading companies and they came into couple parts of Alaska they came into...they ran the business as government...that's the way the Russians did it...and get back into it so to speak and to protect the rights of the people under the laws of Russia. There was some progress on this line by the time the sale (of Alaska to the United States) took place in 1867. So when the Treaty was with Russia and the United States by Secretary Seward there was a provision in it that provided...not a great deal was done about it...the Organic Act of 1884. What did the Organic Act say about rights of the aboriginal citizens here?"

James Hawkins: "Well I think it pretty much that they were to be left in the status quo until future legislative constitute (it), I couldn't explain it any differently."

Assistant Secretary John Carver: "That's exactly right And this form of legislation which is passing the buck...the legislation, they didn't say what these rights are. They just said that whatever they are you still got them. Then in the meantime of course they won the lawsuits on the claims, the Tlinget and Haida case. Isn't that right Jim (Hawkins)? Recognized judicially that these rights could have been taken away by governmental action. They existed as of 1867 or 1884 and then were carved away by someone taking them away for other governmental purposes. There might be compensation, there might have to be money paid for...I had a conversation yesterday morning with the state management of the Bureau of Land Management...if you don't already know, as most of you do, its one of the bureaus that reports to the main desk of the Bureau of Indian Affairs desk here. Of course they have very serious problems in administering these land laws because all of the land managers, and the land managers are a little bit like bankers. They have to be able to put it all down in columns and get it identified and put it into ledger sheets you know make it balance some way or another. This is the way the land managers are. But now the 1884 Act referred to the lands which were used and occupied or claimed by the Native people. What does that mean? To you, use and occupation may mean one thing, in Southeast Alaska it may mean something else. To the examiners of the Bureau of Land Management it may mean something else. And to the Judge of the Federal Court it may mean something else. And the last analysis under our American system it means what the courts finally say it means. And this is a very difficult idea because when administrators, when land examiners know that the final judgment may have to be made by a court, then they automatically become very conservative. If the court decided that they gave out too much then they are personally liable for it. Whereas if they didn't give out enough then they could get it later and nobody could criticize them. It puts them under very difficult pressures. That's what the law says, it said that you could get patent, for the Indians, the Eskimo, a hundred and sixty acres in the area which they used and occupied. They don't emphasize a hundred and sixty acres, they emphasize the used and occupied. And so they say to the applicant, show us that you used and occupied it, prove it, is what they mean. If you can't prove it then you can't expect us to patent it. How do you prove, how do you classify land if you only used the land to hunt on, to gather berries from or to fish on, or lie in wait for game on. They don't know. I don't know how you expect the land managers to know either. Plus it's very clear to me that we are going to have to go to the Congress, we are going to have to ask the Congress to give us some more flexibility. To ask the Congress in Southeast Alaska to allow us to put this land, this hundred and sixty acres in different places, not just in one place. You see what I mean. We are going to have to go to the Congress and tell them that you can't treat land in Point Barrow like land in Iowa.... .We are going to have to give to you the right to get the title that you can file in the courthouse, so to speak, of your village sites. And we are going to have to do it on a basis which will preserve the village integrity. The Eskimo culture there if you want to preserve it. Perhaps it really isn't such a problem here as it is in terms in villages let's say close to Ketchikan surrounding the peninsula where the big pressure is of the Outside, of the non-Indians. The non-Indians trying to take it over from them. The goodwill on my part, to interpret the law, in the same way you think it ought to be interpreted will not be enough. I can't do that. Don't have that much power. I'd like to have that much power. Since I don't have it, because I can't tell a man, you can go to a man who has to actually sign the document saying I order you to sign it. ...this is the responsibility that the law fixes on me. The lawyers tell me what the law is and I can't. The law didn't give me the power to sign it you see. All I can assure you is that we will try when we go to Congress, to go understandingly as to your situation. When we go there we don't, nobody can say 'What do you know about it?' to me. If they said that to me I would be able to say, 'I know this about it. I've been there, I've talked to the people.' I'll assure you that I will present what you expressed here to me today. You know that you have represented here, representatives from about fifteen to twenty thousand Inupiats, Aleuts, Eskimos, citizens of the State of Alaska which may be sixty percent of the eligible voters, isn't that right? That is ten to twelve thousand voters represented here. Ten to twelve thousand voters is quite a fraction of the voters in a small state like Alaska in terms of population and you are able to compete and say...but I don't want you to ever...on a racial basis...it will be bad for you...that's the wrong way. But in terms of using your power to make the politicians understand what the facts are up here, that's what you can ask for. I think you should. It's a long ways to come to Barrow, the people have already said it is expensive to get around...they have to understand what the situation is, that's what has been lacking. Even among the people in Alaska. They all think that because they live in Alaska they know all about Alaska. But how many Alaskans have been to Barrow, to Kotzebue, to Unalakleet or Bethel? Percentage-wise, not very many, have they? But that's all I got to say about that aboriginal rights. Whatever they are, you've got them. But they're not worth much to you until you can get them specified. And I don't think that we can administer laws that specify them as well as we would like to." (End of Tape Two of Three, Side B.)

(Beginning of Tape Three of Three, Side A.) (The opening welcome was given in the Inupiat Barrow dialect by Chairman Guy Okakok. He explains the reasons for the conference. He explains the role of LaVerne Madigan. He explains how Assistant Secretary of the Interior John Carver was invited. He introduces John Carver to the conference. Eddie Hopson serves as interpreter in Inupiaq at each break of Carver's speech.)

John Carver: "Chairman, delegates, and members the Inupiat citizens of Barrow. Thank you very much, Guy (Okakok), for that wonderful introduction. I didn't understand one word of it. (Laughter.) I'm really very happy to be here tonight. To be introduced by my good friend. Guy met me first last August down in Juneau. I had come to Barrow according to the commitments I had made to him that time."

Voice: "John, you have your interpreter out here." John Carver: "Oh, Yes, introduce me to him first." Voice: "This is Eddie Hopson" (Hopson speaks in Inupiat.)

John Carver: "Who is going to interpret for me? It's news to me. With Mr. Hopson up here we have a team working up here. I'll start again by saying I am happy to be here. And I've come here because I made a promise to Guy Okakok that I would come. I saw him last August. You are very privileged to have, to be the host city for a very important convention. Because you have here today representatives, delegates from, from almost all of the Eskimo villages throughout the State of Alaska. Barrow, as the host city, has been a very warm and hospitable place for them and for me. I have been very pleased to meet with Frank and Mrs. (Ada) Degnan and them from so many interesting fine places in Alaska. And I have been particularly interested in talking to the delegate here from Anaktuvuk. When I go back to Washington I will be able to see in my mind such places as Unalakleet, Point Hope, Anaktuvuk, Kalskag and Gambell and all the other Eskimo places in Alaska. Because I have read something of the Bible, I am also happy to know that there is a Jonah here in the audience. The whale, as it is translated. Special, special word of thanks goes to the Association on

American Indian Affairs whose Executive Director is Miss LaVerne Madigan, who has worked so hard to get this convention organized. But it is the Association on American Indian Affairs not the Bureau of Indian Affairs. Today I have a lot of experiences, one experience was to take a jeep ride out to the Point at Barrow with Guy Okakok. On the way back we got stuck in a snow bank.

I want to tell about your Superintendent of Schools here in Barrow, John Gordon. The wheels of the jeep went round and around and around and around and we didn't go. And then Mr. Gordon put his foot under the wheel and we drove right out. Gordon is a very wise and able man. Last night the delegates come here from all over Alaska and had an all night meeting. But I went to sleep. And at four o'clock in the morning, I heard Miss Madigan say in a loud voice, 'It's time to get up.' So I thought that it was very strange that nobody had gone to bed. I heard that, and see there's such a great crowd here because I know your competition is a big party out at the base. We are all very thankful that the man was rescued and brought back to safety. The sea from the Inupiat is a new thing for the Eskimo people. For traditionally the Eskimos have not been able to travel easily from one place to another. While we were visiting some Eskimos in Greenland, over a hundred years ago, over a hundred-fifty years ago. When he got there, the Eskimos thought that they were the only people on the face of the earth. It has always been because the Eskimos have always had to live fairly small groups. Isolated from their fellows. But the Eskimo people lived in the northland all the way to Greenland. If they are not the only people on the face of the Earth. I can say they are among the best of the people on the face of the Earth. Now they have the villages have sent their representatives here to Barrow. That is only the first step. King Islanders will be going to the Seattle World's Fair. They will be there representing all of you, all of the Eskimos of Alaska. And I know that they will be fine representatives. I have come here tonight as a representative of one part of the United States Government. The Department of the Interior. I bring to you greetings to you, special greetings to you and all guests, special greetings from the Secretary of the Interior Stewart Udall and the Commissioner of Indian Affairs Phileo Nash. I have come here for myself and for them, not to tell, but to learn. Not just from the Barrow people, but people from Eskimo villages all over Alaska. I have learned many things about the hopes and aspirations of the Eskimo people. I have learned about their way of life and they are interested in preserving their way of life. I have found you, as other citizens of Alaska,

have the strongest possible interest is a good education for your children. And I have learned that you also want to take part in educational programs for the elderly members of the community to learn the skills so that you can have your share of the jobs that are available in your villages in different programs and construction that comes to your villages. I have learned lessons about how you live and how you hunt, how you whale how you subsistently get your food. These lessons have been a great value to me as I report to the Congress, my superiors in Washington, from, for when all the parts of Alaska are discussed. These lessons that are here to be learned are very important because your problems are not the same as those which face the citizens of your own State or those to the South. Even if they aren't the same, your place in the world is the same as the citizens of Alaska, in Fairbanks, or Anchorage or Juneau or the other large places. Because each of you is a citizen not just of the United States but of the State of Alaska. As a citizen you have a right to vote not only for the President of the United States but for Governor of the State of Alaska and for your own representatives for the Congress and the state legislature. Here again it is important that we have the delegates of so many Eskimo places in Alaska, because meeting together they can speak with a common voice of the problems to the Congress of all the Eskimo villages. But you have a responsibility as you organize as your delegates here to speak as citizens of the United States and citizens of Alaska and not as Eskimos. Because if you always speak as the voice of citizenship then you can not be used by those who seek to take advantage of your Eskimo heritage for other purposes than your good welfare. If you speak as citizens and you vote as citizens and not as Eskimos then you will protect yourselves against those who would like to take advantage of such a large number of people with a common background. The modern world, the world of airplanes, rapid transportation and rapid communications reach into Barrow and other Alaskan villages same time the responsibility of government reach to you. This is why you have a special responsibility because so many of these relationships, so many of these ideas have come, reached into the villages before education itself is reached there. So, in conclusion, I just want to say that this has been a very valuable and exciting experience for me to come to the northernmost city in the United States of America. I would come back very quickly for the hospitality that has been extended to me, to the delegates here. I am very proud to have been involved with such fine Americans. Thank you very much."
(Applause.)

Chairman Guy Okakok introduces the Bureau of Indian Affairs Alaska Commissioner James Hawkins in Inupiat.

James Hawkins: "I am surprised, I did not expect to see quite so many people. I am very glad to be here with you and to be a part of the Eskimo meeting that is here to get a chance to know you as well as all the delegates. I was not born in Alaska, and I am sorry that I was not because I would know you and the problems that face you better than I do. But I have lived in Alaska for twelve years. And during that time I have taught schools, I've homesteaded, I have fished for salmon. I have worked for the territorial government and now the Bureau of Indian Affairs. And since this time, I have gotten to know some of your problems. I know something about the hunting and fishing, that, problems that face you. I have known for a long time that Barrow is in need of better schools. When I first came into the Bureau of Indian Affairs, your representatives to Juneau came to talk to me. Mr. Johnny Nusinginia, Mr. Eben Hopson came to tell me about your need for schools. After their efforts and now you meet and the success of the Bureau of Indian Affairs and Congress, you now see the new school being built. Which represents the efforts of years. And no longer will your children will not have to go thousands of miles from home to do, to complete even the elementary school. In the years to come, I know that the Bureau of Indian Affairs, will continue to do their best to help in every way possible for you to reach your own problems. But the main job is with you because you must see your problems, you must look for solutions, and you must tell us, the State of Alaska, what you want in terms of your own future. I am glad to have been here tonight. I am very glad to be able to see all of you, to see some of you for the first time, to see a lot of you as old friends. And to meet the representatives of all the Eskimo villages who are here. And many of whom I have seen before, for having visited their villages. And whenever you see the red parka coming you'll know that the Bureau of Indian Affairs is in town. (Applause.)

Chairman Guy Okakok: "Thank you ."

Chairman Guy Okakok speaks in Inupiat.

Jonah Tokienna: "Thank you Mr. Chairman, Mrs. Madigan, Honorable John Carver; Assistant Secretary of Interior, Mr. James Officer, Mr. Edward Hopson; President of the Native Village of Barrow Council. Fellow citizens, Inupiat, this is what, it has come up to on our conference here at Point Barrow. The top of the world. A statement of all of these and recommendations, Inupiat Paitot, adopted by the Point Barrow Conference on Native Rights, Barrow, Alaska on November 17, 1961: We, the Inupiat, have come together for the first time ever in all the years of our history. We have to come together in meeting from our far villages from Lower Kuskokwim to Point Barrow. We have to come, from so far, together for this reason. We always thought our Inupiat Paitot was safe to be passed down to our future generations as our fathers passed down to us. Our Inupiat Paitot is our land around the whole Arctic World where we the Inupiat live. Our right to hunt our food any place and times of year as it has always been. Our right to be great hunters and brave independent people. Like our great-grandfathers our right to use the minerals that belong to us in the land we claim. To-day, our Inupiat Paitot is called by Whiteman as 'Aboriginal Rights.' We were quiet and happy and always thought we had these aboriginal rights until last year when agents of Fish and Wildlife Service arrested two Inupiat hunters of Point Barrow. They arrested these Natives because they shot eider ducks for food. They told these Natives they could not hunt eider ducks in nineteen hundred and sixty because of Migratory Bird Treaty with Canada and Mexico. The other men of Barrow. One hun-dred-thirty-eight hunters. All walked up to Fish and Wildlife agents to be arrested too. Each man had an eider duck in hand. Each man said, 'We are all hunters. It is our right to hunt food. If you arrest two, you must arrest all.' When Barrow Natives did this crazy and honest thing, Inupiat, everyone, started to tell of game laws and other laws were taking away 'Inupiat Paitot.' Inupiat, King Island and St. Lawrence Island said Fish and Wildlife agents restricted also hunting of walrus, for ivory and food. Even if these walrus were many more than before passing north. Inupiat of Kalskag and Aniak on the Kuskokwim [River] said agents let them take only one moose a year even if the moose were in large numbers on Inupiat, Inupiat land and the children hungry. Now that we have come together we found that we have hunting and all other problems together. We Inupiat have the same problems in all areas of Alaska. Now we know this and we have joined together to solve these problems. People have thought we did not have problems because we did not say something. But when we get together we found that We Inupiat all share the same problems. Our problems are two kinds. One: Aboriginal lands and hunting rights. Two: Eco-nomic and social development. One: Migratory Fowl. The people that I am representing stated as follows: The primary purpose of the Treaty that is established in that Treaty it intended for the preservation of the game on the part that was taken by the sportsman. The Eskimo and Whites should have equal rights under this Treaty. Those who are below determined economical level should be eligible to take wild fowl.

The action taken by Fish and Wildlife Service is unfair to those who are below economic level. The open season requested in game commission do not apply for this area. The water fowl that are sorely needed, the kill taken by hunters although amount to a good many for Mississippi. It is not anywhere near compared to the kill taken by the sports hunters in the Lower 48 whose livelihood do not depend upon living off the land. But whose livelihood is from definite industrial enterprises that provide steady employment. If they altered it, what we take water fowl for food is like the drop in a buckshot in comparison, when you see taken in Lower 48 taken by sportsmen. In regard to this conservation, Man alone is not responsible. Land animals and birds destroy tremendous number of our game birds. Foxes destroy because of that time that they are rearing their young. Jaegers, hawks, owls, sea gulls kill tremendous numbers. Those predators again were exceeded the numbers that was taken Native people. Kotzebue area recommend, that some bounties be provided for these mentioned predators. Their process are based on the problems of those whose economic levels are low. Their land is very small compared to the land enjoyed year-round and wild. Out of the Eskimo percentage, few jobs that they are able to attain, are seasonal long-shoring and construction. There again, employment is limited to fuel and jobs by way of management of the union. In these construction jobs, many of the men are imported from the States when many of our men are just as capable and qualified. During the last half of the winter there are as many as thirty or forty light planes that come and hunt polar bear that live off the front of the towns on ice. These planes land on ice to make their kill. These planes make their kills, shooting from planes while flying. Their hunters make their kill, take the skins and leave the carcass. Some planes take them out whole. There's hunters, as one person says, that finding their kill is not of the right size they just leave it and stuff. The indications show when dead bears were found drifted ashore with bullet holes, some are found dead on top on the ice with bullets. There are sports hunters who do not kill for eating purposes. As long as planes are being used they are preventing the bear to get close to mainland so the Natives who need the kill will fail to supplement their meager diet and the meat we're eating are being be deducted and deprived of their lives. A man who is hunting for sports is depriving the less fortunate man, Inupiat. This sportsman, who he is also demanding equal rights, is down here shouting and therefore is seeing and therefore describe as he become inconsiderate and is not practicing equal rights. While all the Natives appreciate the boarding schools as Mount Edgecumbe which is being provided for them. More and more they have come to rely on that their loved ones get too far away from them and lose control of their way when they return home.

Kotzebue is the terminal for two big airlines. Distribution center for outlying villages around the Kobuk River, Noatak River and villages around the Kotzebue Sound. All the surrounding areas, our villages are being served commercially by the freight lines, by air and sea. Kotzebue is easily accessible by traveling on boat and dog teams without too much affected by known weather and season. There is good fishing and hunting around this vicinity. The transportation that soaks up or consume expenditures brought forth in the appropriations could become a minority as far as transportation expenditures is concerned. To parents, to all, the students morale would improve knowing that it is not too far away from home. If emergency arises, in matter of a few hours, parents or students would be contacted. This area is also aware of the fact that adult education is a necessity. The people realize the fact that time is speeding up so much and not able to keep up. In fact, everything, economy with a bad foundation would become complex in many circumstances. Number Three Recommendations: Housing. Housing should be made available under disclosure that is being worked out under the Economic Development Plan by the State of Alaska. We understood this program will be worked out for those who need. Those houses to be made available according to the size of the family or you need married couples. And that it be built suitable to withstand severe weather conditions. Many of the Native peoples cannot afford to buy housing in one lump payment, in one lump sum payment. The Islanders are requesting approval to relocate themselves on mainland. Many of the localities on coastal areas from Demarcation Point on to Lower Kuskokwim are the ones who are severely affected by housing shortages. Many of the homes are inadequate and overcrowded which are detrimental to health. Poor materials ordered in sufficiently supplies is not the answer. In other words, poorly constructed house have failed to meet the severe weather conditions are detrimental to health. Under this housing projects, materials from timber areas can be worked out to supply the areas which are affected by housing shortages.

Four: Employment; Such small percentages of men from each village have been able to obtain employment. Very few men in each village enjoy year-round employment. Many of the men from each village have been seeking jobs during summer. Few are fortunate enough to find jobs. Only work for few weeks in long-shoring and in odd and end jobs. Few of our men who are members of the union fill the jobs that are available under construction projects. Contractors of construction projects import many of their workers from the Lower 48. This practice to us is discrimination to men who skillfully operate heavy duty equipment. Men who are competent that can work willingly under proper supervision. We would like to see those building projects, those that have a paying cost of wage, make a way that restores and open up under the Native rights. Reports from Noatak indicate that they would like to have road built from Noatak back to the mountains. The river is low at the time when the yearly store supplies are to be transported by barge. During the ship that remains stable by air from Kotzebue to landing strip at Noatak the freight rate is five cents per pound. From landing strip to community store the long-shoring is one dollar and seventy-five cents an hour. There are other small developments like sawmills. In order to transport these, the sawmills, timber would have to be made available. This road built would keep also provide locals employment. Reports from Gambell also indicated that roads are a necessity. Roads can always be used when travelling by boat is impossible. When travel by air caused by weather conditions. This road also would aid dog team travel. Many times, the streets used for traveling are rough and impossible to get through. In many instances our natural resources are inaccessible because lack of better means of travel. High grade coal in different localities like Kuparok and Baldwin. Coal mines are pretty much inaccessible because of no roads around these areas. So much time is imposed when our people could have time to do some other things to make their living. Fuel being important hunting time is lost because of no roads. Some roads should be provided at timber areas. Canneries be established where fish is plentiful. Safer air landing strip should be built or repaired. One half-maintained air strip; maintaining air strip should be stressed for safety sake. At present there are no air strips at Savoonga, Stebbins and at Buckland. Air strips at Gambell, Wales and Noatak needs repair and maintaining. These air strips are necessary for those who ship reindeer meat for sale, for better mail service and for emergency. These projects, however small will help to provide short term employment that are surely needed for those who are unable to seek employment elsewhere. Number Five: Health; Health under the Sanitation Department of the State, under State Sanitation Department of the State Public Health promotes better water systems. This is especially needed at Stebbins, at St. Lawrence Island and most of the villages. A hospital is needed at Unalakleet, a population center in an area which stages...a hospital is needed over at St. Lawrence Island. The only medical help now available is through a clinic inadequate to meet the needs. Number Six: Artists and Crafts; In many villages, Native Arts is the most important source of cash. It is recommended that there be a survey of the operation of ANAC (Alaska Native Arts and Crafts) with emphasis on the development of new outlets and alternatives to sales by consignment. The latter constitutes a grave inequity, inexcusable hardship to Natives who have to wait many months for compensation for work done. ANAC should be operated by Natives. Arts and Crafts outlet opened by Natives should be established within the villages in connection with tourist industry. Number Seven: Organization; We should be established through which the (Association on) American Indian Affairs should not pay the expenses each time. It is suggested a self-supporting organization be recognized by the conference by paying small fee toward another conference. It is also suggested that a bulletin or newsletter be published and circulated every so often in villages about what is being done, what in the Inupiat organization. This organization should be well established, not to be allowed to all as other organizations have done in the past. All the Native villages should be informed what has been accomplished for the good of those villages. Number Eight: ANICA (Alaska Native Industries Co-operative Association, Inc.); ANICA should encourage the employment of qualified Natives in its headquarters whenever possible. Village Councils should exercise great care in the selection of the managers of local stores. It is recommended that stores be established in villages where Natives, as for example Barter Island and Teller Mission.

Number Eight: Migratory Birds and Game; Under that, walrus, Alaska Natives are being blamed for killing walrus for tusks. By cutting off their head and leaving the carcass exposed on the ice or the beach. Their walrus have been eventually killed by Siberians. And the Fish and Wildlife Service should retract its accusations. Alaska Natives do not wantonly kill for tusk purposes. They kill for food as well. Point Number One: Aboriginal Rights; The rights of us Inupiat has never been explained truthfully and properly to us. They have been refused to us which we Inupiat were entitled to understand. We were told that if the government reserve our aboriginal lands for us we could not be citizens of United States. Could not vote. Would be tied on reservations like a dog. Could not have business come in on our land or set up projects on our land. That was a lie told to us Inupiat to take away our aboriginal lands and mineral rights. Talking at this meeting, about what we were told, about aboriginal rights and reservations we found that each one of our villages were told the same lie. But we never knew that because we never before had the chance to talk to each other. We did not know before what our aboriginal rights are, but now we know. They are our Inupiat Paitot. Our Inupiat Paitot, our Inupiat Rights to own the land and minerals of our ancestors. To hunt and fish without restriction over this land and the sea. Example, at Kalskag on Lower Kuskokwim agents told Natives to pay stumpage fee on timber cut for sale and not for our use. The Kalskag Natives are very poor and they need cash from timber they sell to buy clothes they cannot make from fur and hides. The right to cut timber for sale on their own lands is an aboriginal right for the Inupiat Paitot. Except, at Barrow the poorest families cannot afford to buy fuel to heat their homes and there is hardship. Yet Barrow village sets on top of a great resource of fuel, a great resource of natural gas. The cold people cannot use this natural gas because Federal is the Federal Naval Petroleum Reserve. If the Federal Navy had known about their rights long ago and their aboriginal lands with the reservations then the people could use the fuels, the natural gas. Then some day in the future they could have it developed and have income from it. The natural gas of Barrow is part of our Inupiat Paitot. Congress should not pass a law to take this gas and give it to a private business to develop. The Natives would not get preference that way. The Interior Department should say that the gas belongs to Barrow Natives and should be given back to them when the Navy is through. The Interior Department should arrange with the Navy for the Barrow Natives to use some of the natural gas now to heat their homes. These are examples of things from which we could get income and royalties which we could use these to develop our people. To improve our education, housing and sanitation to make and run, to get better transportation for our villages. We could use the income to keep the independence we Inupiat have always had and want to pass on to our children. Recommendation of Aboriginal Rights: One; When Alaska was first, when Alaska became a State, the United States said, in the Act, that the Natives had aboriginal lands and hunting rights. The United States said Congress would define these rights some day. In Alaska Statehood, the Alaska

Statehood Act also said that the State may take nearly two hundred million acres in the public domain in twenty-five years. If Congress does not define our rights soon this twenty-five years will be up and our Inupiat Paitot will be gone. Congress should act now to settle our Alaska Native claims. Two; All villages should be truthfully informed how our aboriginal lands and hunting rights can be protected by the Interior Department without restricting the Natives freedom and citizenship. And all villages should be allowed to apply for reservations with full mineral and hunting rights. All villages if they want reservations or not should be helped to file claims in the United States Court of Claims for land and rights for which they were deprived. Three; The Interior Department should immediately withdraw from the public domain in Alaska tracts of land around all Native villages pending the establishment of reservations or other settlement of Alaska Native Claims. Natives should be free to hunt without restriction on all withdrawn land and on the sea. We found that we have two problems of our rights which are special. One is the Migratory Bird Treaty with Canada and Mexico. One is the Project Chariot, the proposed nuclear explosion at Point Hope. One; Migratory Bird Treaty. Our right to hunt should not be subject to any international treaty without our consent. We ask the Interior Department to exempt us from this treaty and save us from the need to be law breakers.

Two: Project Chariot; The Bureau of Land Management has licensed the Atomic Energy Commission to do research on Cape Thompson near Point Hope village. These nuclear experimental explosions, the results of this explosion will be very dangerous to Native health and food. The site of this experiment is land claimed by the Point Hope Natives. We deny the right of the Bureau of Land Management to dispose of land claimed by a Native village and urge the Interior Department to revoke the experiments before the experiment is allowed to go and explode. We, the Inupiat, strongly protest and request of the President of the United States of the experiments of the Russians of their nuclear explosions they be discontinued. Mr. Chairman. " (Applause.)

Chairman Guy Okakok speaks to the Conference in Inupiat.

Voice: "My understanding was that the community here would be given a chance to say a word or two if, ah, as they feel. That's my understanding."

Chairman Guy Okakok: ....

324

Voice: "Mr. Chairman, on this Naval Reserve number four, my understanding of the discussion was that, ah, the Department of the Interior would request that the natural gas there would not be turned over to the commercial enterprises. I can just about see a third catalog on that gas when I see it made. As the statement so state that we Natives that we wait and claim gas when the Navy is finished with petroleum number four. How do you know that Navy is going to going to get rid of that petroleum number four that easily? I think that should be reconsidered, on if, on either again request with, that should be reconsidered. But it should be before too long, before any body of recommendations are made by the Department of the Interior."

Chairman Guy Okakok speaks in Inupiat.

John Carver: "I might be able to answer to what he said but I can't answer what you said. (Laughter.) I haven't really understood about this problems...with the gas in Point Barrow but I can certainly see that the people here would feel about it, gas line here only twenty yards out of the village, the gas line going through the town. I will discuss it when I get back to Washington with Senator Bartlett who had a bill in prior to get Congressional action to get gas into Barrow and take it up with the Navy to see it there is any way to do a shorter legislation. But I don't think there is. But I'll try. " (Applause.)

Chairman Guy Okakok speaks in Inupiat.

Voice: "Mr. Chairman, I would like to state what I said earlier in, ah, that language that I speak." (Speaks in Inupiat.)

Chairman Guy Okakok speaks in Inupiat.

Voice: "Mr. Chairman, may I speak in Eskimo, to make it more clear to the group about what we talk about here. I think that Assistant Secretary to Udall was mentioning, referring to the delegates here from other communities. We just consider them as delegates, they are admitting to work out the problems for our people. And I think we should see it as such. There we throw our problems to this committee to be thrashed out for us as towns along the Arctic coast. I think, ah, that should be made to understand to people who really lived up here and I would like to say that some had probably not to have a cross...they just refer to as delegates. But they are committing to represent the people, the Eskimo people from all over the Arctic Slope, wherever the Eskimo is." (Speaks in Inupiat. Applause.)

Chairman Guy Okakok speaks in Inupiat.

Voice: "May I ask what this committee is chartered with?...the reason for asking that is that up here our demands for natural gas up here our demands were based as citizens. We are the kind of people that are thinking they are ... we all want to be citizens, American, citizens of America. We demanded that this case be brought up...now, ah, you're stuck on your charter, that this gas be turned right over to Natives with no departmental advices, I think that is wrong. Except I think you guys got to get a head. I think. I would like to ask...to enter this problem very seriously...we are privileged, as any other places, we are privileged to make demands as tax-paying citizens. We look at it that way...we just ask for private enterprise help we can get that gas. Not just pertaining only to the Natives all the citizens need some...." (Applause.)

Eben Hopson: "I am glad to commend these delegates here who come here to Barrow, to, ah, to make a tremendous policies statement as a group of Inupiat along the Arctic coast. And I want to commend them highly for accomplishing what they have done in a very short time that they have been here. And I think that I am talking for most of the people here. But before Mr. Chairman, I would like move that we adjourn." (Applause.)

Frank Degnan: "Ladies and Gentlemen, LaVerne Madigan, Assistant Secretary...I think we will come back sometimes...we will understand each other better...I know that there is going to be a big dance." (Applause.)

Chairman Guy Okakok speaks in Inupiat. (Applause.) (End of Tape. The conference is over.)

***

Appendix A-3

"The Inupiat Paitot Kotzebue Conference on Native Rights, Kotzebue, Alaska, October 18-20, 1962"

"This year we have met in Kotzebue, the historic converging area where Eskimos of the past have traditionally come to get together to trade and visit.

"This year our purpose of being in Kotzebue is quite different from that of past history. We have come to talk about our problems and to seek solutions to those problems so that we and the Eskimos of the future may have better conditions in which to live.

"Last year's Inupiat Paitot meeting at Point Barrow and this one here in Kotzebue have taught us that by meeting we can see our problems much more clearly than if we had tried to solve them individually. By getting together from many areas of Alaska, we are discovering ways of doing things for ourselves. As we have found in last year's conference at Barrow, if we want our problems solved we have to get up and start doing things for ourselves.

"We are grateful for the help we have had from those who have had interest in our welfare and we still need advice. But still in some cases we should try to work out solutions ourselves.

"In this year's conference we have found that in all areas our accustomed ways of living are being encroached upon by unrealistic laws that do not apply in the native areas of Alaska.

"These laws have been enacted by those who were, and are, ignorant of our way of life; by those who do not take the trouble to find out.

"As a result, hardships are imposed upon the economy of the natives. As James Hawley of Kivalina said in his village report, "These laws are not fit for us."

"I. LAND RIGHTS"

"Congress should define native land rights and pass legislation providing for the settlement of native land claims.

"In any law passed by Congress it should provide that sufficient land be set aside so that the people can sustain themselves, and it should include large enough areas for sustenance on hunting and fishing. In a smaller area around the villages native land title to the mineral as well as the surface should be recognized.

"Until Congress passes legislation dealing with the native land rights the State should prohibit land selection by the state, and the Secretary of the Interior should withdraw land around native villages from state entry.

"The Secretary of the Interior should instruct the Bureau of Land Management and the Bureau of Indian Affairs to prepare a manual of the land laws in effect in Alaska for the purpose of assisting natives in obtaining ownership of land.

"Where land has been withdrawn or reserved for native use and the ownership of minerals has not yet been recognized, Congress should pass a law providing for such ownership so that the minerals may be developed for the benefit of the community."

"II. HUNTING AND FISHING"

"From time unknown, hunting and fishing have always been a means of livelihood of natives in Alaska.

"All the way from Barter Island into the interior, from Nunivak to Aniak in the Kuskokwim, prior to the non-natives coming into this country until today, hunting and fishing have always been a common means of livelihood.

"During the winter time along the coastal areas, seals, oogruks, walrus, whales and fish are the main source of food, while in the Interior and along the rivers caribou, rabbits and other land animals are used as the main source of food.

"The common precautions exist among the natives in all the areas mentioned above that meat taken from kills will not be wasted. "Do not kill animals you do not need" is the usual advice of older natives. Animals, fish and birds caught must be brought home. This means of existence had been carried on all through the life of natives.

"When non-natives arrived, natives began to supplement their meat and fish diet with other foods. They obtained these foods by working wherever employment was available.

"Game laws are now beginning to impose restrictions on the natives. Along the usual routes of migration of walrus, certain people who depend upon walrus are limited to five females and no limits on bulls.

"In some areas, natives are allowed to shoot ducks only during open season in the fall.

"In the northern coast area a hunter is limited to the taking of one polar bear. In certain interior areas there is a limit on beaver trapping. Only one moose is the limit for each hunter per year. These restrictions are causing hardships in many native villages.

"In most villages no other food is obtainable except that which villagers are able to buy from stores and the game that is taken. In most of these villages the raising of vegetables is impossible.

"In larger towns today only a small percentage of natives are employed. Only a small percentage of natives have on their tables well balanced meals.

"Natives during the winter who live on one kind of meat or fish crave other kinds of meat. Natives who live mostly on seals for a certain length of time want a change to fish or to caribou and vice versa. The coming of the ducks is always anticipated with joy because it means a change of diet.

"The need for a change in diet has a great deal to do with the resentment of the game wardens' application of the laws.

"Natives have always been law abiding, but at present time when it affects their food they are used to for a living they are disturbed.

"When we take game for food, we should not be forced to feel guilty because of game laws.

"Many of the game laws are not applicable to natives. "These laws are not fit for us," said James Hawley, of Kivalina.

"RECOMMENDATION; We recommend that the closed seasons should be removed in the case of taking game for subsistence. The primary consideration in making game laws should be the taking of game for food and commercial and sport considerations should be secondary considerations. The seasons should be adjusted in the case of migratory birds, polar bears, moose, beaver, mountain sheep, etc.

"We recommend that when game laws are made or changed, that hearings be held with us in the villages, not just with sports groups in large cities. We recommend that game officials be invited to future meetings of the Inupiat Paitot so they will be able to understand our need to take game for food.

"We Natives are now looking for help. We do not wish to be disturbed and limited in our hunting and fishing. We kill for subsistence; we do not kill for sport. We want to hunt and fish like we always have from time unknown."

"III.   ARTS AND CRAFTS"

"Arts and crafts is still a main source of living in many parts of Alaska. Arts and crafts should be continued so that the younger generation may carry it on as a part of our heritage. Arts and crafts is a means whereby natives can be self employed. Improved marketing of arts and crafts would be very beneficial to natives of Alaska. Eskimo women are some of the best seamstresses in the world and their talents should be developed. With training in supervision and with financial assistance arts and crafts could be and should be stimulated. Perhaps arts and crafts can be tied in with vocational training."

"IV.   ECONOMIC DEVELOPMENT"

"We Inupiat want to better our lot in life; we want jobs to provide the ever increasing need for cash in our economy. We want industries and small businesses but need help in getting them started.

"In order to have economic development, many of our villages need improved water and sanitary disposal systems. We need aid in getting these systems for our villages."

"V.   ORGANIZATION"

"The Inupiat Paitot at this meeting unanimously adopted a set of by-laws under which the Inupiat Paitot organization can operate year around. The by-laws provide for a president, an executive secretary, and an executive committee composed of the President, executive secretary and three additional members elected by the organization meeting in convention. Decisions between meetings will be make by vote of the executive committee, in person, by proxy, or by mail. Membership in the Inupiat Paitot is open to every Eskimo village in Alaska."

"VI.   HEALTH"

"We, Inupiat, would like to stress the importance of sanitation. Better water systems and systems of waste and garbage disposal in many of our villages are needed. We would like to cooperate more and more with the State Department of Sanitation so that such facilities can be made available to us. We need technical and engineering assistance.

"We, Inupiat, would like to see non-natives be given hospitalization privileges on emergency cases and therefore recommend that policy of the United States Public Health Service be changed so that non-natives be allowed to buy this service."

"VII.   HOUSING"

"A good many of the delegates of the Inupiat Paitot have expressed their desire for better housing. The houses they live in are too small and inadequate for big families. Living in such small quarters often creates unsanitary conditions and illness. Inadequate housing often interferes with the work that health officials are attempting to promote. The efforts that have been spent by health officials are practically nullified."

"III.   LAW ENFORCEMENT"

"We Inupiat would like to stress the need for greater law enforcement for the villages. Kotzebue particularly stresses the need for more law enforcement since the establishment of a liquor package dispensing store in that village. Kotzebue has secured part-time services of the state policeman stationed there but sometimes he is required to be away from Kotzebue for long periods of time and at those times the need for law enforcement increases."

"IX.   EDUCATION"

"Although we have some very good schools, thus far the educational facilities in Alaska have been inadequate.

"Most Alaskan natives attend the BIA schools. The BIA has only one high school in the state which is greatly insufficient. More than 700 students ready for high school will not be able to attend this year. In the future, more high schools should be established in the Barrow, Kotzebue, Unalakleet and Bethel areas. These schools should be boarding schools large enough to accommodate the local high school population, plus the high school population of nearby villages. The buildings should be constructed to provide for future expansion (taking into consideration the population projection) so that schools will not become outmoded so quickly.

"A vocational school should be established to provide specialists needed in Alaska. The vocational school should offer courses in the basic trades such as carpentry, auto mechanics, heavy-duty equipment operators and the like. A prerequisite for entrance should be a high school education or high mechanical aptitude and interest.

"On-the-job training is recommended for older people instead of attending the vocational schools or in addition to the vocational school program. A broader adult education program should be initiated by the BIA."

"X.   WELFARE"

"The welfare is tied in with education and economic development in our native areas because welfare economy becomes a part and parcel of our livelihood when both education and economic development are lacking and inadequate.

"Welfare is a necessary evil. It is necessary when we are destitute and in need because of our inability to support ourselves through lack of employment or unfortunate circumstances of illness. But it is beyond our dignity to resort to relief measures when other means can be available by which we can support ourselves and our families.

"The natives of Alaska are tired of welfare. In most cases, the natives now receiving welfare aid would much rather earn money through employment or other gainful means. The natives are proud people and sanction the product of labor as their reward in all pursuits of livelihood. Higher education, gainful employment and opportunities for self-determination are long sought goals. Welfare has its place in our way of life but this should not be the answer to our way of life."

"XI.   EMPLOYMENT"

"At the Inupiat Paitot meeting delegates from different parts of Alaska have expressed their views so that the several officials from Washington, D.C., Juneau and Fairbanks who have come to attend might understand. Unemployment was very much mentioned. Villages have few jobs. Example: At one village out of 85 employable people only four had jobs. This gives an idea for the Economic Development Board for the need here in Alaska for employment for Eskimo people. We, in turn, have heard these officials say they are working on economic development and employment and we are very grateful to hear of this and hope these problems will be solved soon.

"RECOMMENDATION: Unalakleet-housing in this big village is acute. Most of the houses are old and are impractical to remodel. They are health hazards. At present, there is no way of financing to build new housing. the only ones who can afford to build new houses are permanently employed people and there are few of these. Out of 600 people at Unalakleet, only 13 have steady jobs. 150 people of this village can be classified as the working force but work is practically non-existent.

"Unalakleet has a reserve of two square miles. This reserve is getting crowded with 600 people in the village. Unalakleet wants to expand its reserve under native land claims extending north to Kateel, east to the Yukon River, and south to the Black River on south mouth of Yukon River. Unalakleet asks that mineral rights be included in this land claim.

"RELOCATING OF VILLAGES: During the first meeting of Inupiat Paitot at Barrow in November, 1961, delegates from the King Island people made known their need to relocate their village to the mainland from their island homes to Cape Wooley, 45 miles west of Nome. Cape Wooley, according to the delegates, is a good place for hunting and fishing. In establishing this village King Islanders desire to live in better sanitary conditions.

"The delegates again this year brought this matter to the attention of the Inupiat meeting. King Island people still want to move. Part of them are living in Nome and part of them at the island.

"For economic reasons, the King Islander feel better procurement of supplies would be easily attained at the new site. They believe they would be in a better position for obtaining airplane services. If a school is established, their children would be able to go to school 180 days of the year. Seal hunting is good and the people would be able to pick more berries to supplement their meat diet.

"The Inupiat Paitot support the King Islanders in their desire to move to Cape Wooley.

"RECOMMENDATION: Kaktovik (Barter Island) wishes to move the village from the present site 600 yards to higher grounds. The present site is swampy in summer and unsanitary.

"There is danger from air traffic because the end of the runway is practically on the edge of the village and there is little room for expansion.

"The proposed site would be near fresh water and would be high enough to provide adequate drainage.

"The Inupiat Paitot supports the village of Kaktovik in their desire to move to a new location near their present village site."

"DELEGATES: Guy A. Okakok-Barrow, Alaska. David Kagak-Wainwright, Alaska. Herman Rexford-Kaktovik (Barter Island), Alaska. James Hawley-Kivalina, Alaska. Tony Joule-Kotzebue, Alaska. Jack Jones-Kotzebue, Alaska. Fletcher Greg-Kotzebue, Alaska. Joe Carter-Noorvik, Alaska. Felton Comack-Kobuk, Alaska. Emma Willoya-Nome, Alaska. Paul Tiulana-None-King Island, Alaska. David Saccheus-Elim, Alaska. Frank Degnan-Unalakleet, Alaska. George I. Dan-Stebbins, Alaska. Bill Amouak-Marshall, Alaska. August Seton-Hooper Bay, Alaska. Willis Walunga, Gambell (St. Lawrence Island), Alaska. Timothy Kameroff-Aniak, Alaska. Howard Rock-Pt. Hope, Fairbanks, Alaska. Charles Degnan-(Unalakleet) College, Alaska. Martha Teeluk-Kwiguk and College, Alaska (convention secretary). Vern Eutuk-Shishmaref, Alaska. Herbert Onalik-Noatak, Alaska. Simon Paneak-Anaktuvuk Pass, Alaska. Willy Goodwin-Kotzebue, Alaska. George Washington-Buckland, Alaska. Edward J. Shavings-Mikoryuk (Nunivak Island), Alaska. Emily Ivanoff Brown-College and Kotzebue, Alaska.

"HONORARY GUEST: Alfred Ketzler, Chairman, Dena Nena Henash, Indian organization, Interior Alaska.

"OTHER GUESTS" James Officer, Asst. Commissioner, BIA, Washington, D.C., main speaker. Dr. Paul Phillips, Dr. John Abrahamson, Ross L. Miller, Prentiss Gazaway, Dan Jones, Ross Youngblood, Charles Hall, R. D. Hollingsworth, and Arthur Nagozruk."

***

Appendix B

"The Conference just concluded was a historic step for the Native people of Alaska. For the first time, leaders representing the state's 43,000 Indian, Eskimo and Aleut people joined hands to discuss their common problems.

"The Conference will be remembered, and perhaps honored, in commemoration, by future generations of Natives, as the beginning of self improvement for our Native population.

"It will be remembered as a beginning of understanding between the Indian, Eskimo and Aleut people; an understanding that will have far reaching results. It will be remembered for the beginning of Native political responsibility that has not been given proper emphasis heretofore.

"The benefits from this and subsequent gatherings will enrich our Native population, thus reflecting on the well-being of our great state of Alaska and the nation."

"ORGANIZATIONS REPRESENTED
Cook Inlet Native Association
Alaska Native Brotherhood
Inupiat Paitot
Fairbanks Native Association
Gwitchya Gwitchin Ginkhye

"VILLAGES REPRESENTED
Tanana
Noorvik
Kotzebue
Point Hope
Unalakleet

I. UNITY

"The Conference emphasized the continuance and strengthening of local, regional and statewide conferences and organizations to unite the Native people of Alaska. One of the chief methods stressed to bring about better unity was improvement of communication on a year round basis.

"John Hope, Grand President of the Alaska Native Brotherhood and chairman of the meeting, pointed out that jealousy and sectionalism are detrimental to unity among Natives. On the other had, conferences of all the Natives are extremely beneficial toward lessening sectionalism and rivalry.

"Leaders of any organization, whether it be on the village, regional or state levels should not entertain their responsible offices as stepping stones for personal ambition at the expense of their organizations and people."

II. POLITICAL ACTION AND EDUCATION

"Each Native community is urged to take an active part in politics by joining existing political organizations. Where these organizations do not now exist in the villages, these villages are encouraged to initiate them.

"The importance of joining political parties and working in them at the precinct level is emphasized because political appointments, such as postmasterships, can thereby be obtained.

"Women can play an important role in making each locality or area more aware of the importance of political affairs. They can help to make political organizations work more effectively by their participation in all political activities.

"It is important for villages to form political information or action committees to acquaint all the Natives of the mechanics of voting, of the issues that are important to a given area, to the history of a candidate. Voters of limited education should be assisted in classroom-type instruction in learning how to sign their names, how a ballot looks, should be given sample ballots, should be taught to recognize the candidates' names and should be taught how to mark their ballots.

"It is urged that the Native become acquainted with the candidates for office and acquaint the candidates with the needs of their areas.

"The potential political power of the politically educated Natives was stressed with 20 per cent of the total vote of Alaska in Native hands."

III. EDUCATION, HEALTH AND WELFARE

"Education is a key to the solution of the economic, social

and political problems now facing Alaska Natives. The living standard of the Native will be raised by the degree of his education level. A great part of the responsibility for increasing the educational level of Natives, lies with parents. Parents should insist that their children attain the most education possible.

"Certain educational standards must be met before positions can be filled on the local, state and national level both in government and private industry.

"The Fairbanks Native Association is conducting a state-wide survey of educational problems and needs and leaders in various sections of Alaska were urged to help in conducting the survey.

"Because of an inadequate state budget in dealing with problems of sanitation, local leadership is vital in this area. Leaders should work in each community to assure a good supply of drinking water and a safe and sanitary sewage disposal system."

IV.   WAR ON POVERTY

"The Conference is enthusiastic about President Johnson's War on Poverty and felt it had much application in Alaska. The villages and organizations are urged to become fully aware of its programs and to be able to take full advantage of anti-poverty legislation. In view of the feeling on these matters, the conference passed the following resolutions:"

V.   RESOLUTION

"WHEREAS, The President of the United States, Lyndon B. Johnson, has proclaimed a 'War on Poverty'; and

"WHEREAS, a condition of poverty, or near poverty exists in certain sections of Alaska, especially among our Native villages; and

"WHEREAS, no relief is in sight for the immediate future; and

"WHEREAS, the plight of Indians of America has been given special attention by President Johnson, in his State of the Union message and subsequently in speeches across the nation; and

"WHEREAS, Alaskan Natives will benefit materially from programs now being advocated for Indians of the united States, by various Federal and State agencies;

"NOW THEREFORE BE IT RESOLVED, by the Conference of Native Organizations, representing the forty-three thousand Natives of Alaska, assembled in Fairbanks, Alaska, on this 27th day of June, 1964, respectfully request the Bureau of Indian Affairs, Governor William A. Egan, Senator Ernest

Gruening, Senator E. L. (Bob) Bartlett and Representative Ralph J. Rivers, include Alaska in any program federal or state, to improve the economic condition of our original Americans.

"BE IT FURTHER RESOLVED, that the Conference of Native Organizations endorse and support the EQUAL OPPORTU-NITY ACT of 1964 now before the Congress of the United States."

VII.   IMPACT OF CONFERENCE

"Conference delegates were unanimous in their enthusiasm for the results of the Conference and recognized it as a major step in the uniting of the Native peoples of Alaska for their common good. The delegates unanimously agreed that this type of conference must be carried on as an annual occurrence.

"The Cook Inlet Native Association of Anchorage made a tentative invitation to host next year's conference.

"In recognizing the importance of the conference, the delegates hereby request all villages and organizations to plan and work throughout the year toward financing delegates to the forthcoming conference."

VIII.   MESSAGES

"Delighted to learn of leadership meeting. Uniting Alaska Natives is the necessary first step toward solving many of the existing social, economic and educational problems. For in unity there is strength and from a position of strength, decisions can be made-decisions which can come only from within the Native groups and not from outsiders, no matter how well intentioned they might be. It is not only desirable that leadership of Alaska Natives unite but it is their responsibility to do so in order that those they represent might look forward to a better life. The future of Alaska is highly encouraging. Whether the Native people of the state will be able, as a group, to reap the benefits of the expected growth and prosperity will depend, in the main, upon inspiration and the responsibility of their leaders, I send you my every good wish for a fruitful and productive conference. —E. L. BARTLETT, (United States) Senator"

"Please extend my warm regards to all who are attending the leadership conference of Native organizations in Fairbanks and express my best wishes for a good and productive meeting. —ERNEST GRUENING, United States Senator"

"I welcome this opportunity to send greetings and best wishes to those who are participants in this first statewide leadership conference of Native organizations. Each of you is a leader of our state. The discussions you are about to embark upon are indicative of an increasing awareness that Alaska progresses only when each among us likewise advances. I strongly commend you for the leadership and interest which each delegate had exemplified in working toward a better life for Alaska's Native Americans and extend every good wish for a successful conference. —WILLIAM A. EGAN, Governor of Alaska"

"I take this means of sending my warm greetings to all in attendance at the leadership conference of Native organizations and my best wishes for good progress toward the goals of unity and political responsibility. Various Native groups have already proved the strength that goes with organized effort in dealing with legislatures as well as federal agencies that render reports on legislation in favor of Native communities and individuals such as my bills to secure natural gas for fuel for Barrow, enabling establishment of town sites on public domain in areas classified as mineral including Petroleum Reserve Number 4 on the Arctic Slope, establishing a town site for the Klukwan Indian village, authorizing sale to the city of Saxman of unoccupied federally owned lands within the town site, and other bills involving Yakutat and Tyonec and the Tlingit Haida communities which are supporting my bill to amend the jurisdictional act to allow per capita distribution of the money soon to be adjudged in our favor. Will welcome receipt of the resolutions adopted by the conference. — RALPH J. RIVERS, U.S. Representative"

"I wish to extend greetings from the Bureau of Indian Affairs to the conference of native organizations. It has been my pleasure to observe the beginning of growth of the Inupiat Paitot, Dena Nena Henash, and the Association of Village Council (P)residents of Bethel, Alaska and to observe the Alaska Native Brotherhood and Sisterhood at work at their conventions. These developments have provided a forum by which many of the Native people of Alaska can be heard. The joining of the Native organizations is a big step forward in providing the opportunities for the Native people to speak with one voice on matters which pertain to all of us. I wish you a very successful conference and congratulate you on the leadership and vision which has led to this first conference of native organizations in Alaska.—ROBERT L. BENNETT, Alaska Area Director Bureau of Indian Affairs"

"Whether we choose to stay away from politics and whether we like it or not, we are going to have to put up with it at every level of government-Federal, State and local.

"To some extent, every one of us deals with politics in our own villages. When we elect our councilmen, deal with our merchants and other business people in our town—all of this is politics. Those of us who have been exposed and involved in local and State politics should make every effort to educate our people at home by telling them of their rights and privileges as citizens of this State.

"One of our very weak points in exercising our rights is in our annual visits to the polls during the State primary and general elections, and in our local elections.

"Everyone nineteen years of age and over has a right to vote in this State. The Native people in general have got to realize now that unless they come out and vote for their candidates, the will not get the proper representation in the State legislatures. The same holds true in local elections. This is the basic right which we in America have fought for time and again and which many of you, including myself, have had a share of fighting for. To fight and shed blood for something and then not make full use of it is senseless to me. Let us make use of that something by exercising our right to vote. Vote for a person of your choice and on an issue according to your own convictions, but come out and vote. If we come out in numbers we will prevail.

"Another good point to remember in politics is unity. When several people get together and start discussing an issue, each one can express his own views and probably come up with a different one each time. This is good. But before a final decision is made, most differences should be ironed out to the best interest of all and when the crucial vote is taken, come out with a united front. There is nothing more important than to have a large group of people to press for something all united. Then, those in responsible government positions have no alternative but to comply with the wishes of the people. Battles in politics are not won overnight. As a matter of fact, the are not always won. Merely because on fight is lost does not indicate or does not mean that the battle is lost forever. What I am saying in effect is, battles in politics are a continuing process and unless we pursue it continuously, we may never succeed.

"Unity is of the utmost importance and results in a united front so impressive to the responsible people in government that it gives them no alternative but to comply with the wishes of the people. —EBEN HOPSON, State Senator, Barrow, Alaska"

IX.   DELEGATES

"**Mardow Solomon**, President,
Gwitchya Gwitchin Ginkhye, Fort Yukon
Peter Simple, Vice President,
Gwitchya Gwitchin Ginkhye, Fort Yukon
Guy Okakok, Chairman, Inupiat Paitot, Barrow
Bernard Nash, President, Village Council, Point Hope
Tony Joule, Member, City Council, Kotzebue, Alaska
Robert Newlin, President, City Council, Noorvik
Barbara Trigg, Representative,
Arctic Native Brotherhood, Nome
Alfred Grant, Representative, Tanana
Nick Gray, Vice President,
Cook Inlet Native Association, Anchorage
Ralph Perdue, President, Fairbanks Native Association
John Hope, Grand President,
Alaska Native Brotherhood, Juneau
Frank Degnan, Mayor, Unalakleet
Alfred Ketzler, Representative, Nenana
Ed Lutsen, Representative, Fairbanks Native Association
Howard Rock, Executive Secretary, Inupiat Paitot,
Fairbanks"

X.   HONORED GUESTS

"**William Byler**, Executive Director,
Association on American Indian Affairs, Inc.
Jay A. Rabinowitz,
Judge of the Superior Court, Fairbanks Alaska
Herbert Soll, State District Attorney, Fairbanks
Satyendra (John) Mathur, Division of Sanitation,
Alaska Department of Health and Welfare, Fairbanks
Roy Peratrovich, Tribal Operations Officer,
Bureau of Indian Affairs, Juneau
***

Appendix C

December 13, 1962 Senator E. L. "Bob" Bartlett interviews Frank Auvnue Degnan in Fairbanks, Alaska, a verbatim transcript:

Frank Degnan: "My name is Frank Degnan. I am now in the office with Bob Bartlett. Repeating a story I told them five years ago. It is now December 13, 1962. This story happened back in 1918 in the lower Yukon. I was buying furs and interpreting for Archie Grant and Mrs. (Franklin) Moses. They had a trading post and store in St. Michaels. So we thought we could make some money by buying furs on the Yukon. This was Alakanuk (A-lugn-naq.) A-lugn-naq is on the Yukon. They were a Native village of about sixty or seventy. While trading there, the people spoke the Eskimo dialect. The lower Yukon dialect. And when you asked a question, the answer would always be 'Na-me-kee-kah.' The folks there would come into the trading post there and I would ask them the question, 'What do you want?' in Eskimo and they would always answer 'Na-me-kee-kah.' And a little child would come in and I would ask the same question and the answer would be 'Na-me-kee-kah.' So I figured there would be only one way to cure 'Na-me-kee-kah.' About midnight I come out with a shotgun and I shot into the air. The Eskimos were so surprised they come out and they asked, 'Jul-lit, Jul-lit,' which means 'What you do?' I hollered, 'Na-me-kee-kah.' The next day, the first person that came into the trading post, I asked him a question, I got an answer right now. So they told me that they had a medicine man there. This man's name was 'Ah-yung-nak,' I believe. One of the lads was in there, they were playing poker in a kashim. He said, 'Now we are going to show you this medicine man will do a trick, he is going to find the twenty dollars one of our boys lost, he is going to show us the thief.' I said, 'Okay. Let's find out. I want to see a medicine man do his tricks.' So I walked in. Everyone was crawling around. The medicine man got up, he said a few words, of foreign tongue, that I couldn't understand, even in Eskimo. He marched forward and he marched backward, he looked around, he was going to point at the man that stole the twenty dollars. He spotted me, he let out a big yell, he said, 'That the devil has left me.' So he couldn't find the twenty dollars. So as time went on there was another medicine man, he come into the place. He says, 'I could do anything.' I asked him, 'What can you do?' He says, 'You know, I can take a gun and shoot without shells. I say, 'You have to show me.' He says, 'You can take me and take all my clothes off and put me in a kashim and start a fire and I will not even burn.' I says, 'I do not believe you.' So he said, 'Ahm.' So I said, 'I'll make a deal with you, I'll give you forty dollars, for a price of a fox if you show me your trick. In the first place I says I don't believe you.' We happened to have, they were taking a census that year, Sullivan the Irishman, Johnny Grant, he was also an Irishman. Peterson was the lad that was interpreting and translating for Sullivan. He says to me, 'You know these Eskimos do have magic. They are medicine man, you had better be careful. I lived with them all my life.' I said, 'They'll have to show me. I said, 'I don't believe in medicine man, meaning 'Doong-galek,' meaning the man with the devil, has the devil's powers. So we went into the kashim, a house under the ground. In fact, it was probably the first bomb shelter was built, it was built, it was underground. We went in through a tunnel, and after you went through the tunnel you come through the center of the floor. And they you went to the side where there was benches. So he come in and this Eskimo said, 'We are now going to show you that I can shot out of an empty gun. Well I said, 'I don't believe you. Peterson says, 'Frank, Please don't do that, he's a medicine man.' I said, 'I don't believe it.' So the medicine man sat down, he was just stark naked. He come to me and says, 'Frank, you get a gun.' I said, 'What kind of gun do you want, a 30-30?' He said, 'Yes.' So I went out and got a 303, something he didn't want. There was no shells to be got. I tossed the gun to him. He caught it. So he sat down. He was naked. There was low coal oil lamps around. They had their tom-toms. And Peterson kept whispering to me. He said, "Frank,' he says, 'You should never answer that man the way you do. He is dangerous.' I says, 'Well,' I says, 'He's got to show me,' I says, 'He's only a man like myself. How can he be so powerful?' So this man, without any clothes, takes this gun, it was lever action. So, they had their tom-toms, each one, in a minor tone they hummed, and they beat their drums, with a stick. And as they beat the drum, he pat the gun, he lowered the lever and pulled it back. Nothing happened. Believe me, I smiled! I says, 'A medicine man like that I didn't think much of him.' So I said to Peterson, 'Did you see him?' He says, 'Be careful sonny.' Just about that time he takes his gun, he pats it a little, and he lowers the lever. and sure enough, I could hear that shell go into the chamber of the gun. I know it was loaded! So he stands up and he points and he takes the gun, cocks the hammer, then he goes around and then he points the gun right between my eyes. I looks at him and I smile. And Peterson, Sullivan and Grant froze right in their seats. It kinda, the Eskimo turned white and the Whiteman turned red. so he come around and he make the circle and he pointed to the corner of the kashim. Bang, off went the gun! It was loaded. So they kept a pounding on their tom-toms, he sat down and give it another pat. Sure enough, it loaded the second time, he shot the other corner. When he unloaded the gun I jumped down, I say, 'I would like to see what kind of shells he had.' I grabbed them up. They were regular shells that fit the gun, manufactured shells. And how in the world he ever got those shells, I do not know! He was stark naked, hands on his hip. He shot four times, and Peterson says, 'Did you see that?' 'Well,' I says, 'I haven't seen him burn at the stake yet.' So when that was over, well he was somewhat like Houdini the Magician that I read about. So he asked me to tie him up, in all knots. And I know quite a few knots because I had been with the sailors. I know bowlines, half-hitches and half-knots and so forth. So we sat him under the floor, tied his hands behind his back and you know so he couldn't move. There was only about sixteen inches underneath of clearance, just enough for his body, so he could lay down. And he had one Eskimo holding on to the rawhide, it's a thick rawhide, come off an oogruck skin. He was hanging onto that with two hands and he bounced through the air to one end of the kashim and he bounced back. And just about that time that medicine man jumped up out of the middle of that floor, he pushed the boards back, and then he looked at me and said, 'That isn't all. I will show you one more trick.' So he picked up some of these reindeer horns that they use, has two holes, you know, they are about four inches long, and they use them for weights on these nets. So he sets them down on the floor and he had a nail stuck on the wall and a string to his hands, you know. He said he was going to thread those sinkers, reindeer horn sinkers. And we sat there, while he was using a tom-tom. He set his back and start singing. Everytime they hit the tom-toms with the stick, one of those weights would jump up and the string would be right through it, you know. You could see it. and, ah, well, one of the four of em, that tied him there, he come over to me and he smiled and said, 'You satisfied?' I said, 'No, I said, 'You said you promised me you'd burn. And you haven't.' 'You see,' he said, 'That's as far as I will go tonight.' So I said, 'Thank you. I owe you forty dollars.' That was the end of the story."

Bob Bartlett: "Frank, do you recall any others?"

Frank Degnan: "Well, that ah, the only story I can repeat, they were really superstitious. And I thought there that those people that spoke in the Eskimo dialect that they couldn't understand a word of English. But I found out that some of the people there could read and write better than I could. But they wouldn't show it."

Bob Bartlett: "Why?"

Frank Degnan: "They had gone to school at Akulurak, that's a Catholic institution. But they would never let anyone know that they could read and write."

Bob Bartlett: "Why do you think that this was so?"

Frank Degnan: "Well, it was that people come and go, they wouldn't let you know they knew what you was taking about. They just figured that you were a foreigner and they, ah, talked amongst themselves. But, ah, to think that they were people that didn't understand you, you'd be fooled. They acted somewhat like the Chinaman, or the Indian. I read about an Indian attorney in New York one time. He got tired, he had so much business. He got so tired of being pestered by the people and he had so much money. He had the telephone, the business was so much and the money didn't do him any good so he went back to the reservation. When he got back to the reservation, he would ride his pony. He made his hair grow long and he had his blanket on and the tourist come around. They asked this Indian questions and the Indian say, 'No speak English.' A graduate from college and a professional attorney."

Bob Bartlett: "Well, Frank, would any of these people be Catholics out of the Catholic school?"

Frank Degnan: "They probably would. But that's their way of life, they didn't let on, they were Christians at heart and also they would not molest the people that believed in it. They were a sort of a people that agree with anyone if they wanted to believe that way that was their business and they had their own thoughts. I was the only party there that kinda confused them. I could speak their language and act like they could and eat what they could. But they were really superstitious. One Eskimo come in one evening and he come in, and there's a story. We had some dead people that died during the flu. They were piled up in a stack there. And the dogs were eating them, you know. They weren't buried yet. Of course, they were on the surface. So what happened? Every time I see a dog come by, you know, fed there, I couldn't figure out why the Natives didn't bother them. I come out with my thirty-aught-six, I mean my gun, and I would shoot every dog that I saw that was feeding on the peoples there. So one evening, I've heard my mother tell me that if something landed and you were alone in the house you had to be very quiet. It was, ah, Spirit. you could feel it when it landed on the outside of the house. (Frank pounds out the sound, a sharp distinctive thud.) Like that! Then it would drag the circumference of the house. and there would be a white vapor come in and there would be a ghost there. So, ah, I didn't believe that either. So while I was there something did happen. Back of this old trading post, I had a female dog, was a great pal of mine, you know, good company. and sure enough you could hear it creaking on the ground, circling the house. And my dog was so scared, the hair stood up, and start barking. So when the dog went out this Eskimo froze in his tracks. And I opened the door and let the dog out and I grabbed my gun and I ran out. I circled the house to see what kind of ghost there was, I wanted to see him. and I come back in. This Eskimo was so scared! He says, 'You can't sleep here. You got to sleep in my igloo.' You know I had to go with him. so I went to his house to please him. When he went to sleep I got up and went back to my trading post. I was just as safe as my pet dog, or my leader, in that house because I never saw a ghost."

Bob Bartlett: "You never saw any of the white vapor?"

Frank Degnan: "No. The only time I see the white vapor is when a person is smoking a cigarette."

Bob Bartlett: "Ah, touché. Ah, do you think that some of these people back in 1918 would be Catholics and still believe in the medicine men?"

Frank Degnan: "Well, I believe that if they were good Catholics, they'd, ah, if they believed in spirits, they'd tell you there's a spirit, they'd believe that the medicine man had a spirit, maybe a bum spirit. Naturally."

Bob Bartlett: "They could see the same things you say, would they attribute them to some unusual powers to him at any rate?"

Frank Degnan: "Well, this one medicine man, he was unusual. He had an operation. He operated a woman for appendix, really cut with a knife. And requested that they never touch the food and you know, to be careful and yet that woman survived. But he just didn't cure her by touching her, he operated."

Bob Bartlett: "He was a surgeon."

Frank Degnan: "He was a surgeon. But he made a living at it too, I guess. He charged them so much. He was a business man."

Bob Bartlett: "Well, Frank you were telling me earlier today that there were about six hundred people in Unalakleet now. Now, ah, substantially all of those are Eskimos?"

Frank Degnan: "Yes, the biggest majority of those are Eskimos."

Bob Bartlett: "Of the Eskimos, how many of them would you say don't speak English at all?"

Frank Degnan: "Well, the all, you see that's been we say seventy-five years ago a minister come into Unalakleet. The Eskimos called him 'Eez-gha-liq,' and I believe his name was (Axel E.) Karlson. And he come there when Unalakleet was strictly Eskimo. they were, ah, very, ah, in their old customs when they had potlatches. You see, each community has a chief. Ah, they may be two chiefs. They may have competition. In order to be a chief you must be athletic and wise. And I believe the reason that they had two wives is that because the chief was such a good hunter, one wife couldn't take care of everything. You know as a servant. That was their tradition. But today there's a few. They all understand, mostly understand but they, they'd probably look at you and not answer you. But there is a very few. Through education. Many times I've seen, ah, our folks there, I say our folks, because I am Eskimo."

Bob Bartlett: "Are you full blood?"

Frank Degnan: "I am half Irish. You see, my dad."

Bob Bartlett: "I set that down for tape only, I knew it."

Frank Degnan: "I beg your pardon."

Bob Bartlett: "I was getting that remark for the tape only. I knew you were half Irish."

Frank Degnan: "You know, they asked my dad one time, why he'd married an Eskimo woman. He said he was captured by the Eskimos, forced to marry an Eskimo princess, and that was that. Then they asked him why he was bald-headed. 'Well,' he says, 'Up there in Arctic, crawling in and out of them igloos,' he says, 'the polar bear hides wore the hair off the top of my head.'"

Bob Bartlett: "Well, ah, a while ago you said, 'Shall I speak Eskimo in the lower dialect or the Arctic?' How many dialects are there in Eskimo, a whole lot aren't they?"

Frank Degnan: "Well, back in 1923, Knud Rasmussen crossed the Arctic. And he had three Eskimos, I believe, with him, to write a book on the Eskimo. So he come from Greenland. He was. His mother was an Eskimo and his dad was Danish. So he had learned to read and write the Eskimo and speak it fluently. So he was supposed to master all dialects in the Eskimo language. When he got to Nome I was court interpreter. And I spoke the Lower Yukon dialect. And, Ah, Hooper Bay, and Nunivak."

Bob Bartlett: "Three different ones."

Frank Degnan: "They, ah, they is so much similar and that is why he thought that he could speak that language. But he couldn't understand them so they hired me. I being able to, ah, understand it. And it was a lucky break for me that he spoke Danish and English. I had to question him in a few words in the Eskimo Greenland dialect. You know, they were similar but they had words that was, that I didn't understand, that they didn't really use on this side of the, from Greenland to the North American Continent."

Bob Bartlett: "Well, Frank, ah, let's say for a fellow living at Unalakleet, can he understand the Barrow man?"

Frank Degnan: "They can understand the Barrow people now because it's conglomerate, because its from all over. It's been that way for many years. But I have seen people from one village to the other and they wouldn't understand the different dialects. We have three dialects, I mean, the Lower Yukon dialect, ah, Golovin Bay, and Elim, they is similar. But they have some few words that differ. Then you take, ah, from St. Michael, from Stebbins down to Hooper Bay there they seem like it is one dialect. they are a little slower. Then you take, ah, Nunivak Island, its the same dialect, but it would be somewhat like the English-Eastern, like if you are speaking that Yankee dialect and an Englishman comes along, it would be somewhat, some difference."

Bob Bartlett: "Did you speak all of these dialects?"

Frank Degnan: "I don't speak them fluently but I can make myself understood and I understand most of them. There is one place that I have never been. I was hired by the Danish Government to translate for Knud Rassmussen. I have never been on the St. Lawrence Island. But listening to the radio, I heard, ah, Slwooko translate the Bible over the KICY, (Covenant Mission Radio Station in Nome, Alaska) he spoke in the, ah, St. Lawrence dialect. And I have never been there, but do you know, I understood every word he said translating the Bible, maybe it's because I know something about the Bible. But

I think that is one dialect that is never been contaminated by other dialects. I think that is an ancient dialect that is handed down for generations."

'Bob Bartlett: "Why don't you do this for us, why don't you take, Oh, just a simple sentence, ah, such as 'We are going to have a good summer,' say that in some of the different dialects and then tell which one you said it in. In each case."

Frank Degnan: "Well, you see, in our language, sometime we have the cart before the house, if I should tell you, ah, say 'Come in the house,' I would say, 'House, come in.' so sometimes it is not so easy."

Bob Bartlett: "You make one up."

Frank Degnan: "Now I would have to get one that is similar. Now supposing I said, Ah, 'Qu-yan-nah,' and 'Ee-leg-a-na-meek.' Means same thing. 'Qu-yan-nah,' and 'Ee-legh-a-na-meek,' that mean 'Thank You.' I say I speak all dialects, but I have so many dialects I get confused in wording them. I would have to be in one community maybe for a week or two and then it would come back to me and then I would almost speak it fluently. you see, I was down to, down to the cannery, and the name of it was 'dead people,' for the Libbey's we had, ah, Quinhagak dialect, Hooper Bay dialect, and you know that the Quinhagak Eskimos could read and write their own language."

Bob Bartlett: "I did not know that, I did not know any kind."

Frank Degnan: "They wrote it, they have Bibles translated into Eskimo."

Bob Bartlett: "Who did that?"

Frank Degnan: "Quinhagak."

Bob Bartlett: "Who did that for them?"

Frank Degnan: "That I wouldn't know. I have a trans-lated. And the other one, the songbook is 'Yau-ghoot,' meaning 'songbooks.' they have songbooks. They sing in English and Eskimo. it's wonderful to hear them. and they preach in their, their language. and, ah, if I went to, ah, ANS Hospital (Alaska Native Service) in Anchorage, if I come into a place, and I see an Eskimo parky or pair of mukluks, I would almost know where he come from."

Bob Bartlett: "From his dress."

Frank Degnan: "From the dress. So I went into the room one time, and in this room, they were all Indians. There was just one Eskimo in there. So when I come in, I said, 'Chau-pete Nau-gaum-dutch-cul-nut-coo-thlut-kai.' that Eskimo got up and sat down and he laughed. and then I spoke to him in his dialect. And after, when I got ready to go, one Indian said to me, he says, 'That man laid in that bed, he wouldn't even eat or talk to anyone for three days.' He says, 'You were the only one that ever brought him back.'"

Bob Bartlett: "What did you say to him?"

Frank Degnan: "Oh, I says, 'This, What, Seagull, Crane, Coo-thlut. I make noise like a crane, Coo-thlut, Coo-thlut, Kai' Just some words made up just to be funny."

Bob Bartlett: "Uh-huh. Frank, let me tell you a story, makes me think of St. Lawrence Island. I was over in Gambell, on the island in October, and this is the story they told us, thirty-eight miles from there, on the Sibe-rian mainland, there's a Soviet radio station and twice a week, Sunday's and on Wednesday's they aim a broadcast at the St. Lawrence Island Eskimo. Propaganda. Pure and simple. To convert our Eskimos to their way of thinking. And this is an Eskimo dialect and they had themselves a special announcer over there. But one day, oh before I tell that part, I must say that, Ah, the man that told me about this said that their propaganda was very rude, raw and crude. And altogether ineffective, waste of time and money on the part of the Russians. For they weren't converting anyone on St. Lawrence Island. But anyway, ah, this announcer was telling one broadcast, said in Eskimo dialect, he said, 'I don't believe what I am going to tell you but this is the way it is written for me to read and I am going to read as it is written.' And he did. And that is the last time they heard from that announcer."

Frank Degnan: "You know, we, ah, my mother of course was raised and they traveled in skin boats. My grandfather was a chief. So they'd paddle up to Wales, they even went over to Siberia. And they come back. My mother claimed that the first time she ever, she went to Port Clarence, and looked around, she never seen so many boats. It looked like a forest. The whaling boats was in there. And while she was there, her dad was trading, and while they were trading she was walking around. And the skin boat was probably twenty feet below the ship. She saw her first colored person. She said she was so scared. She jumped out of that sailing whaling boat into the skin boat and covered herself up with caribou hides. Before they had reindeer in Alaska. And she found out that they were people too later on. But, ah, you have many names you inherit. You know every time a child is born or every time someone is dead and a child is born, there may be several children, and they're named after that person that died. And I have, mother said, I have some names. My name is 'Nook-too-yii,' that's in, that's a Siberian name. In the Siberian language, I am not a Siberian but I inherited that name because they had traveled and they had friends. Probably someone, of our forefathers that traveled had that name. My Eskimo name, I am named after my grandfather 'Auvnue.' 'Auvnue,' means 'cottonwood bark.' And my son (Chuck) has gone to the University of Alaska and his name is 'Qaiguq,' that's "birch bark.' Not cottonwood bark but birch bark. And how he happened to inherit his name, was, there was, ah, a man that lived in Golsovia. A man that people loved so much. He had died. His name was 'Qaiguq.' And after he had passed away, my wife named my son 'Qaiguq.' Because this old man used to come in and bring his parky and ask my wife, and you know, my wife was pregnant, you know, he'd bring his parky and he says, 'You mend this for me. And you do this and mend my boots or something.' And she remember that and she thought it would be nice to name him 'Qaiguq.' But many funny things happen in the Eskimo custom. 'Qaiguq had a friend and his friend's name was 'Tetpon.' And do you know, my son, when he was, when my son was born, he was a blonde. My wife is half Swede, Eric Johnsson. So when my son was born he was blonde as any Swede you ever seen. And I used to call, 'Hey, Swede,' some people used to look at me and say, "You can't say that.' I says, 'He's my son, I can say anything.' But when he grew up he has dark hair."

Bob Bartlett: "He's the boy that met the airplane?"

Frank Degnan: "That's right. So Qaiguq, he was a gentleman. He used to go out fishing tomcods. Do you know at one time, a mountain sheep come down there. And stood in front of him. While he was fishing tomcod. Oh yeah, you know, on the ice. He looked at him and the mountain sheep took off. He had a gun. He wouldn't shoot even him. And the folks around there said, 'There's a seal down there Qaiguq, you go get him.' 'You know that poor feller has got to live too and he's resting and he's taking a sunbath,' he says, 'I don't want to kill him.'"

Bob Bartlett: "Frank tell us something about the history of Unalakleet, will you? How it got started, why and all the rest of it."

Frank Degnan: "Unalakleet, I believe means Unaliqlegmuit, Unaliqleq means 'Southerly.' Maybe it's the Southerly village. It could be Unaluq, we have the Southeastern winds there blowing all the time. It could mean the Southeastern winds. But Unaluqleet means, "the last village towards the South,' in that dialect. It was a village that was on the coast, and I believe one of the first, one of the first villages to smell a ship before they saw it. They smelt this ship before they saw it on the horizon. They probably were burning coal and they were not accustomed to that. And pretty soon, as this ship kept coming towards the land. First they saw the big sail, it was such a mammoth ship that something that they had never seen before in their life, they thought the Devil himself was coming. So they took off into the hills. They says, No, there was one man there, he says, 'No,' he says, 'I'd like to see the Devil,' he says, 'I am not afraid of him. I want to stay here. I am kinda useless anyway so I'll stay here.' And the rest of 'em took off to the hills. They come in on their rowboats, you know, something they have never seen before. So this, when it went away, the folks come back. And he had many stories to tell them: They give him cloth, they give him tobacco, they give him many things.' Oh they did not even know what they were for. They probably didn't need them. The thing that was most valuable was the cloth or the leaf tobacco. They were used to leaf tobacco because they used to go over to Siberia to get that. Way back in the early days. So he had a great story to tell. So he said, 'They were very nice people. They had glass eyes. Meaning bead color, you know, call glass eyes. They had very white skin and they had fox fur. (They had red whiskers.) So, Ah, and they were quite happy, but they had an interpreter with them and he happened to be from the lower Kuskokwim somewhere and they probably had taken him over to Kodiak and when that was the first capitol, probably. And, ah, from that time on the Natives lived there they had good relationships with the Indians. The Indians used to paddle down, from the Yukon, mind you, come down the Portage and come all the way down to Unalakleet. Mother claims that when they come they were happy. Because they brought chewing gum. And the chewing gum, it's spruce gum. Chewing gum was the pitch that they put on the seams of their canoes. The Eskimos used to go out and chew that pitch and that was their chewing gum and they remember that. The Indians were not very happy about it. But the kids had a lot of fun. So they really, ah, had good relationships. The Indians and the Eskimos. They bartered and they traded. ah, the Indians, ah, probably, ah, lived on top of the ground and the Eskimos lived underground and they had lived in these old igloos. Ah, when you hear of igloos, you probably think of an ice house. But an igloo is a house. Just igloo means house. If you say, 'Iglutalik,' it means 'a place where there's a house.' So, as time went on, the, ah, the Eskimos are very busy people. They prepare for the winter, the hard winters, for survival. And the Indians were busy too. In their own way, their mode of living. But some times they, ah, they run short of food and they come down and sneak in on the Eskimos. And what they want. Sometimes they catch them inside their kashims, probably set fire to it, pour seal oil on it. From what I hear, I don't know how true it is. It probably is true. So the Eskimos is always on the alert. The last time they almost had a war, the chief was there. The Eskimo chief. He say, 'There's Indians here. We're going to have war. There's very few of us. We have got to do something. So, ah, by day he organized them, he organized all the children. All the old folks. And everyone in the community to travel from their igloos to their fish holes. And they had a continual stream. Mind you, they were just a handful of Eskimos there. But they had a continual stream going back and forth. The Indian watched them for a couple of days. He says, 'Too many Eskimos down there.' So they won the war without firing a shot."

Bob Bartlett: "When do you think that might have been, I mean when they were fighting?"

Frank Degnan: "Well, it couldn't have been too many centuries ago. I believe, oh, maybe a hundred years ago."

Bob Bartlett: "When was Unalakleet founded?"

Frank Degnan: "Oh, Unalakleet at the present time was founded probably back in, the present place, probably founded, in the early, about 1830, probably. But there has been villages there. For centuries. There's one place at the north of the runway, I believe there was about twenty-five hundred Eskimos. I judge that because I know from these dugouts, the kashims, and the tunnels that they have, you don't see no wood there or nothing. But it has been there, probably, ah, oh maybe three hundred years ago. They were a population, and the channel probably went out where the FAA (Federal Aviation Agency,) is now. You see, the Eskimo goes to a, he lives on the coast where there is fish, seal, tomcods, and the herring. All the food that they have. The reason why they live on the coast. they claim that, ah, there is more vitamins in seafoods than in they do in the land animals. So, ah, we'd say back in 1855 the Russians, ah, were there, they had their forts and they, ah, had their compound there. They, ah, used to flog the Eskimos for coming inside there. And, ah, they really didn't like that. And there was one Eskimo. And he, ah, figured he had enough so he had a jade knife and he yanked that out and he says, he really wasn't going to fight the Russian, he was going to commit suicide. But the Russians thought he was going to put on a royal battle so they were pretty nice to him and they turn him loose. So as time went on, they, ah, was so mean, the Eskimos organized. They had medicine men, you know. In fact, I think, my granddad worked for them at one time, inside, when he was a young man. So these, ah, these, ah, Eskimos got together. They had their bows and arrows and spears because they had no modern equipment to fight with. They walked over to this, this Russian fort. The Russians, they probably had a pretty good chief or general, whatever he was, the man in charge. He thought he'd scare these Eskimos by firing a cannon. So he takes his cannon. He sets the cannon up to scare these Eskimos away. They come with their bows and arrows and spears and they kept a coming. So he sets his cannon and points it at a, at a cache. You know, where they kept their dried fish and food up there. So they fired the cannon. The Russians thought that he'd a gonna run. The big boom, the big smoke and the cache blew away. But the Eskimos never run. I asked them why they didn't run. The Eskimos thought that he was a medicine man. They says that we could do just as good a medicine as the Russians would do."

Bob Bartlett: "Now..., do you have a question or two to ask?"

Response: "I am so wrapped up in this I can't think of anything at the moment."

Frank Degnan: "So as time went on, this place across the river from the present location. On the other side. There's a mound there that the Eskimos built. And this mound was more of a protection. They made it higher than the other side. They built their, their ah, their log igloos in there and they had tunnels for, in case of war or something, hidden in there. And the water level. This is the story that I, was told to me. There was a lot of, many stories told. But a few things I never paid much attention because I figured they were just stories to be passing time. If I jotted down what I heard my mother told me, I, ah might had some great stories. So, ah, here's what happened. They had us. The Russian's had the small pox and they brought in the clothing and distributed amongst the Eskimos. And the whole village had small pox. And the older people all died off. And I believe that my mother's uncle was one of them. He said that he hauled, he had a oogruk hide. He put the dead person in that then he hauled them over into the high, ah, higher banks to, you know the Eskimos never buried the dead. They lived underground and kept the dead on the surface. So, ah, he hauled them over there and all the ones that were left were the children. So he took the children and moved on the other side. The main village we have now. And, ah, my mother inherited a bow. You know one of these bows for drilling. It was given to her and she give it to Frank Insall, a man in Shaktoolik, he died, oh about ten years ago. [Note: My father told me that the man was Frank Insall of Shaktoolik known as 'Da-ghou-ah.'] She said, 'I am a woman. You have more use for this bow.' And she give it to this man. And do you know, before he died he sent it to me. I still got it. It was one of these things, you know, they have a rawhide on it, and a stick and a mouthpiece. And they can drill pretty fast. In fact, some of the King Islanders use it and they think it is even faster than a regular electric drill.

You know, when they know what they are doing. Precision. So, ah, this new village is the present day village. And I think we should preserve that, ah, old village for a future date. I think we should, ah, there's a string of beads in there somewhere. You know, beads was their money. My mother was wealthy, she had a lot of beads. That was handy, you know, there is certain type. There is one type that is real blue they find in the mountains she claims. There's another type with, ah, with a little white spot inside. She used to tell me each one had a price and very valuable. It was a means of exchange. And she wore them around her neck and on her ears. And my mother had tattoo marks on her chin. And the menfolk had holes in their lips and they, ah, call them 'Doo-tak.' This is 'Dum-thlu-um.' which means mark on the chin. And I, ah, do not know why they had the holes on their lips, they must had some reason. I know my mother used to tell they used to have ivory buttons in them and they used to suck on them, you know. Maybe style. Something like those Africans , they have their big lower lip, you know. I've, ah, everything I've heard about the Eskimos. They are very friendly people. They have a lot of love. And mother claims that people never died much before the, what they call the civilization. They, ah, she said that before the Whiteman come, they lived underground. They had the nicest house and the warmest houses and it was air-conditioned and in fact it was the first bomb shelter. And they, ah, didn't bury their dead they left them on the surface. And of course, one day I was questioning, I says, 'Why did you live underground? She say, Well she lived underground to keep warm. Why didn't you bury the dead? She says, 'The ground was frozen, we didn't bury them.' I says, since the missionaries come, preach to them, I says we come out of the ground, the Eskimos come out of the ground and took the dead and buried the dead and put it in reverse. That's the civilization for you. Well I thought, ah, then the ministers wife asked me, she says, 'Why did they bury them on the surface?' I told them, well, I says, 'So that they would be prepared when Gabriel blows the bugle,' I says, they didn't have to kick up the dirt. They would be ready to go.' I don't believe, I, unless you have any questions?"

Bob Bartlett: "No I don't. Do you have any questions, Roy?"

Roy: "No, ah, did they have any particular ceremonies or anything concerning the old people. People that had, maybe lived their life and were crippled or unable to work, was there any procedure or any way to come to the end of life that you heard any stories about?"

Frank Degnan: "No, I haven't heard of any stories. But the people lived, and they lived over a hundred years old. Because mother told me that the people used to live till they got a new set of teeth and their gray hair turned black."

Bob Bartlett: "Those were the times."

Voice: "Those were the good old days."

Frank Degnan: "Don't know how good they were but I've seen em. You know I used to haul water for them, pick a little wood. And they thought I was a pretty nice lad. He says, 'I hope you live as long as I do.' I says, 'Me? No!'"

Bob Bartlett: "Frank, did they believe in an afterlife? Those old people."

Frank Degnan: "You know, there was a question I asked my mother. My mother was educated. My mother was, I think, one of the greatest Girl Scout leaders in the world. In fact she saved my life, and my Dad's life. You see, I asked many questions. I asked my mother, I says, 'How come you Eskimos don't read and write?' 'Huh,' she says, 'We got a wonderful memory. We remember everything.' She says, 'We don't have to put it on paper.' She says, 'We've got it in our minds, it's in our head.' She says, 'These people are so absent-minded they have got to put it on paper, and they look for it here, they look for it there and if they didn't have it with them they couldn't remember what it is all about.' So I thought it was kinda cute. So I says, 'Now,' I says, 'Ah, you know when Christianity come, they preach about Jesus Christ and God.' I says, 'What did you have before, ah, what happened to the Eskimo when he died?' She said, 'You know son, when the Eskimo dies, his body leaves his soul. His spirit goes clean around the world and when it comes back to its Earth birthplace then it goes up to Heaven. Where the Sun never sets and the grass is always green. I asked mother, I says, 'How come,' I says, 'the Whiteman don't, they thought the world was flat. Columbus went out and proved it was round.' I says, 'How did you know it?' 'Oh', She said, 'We just know it that's all.'"

Bob Bartlett: "Well, did they believe in a life after this one?"

Frank Degnan: "They sure did. There in that new life that they had, it was peace and harmony. Nothing to worry about."

Bob Bartlett: "Well, is it true, as you sometimes hear, as you often times read, that when a person would get old and crippled or the like, that they'd take them outside and they would die?"

Frank Degnan: "They probably do that in different tribes, they had different systems. You take up in the Arctic, where it is so tough, they'd probably. I've heard stories that, ah, if a person that lives so long, it was an honor to die. But it had to be, he had to request it. He made the request to his son. Then it was an honorable death. Otherwise if he commit suicide it was, it was no good."

Bob Bartlett: "Then it never happened because they didn't want to take care of the older people?"

Frank Degnan: "No that wasn't the case. It was, ah, that, ah, it was just visa-versa. It was the, the party requesting that they, ah, want to rest. But they can't commit suicide because it was dangerous. Because it could be with them all the time. So it was honorable to ask his own son or someone. That was the tradition centuries ago. They don't practice it, I've never heard it, you know."

Bob Bartlett: "Not in your time?"

Frank Degnan: "Not in my time."

Bob Bartlett: "Did they ever do it in the southern, ah?"

Frank Degnan: "They probably had customs. I've never paid much attention. I was kind of a, oh, I don't know, probably little too much Irish."

Bob Bartlett: "Well, ah, were you born in Unalakleet, Frank?"

Frank Degnan: "I was born in St. Michaels. I was born in nineteen hundred and one. You know something happened. My mother. I think this is what happened in Unalakleet. This is something I, I have always kept to myself. My Mother told me, my granddad was a chief, a big chief. And he liked his spirits. You know you got two kind of spirits. One you get from the minister and one from out of the bottle. So, ah."

Bob Bartlett: "[Laughter.] So he wasn't concerned about the minister?"

Frank Degnan: "Well. When he was a chief there weren't too much Christianity. They didn't know anything about it. They probably got it from the Russians. They were, you know, Greek Orthodox. So, Ah, he had his own still and my mother run the still she told me. She says, 'You run that, Ah, stuff through and when it lights with a match, it's cured.'"

Bob Bartlett: "And it burns."

Frank Degnan: "So, ah, my mother moved. So, ah, the Irish lad that come from the States in ninety-eight. On the Moran Fleet. He had a mother too. His mother come from Dublin, Ireland. She sailed around the Horn, for eighty days to make it from Dublin, Ireland to the State of Washington, to Port Townsend. So when my granddaddy died, the first minister was there. When Momma heard that Grandpa died at home she went over to get her inheritance. She had several caches full of furs. He had the most modern guns, shotguns, and rifles in his day. Being a chief and a trader. Believe he traded for the AC Company at that time. So, the Natives disowned her because she married a Whiteman."

Bob Bartlett: "Oh."

Frank Degnan: "Probably was. Don't know for sure. But she said she come home to, to get her inheritance. Because she worked. You see, there, in the olden days, the women done the work. The men went out and hunted. They shot the seal, the bear, or the whale. They just tell them where it's at. So the younger generation, the womenfolk, they'd go and get it and bring it back. So she figured she is entitled to inheritance. She come in there, to the village. They lived in igloos and some maybe, some board and log houses. Dad was there. He couldn't understand a word of Eskimo. But there happened to be that first minister come in (Axel E. Karlson) and they were debating. And, ah, I think it was (Stephan) Ivanoff was, ah, the interpreter."

Bob Bartlett: "Paul?"

Frank Degnan: "The old man."

Bob Bartlett: "Oh, the old man."

Frank Degnan: "Oh, that's back in, oh, nineteen hundred, nineteen hundred, he was a young man then. And, ah, Ivanoff's dad (Sergei Ivanoff) was a baker for the Russians when they were a colony, colonized here. Mother claims every time she saw Ivanoff's dad, the old man Ivanoff had clay on his hands. You know, he was a baker, that was the flour that she thought was clay. So, ah, the only time that my dad understood when this, ah, this

(Stephan) Ivanoff was translating in English to this, ah, minister (Axel E. Karlson). My dad got up, Momma says that's the first time he spoke to the minister. He says, 'Do you know,' he says, 'the oldest person in the family is legally entitled to inherit everything his folks had.' They probably had something to do with it I don't know. So they moved. I've shot that ten gauge shotgun, one of the oldest...I believe, had a telescope sight I played with. They, ah, disowned my mother. Now I've come back. I don't use that against those folks. I've been the chairman for about seventeen years."

Bob Bartlett: "Chairman of the Village Council?"

Frank Degnan: "Yes."

Bob Bartlett: "Frank, we are about at the end of the tape. Why don't you, ah, conclude, give it a fine closing touch with a minute or two in Eskimo. Say anything you want to say, wind it up."

Frank Degnan: "Ah, Bob Bartlettum, Oonis-kauz-kauna, oonis kaun-neu-gha, onif-kau-ghna, oopit-kah-ghlaa. Ka-yu-ka Unaliqlegmuite ping-gh-ghlet. Yu-peet-Juhlee, kung-ghoo-gee muluk-lu-gee pic-king-ite. Oom-zuu—wuk-tu-ta-sin-wa-kin-taut Oonif-kies-kin-ite-taut-Oonif-ka-ghain-ah. Quanna-its-sple-chee, Nee-cho-il-ghainne. Auvnue we ghainne. Thank you."

Bob Bartlett: "Thank you, Frank (Degnan.)" (End of Tape.)

About the Author...

Frances Ann Degnan is an Unalit/Kawerak woman. She was born in Unalakleet, Alaska on May 26, 1943. She is still living and sleeping on the spot where she came to Earth in her Unalit homeland. Frances has always followed in the footsteps of her parents, Frank and Ada Degnan. Like them, she loves her homeland. She became interested in the life and changing times of her people at the age of twelve. Along with her father, she served in the Alaska Federation of Natives organization in 1970 and through the passage of the public law settling the Alaska Native Land Claims on December 18, 1971. Frances continues to serve on several boards that affect the village and region.

Frances was educated at the Unalakleet Day School, Mount Edgecumbe High School and the University of Alaska in Fairbanks where she received her Bachelor of Arts degree in Psychology and Sociology in 1964. She then returned home and is now self-employed.

Frances's favorite activities include smoking fish and other subsistence activities, knitting musk ox wool, and being out in the country.

This is her first book. She wishes she could have named all the people of Unalakleet and included a short biography of each in this book as they all are very important to the history of Unalakleet.